The United States and the Middle East: 1914 to 9/11

Part I

Professor Salim Yaqub

THE TEACHING COMPANY ®

PUBLISHED BY:

THE TEACHING COMPANY
4151 Lafayette Center Drive, Suite 100
Chantilly, Virginia 20151-1232
1-800-TEACH-12
Fax—703-378-3819
www.teach12.com

ISBN 1-56585-686-4

Salim Yaqub, Ph.D.

Assistant Professor of History, University of Chicago

Salim Yaqub received his Ph.D. in American history from Yale University in 1999. He is currently assistant professor of history at the University of Chicago, where he teaches American, international, and Middle Eastern history. His area of research specialization is the history of U.S.-Middle Eastern relations since 1945. Dr. Yaqub's first book, *Containing Arab Nationalism: The Eisenhower Doctrine and the Middle East*, will be published in 2004 by the University of North Carolina Press. The dissertation version of this work received the John Addison Porter Prize and the George Washington Egleston Prize from Yale University in 2000.

Dr. Yaqub gratefully acknowledges the assistance of Elizabeth Teare in preparing the lectures for this course.

Table of Contents

The United States and the Middle East: 1914 to 9/11 Part I

The United States and the Middle East: 1914 to 9/11

Scope:

This course examines U.S. relations with the nations of the Middle East since 1914. Although the structure of the course is mainly chronological, four central themes recur throughout the lectures.

The first theme is the growing involvement of the United States in the affairs of the Middle East, a consequence of America's increasing global power. In the first four decades of the twentieth century—except for a brief but important flurry of activity in the late 1910s—U.S. interests in the Middle East were almost entirely missionary, philanthropic, educational, and commercial. This started to change with America's entry into World War II, which caused U.S. officials, for the first time, to see the geopolitical orientation of the Middle East as vital to American national security. During the war, U.S. military forces occupied large portions of the Middle East, turning Iran into a corridor for supplying the Soviet Union and North Africa into a staging area for invading fascist Italy. After 1945, the Middle East remained vital to U.S. security, both as a staging area for a possible war against the Soviet Union, America's new adversary, and as a source of oil for Japan and the nations of Western Europe, America's new Cold War allies. For the first decade and a half of the Cold War era, the United States generally deferred to Britain as the preeminent Western power in the Middle East, but following the Suez crisis of 1956—which demonstrated that Britain could no longer play this role—Washington stepped in to take London's place. For another couple of decades, the United States and the Soviet Union vied for political and strategic advantage in the Middle East. In the mid-1970s, however, the Soviet position in the region began to decline, foreshadowing and, in a small way contributing to, the demise of the Soviet system in the early 1990s. Now the sole remaining superpower, the United States wields unparalleled power and influence over Middle Eastern affairs.

The second theme of the course is Middle Easterners' ongoing quest for political independence and self-mastery. In the early decades of the twentieth century, Turks, Arabs, Jews, Iranians, and Kurds sought to gain political control over portions of the region, often in opposition to the imperial agendas of European powers. By mid-century, most of these groups, with some important exceptions, had succeeded in establishing formal national independence, but Middle Easterners remained preoccupied with combating external domination, real and perceived. After 1945, as the United States grew more involved in the region's affairs, it increasingly became the object of indigenous resentment. In Iran and the Arab world in the 1950s and 1960s, secular nationalists resisted American pressure to side with the West in the Cold War, while Arab nationalists in particular tried to defeat or contain Israel, which they saw as an instrument of Western power. By the 1970s, secular nationalism was a declining force in Arab and Iranian affairs, increasingly giving way to political Islam, whose rejection of Western influence was far more profound. In the decades since, Islamists have been generally unsuccessful at seizing state power (the Iranian revolution is the major exception to this rule), but they have posed a formidable challenge both to the United States and to existing regimes in the region. Of all the Middle Eastern nations, Turkey and Israel have enjoyed the closest relations with the United States, but they, too, have sometimes chafed under Washington's restraints on their freedom of action.

The third theme is the difficulty the United States has experienced in balancing diverse, and sometimes conflicting, interests and objectives in the Middle East. After 1945, America's primary objectives in the region were securing Western access to Middle Eastern oil, preventing the Soviet Union from reaping political or strategic advantage in the area, and ensuring Israel's security. Pursuing the last of these objectives often complicated the pursuit of the other two. Washington's close relations with Israel generated anti-American sentiment in the Arab world, providing the Soviet Union with opportunities to increase its political influence in the region. Similarly, during the Yom Kippur War of 1973, President Richard M. Nixon's decision to airlift military supplies to Israel prompted oil-producing Arab states to impose an embargo on oil shipments to the United States and some European countries, causing major dislocations in the global economy. As the Cold War drew to an end, the imperative of containing the Soviet Union gave way to two new objectives: combating international terrorism and preventing "rogue" states—such as Libya, Iran, and Iraq—from challenging U.S. policies in the region. Both of these objectives have acquired fresh urgency following the terrorist attacks of September

11, 2001, but Americans disagree over whether the two goals can, or should, be pursued simultaneously. While President George W. Bush argues that the necessity of disarming Iraq (and, perhaps, overthrowing its government as well) cannot be separated from the effort to defeat Osama bin Laden's al-Qa'ida network, others insist that Bush's preoccupation with Iraq has diverted precious energy and resources from the war against al-Qa'ida. As in previous decades, Washington finds no easy formulas for pursuing its diverse objectives in the Middle East.

The fourth theme is the rising antagonism between Americans and Middle Easterners. In the first four decades of the twentieth century, the United States had a relatively benign reputation among Middle Easterners, who appreciated that the United States had no imperial ambitions in the Middle East and who were grateful for the educational, philanthropic, and humanitarian services Americans provided in the region. But once the United States emerged as a global superpower and began pursuing policies that antagonized the broad currents of regional opinion, much of that goodwill turned into bitter resentment. On the American side, there has also been a rising tide of suspicion and anger directed at the dominant cultures of the Middle East. Orientalist stereotypes of Arabs and Muslims have long proliferated in American culture, but in the early years of the twentieth century, those images were relatively benign, romanticizing Middle Eastern society as often as they vilified it. It was only in later years, as the substance of U.S.-Middle Eastern relations grew angrier and more violent, that popular images of Middle Easterners became more uniformly threatening.

Lecture One
A Meeting of Two Worlds

Scope:

The first lecture establishes the thematic and historical underpinnings of the whole course. After setting forth our four main themes—increasing American power, indigenous political aspirations, conflicting interests and goals, and rising mutual antagonism—the lecture briefly outlines the political situation in the Middle East before the First World War, describing the decline of the Ottoman Empire and the growing military, political, economic, and cultural encroachment of the European powers into the empire. We then discuss Americans' private interactions with Middle Easterners up to 1914, paying particular attention to the activities of American Protestant missionaries. Next, we describe America's growing international assertiveness following the Spanish-American War of 1898. We end with the outbreak of World War I, an event that will bring Washington into the center of great-power deliberations over the political fate of the Middle East.

Outline

I. Although the structure of the course is mainly chronological, four central themes recur throughout the lectures.

   A. The first theme is the growing involvement of the United States in the affairs of the Middle East, a consequence of America's increasing global power.

      1. During World War II, U.S. officials came to see the geopolitical orientation of the Middle East as vital to American national security and began, for the first time, to devise deliberate Middle East polices.

      2. After World War II, the United States gradually supplanted Britain as the preeminent Western power in the Middle East; it then vanquished the Soviet Union, emerging at century's end as the sole remaining superpower, wielding unparalleled power and influence over Middle Eastern affairs.

   B. The second theme of the course is Middle Easterners' ongoing quest for political independence and self-mastery.

      1. From the 1910s on, Turks, Arabs, Jews, Iranians, and Kurds have fought to acquire or maintain political

control over portions of the region, often in opposition to the designs of outside powers.

2. After 1945, as the United States grew more involved in the region's affairs, it increasingly became the object of indigenous resentment.

3. By the 1970s, secular nationalism was a declining force in Arab and Iranian affairs, increasingly giving way to political Islam, whose rejection of Western influence was far more profound. These Islamists have, however, been generally unsuccessful at seizing state power, though they have posed a formidable threat to the United States and to existing regimes in the region.

4. Though Israel and Turkey have enjoyed the closest relations with the United States, they have sometimes chafed under Washington's restraints on their freedom of action.

C. The third theme is the difficulty the United States has experienced in balancing conflicting interests and objectives in the Middle East.

1. During World War I, for example, Woodrow Wilson's devotion to the principle of national self-determination conflicted with the imperial agendas of his wartime allies.

2. After 1945, America's primary objectives in the region were securing Western access to Middle Eastern oil, preventing the Soviet Union from reaping political or strategic advantage in the area, and ensuring Israel's security.

3. During the Cold War, America's close ties to Israel made it harder to convince Arab countries to side with the United States against the Soviet Union.

4. As the Cold War drew to an end, the imperative of containing the Soviet Union gave way to two new objectives: combating international terrorism and preventing "rogue" states—such as Libya, Iran, and Iraq—from challenging U.S. policies in the region.

5. Following the terrorist attacks of September 11, 2001, however, Americans disagreed over whether seeking "regime change" in Iraq would advance, or detract from, the effort to defeat al-Qa'ida.

D. The fourth theme is increasing antagonism between Americans and Middle Easterners.

   1. In the early decades of the twentieth century, the United States had a relatively benign reputation in the Arab world.

   2. As the United States emerged as a superpower, however, and began wielding powers in ways that conflicted with the interests of many Middle Easterners, much of the goodwill turned to bitter resentment.

   3. The United States played a key role in bringing the state of Israel into being, a development that infuriated the Arab world, especially as it resulted in the uprooting of an existing Palestinian Arab society.

   4. Americans, for their part, have always harbored Orientalist stereotypes of Arabs and Muslims, but in the early-twentieth century, those stereotypes were often romanticized and benign.

   5. In more recent decades, however, popular American images of Middle Easterners became far more threatening.

   6. Americans and Middle Easterners have drawn ever closer to each other in recent years as more Americans have lived and worked in the Middle East and more Middle Easterners have emigrated to the United States.

   7. It is hard to avoid the conclusion, however, that in the aftermath of September 11, negative impressions, on both sides, significantly outweigh the positive ones.

II. In the late-nineteenth and early-twentieth centuries, two simultaneous developments—the accelerating decline of the Ottoman Empire and the emergence of the United States as a world power—created the conditions for increased U.S. involvement in the Middle East.

   A. For several centuries before 1900, almost all the societies of the Middle East were under the control of the Ottoman Empire.

   B. For the last two or three centuries, the power of the Ottoman Empire had begun to decline relative to that of the European powers.

1. In the nineteenth century, a number of those powers, especially Britain and France, had started to encroach on portions of the empire, though in many cases, Ottoman authority remained formally intact.
2. Iran enjoyed nominal independence, but it was heavily dominated by Russia and Britain.

III. In the nineteenth century, the U.S. government had no real interest in the politics of the Middle East.

   A. The government did, however, have an obligation to protect the lives and property of American citizens who traveled or lived in that region.

   B. Of these Americans, Protestant missionaries made up the largest and most prominent single group. They lived and worked throughout the lands of the Ottoman Empire and, to a lesser extent, in Iran.

   C. In the second half of the nineteenth century, most of the attention the U.S. government devoted to the Middle East was aimed at ensuring that local governments did not trample on the rights of these American missionaries.

IV. In the early years of the twentieth century, however, the U.S. government began to involve itself in political questions in the Mediterranean region.

   A. A case in point was the Moroccan crisis of 1905–1906, in which France and Germany vied for influence in that country.

   B. In early 1906, Roosevelt convened an international conference over Morocco in Algeciras, Spain, the outcome of which was a general affirmation of France's dominant position in Morocco.

   C. For Roosevelt, the substance of the dispute was far less important than the opportunity for the United States to signal its growing willingness to take part in great-power deliberations, even in an area as peripheral to American concerns as the Mediterranean region.

V. In the following decade, the United States would thrust itself into great-power diplomacy over the Middle East itself. The occasion for this involvement would be the political disruptions resulting from the First World War.

A. To a considerable degree, World War I has its origins in the Near and Middle East.

    1. The Balkan crisis that sparked World War I was intimately connected to the simultaneous unraveling of two major empires, the Ottoman Empire and the Austro-Hungarian Empire.

    2. The combination of growing instability in the Balkans with the existence of a rigid European alliance system eventually sparked the First World War.

B. In the summer of 1914, Archduke Francis Ferdinand of Austria was assassinated by a Serbian militant with informal links to the Serbian government. The resulting crisis activated the mutual security obligations among the major powers, plunging all of Europe into war.

C. In late 1914, Turkey joined the war on the side of Germany and Austria, causing the conflagration to spread to the Middle East.

VI. World War I had a devastating effect on Middle Eastern societies, less from the battlefield carnage itself than from the immense demographic and economic dislocations the war brought about.

A. Hundreds of thousands of people were uprooted from their homes, forced into exile, or in some cases, subject to mass killings.

B. Millions more fell victim to poverty, famine, and disease because the war effort disrupted trade, transportation, and sanitation systems throughout the Ottoman Empire.

C. These dislocations would contribute to the collapse of the Ottoman Empire as a whole.

D. That collapse, in turn, would bring Washington into the center of great-power deliberations over the political fate of the Middle East.

Suggested Reading:

Daniel, Robert L. *American Philanthropy in the Near East, 1820–1960*. Athens, OH: Ohio University Press, 1970.

Hourani, Albert. *A History of the Arab Peoples*. London: Faber and Faber, 1991.

Little, Douglas. *American Orientalism: The United States and the Middle East Since 1945*. Chapel Hill: University of North Carolina Press, 2002.

Questions to Consider:

1. In what ways did the accelerating decline of the Ottoman Empire set the stage for increased American involvement in the Middle East?

2. What developments in nineteenth-century American life—cultural, political, industrial, and economic—caused Americans to take an increasing interest in Middle Eastern affairs?

Turkish Ottoman Empire circa 1914

Lecture One—Transcript
A Meeting of Two Worlds

This is the first of twenty-four lectures on the United States and the Middle East, covering the period 1914-2001. We begin in 1914 because that year marked the start of World War I, the conflict that resulted in the collapse of the Turkish Ottoman Empire, and thus in the emergence of many of the present-day states in the Middle East. World War I also was the event that drew the United States, for the first time, into great-power deliberations over the political fate of Middle Eastern countries. To be sure, the United States soon returned to its previous position of aloofness from Middle Eastern affairs, but in the 1940s it again became vitally interested in the political life of the Middle East, a posture it has maintained ever since.

We end in 2001 because it was on September 11 of that year that the territory of the United States came under devastating attack, by a band of shadowy terrorists, most of them Saudis, presuming to act on behalf of an aggrieved Muslim world. This attack put an end to the sense of physical security and impregnability that Americans had experienced for most of the nation's history.

The eight and a half decades lying between these two milestones represent a remarkable transformation in America's role in the Middle East, from a rising power with enormous potential for world leadership, but with little official interest in the political fate of the Middle East, to a world colossus so prominent in the political, economic, and cultural life of the Middle East that it was the unquestioned target of those bent on attacking the West for its perceived offenses against Islam. How we got from there to here, and what that evolution tells us about American politics and society, will be among the central questions of this lecture series. There are, of course, no easy answers to such questions, and I certainly won't attempt any glib answers here. Instead, I'll be presenting a narrative history of U.S. political involvement in the Middle East in the eight-plus decades following 1914, hoping to do so within a framework that allows you to seek answers of your own to these questions and to others like them.

Although the structure of the course is mainly chronological, four central themes recur throughout the lectures. What I'm going to do in this lecture is discuss those four themes, and then turn to the historical background for U.S.-Middle Eastern relations after 1914, looking mainly at the late-nineteenth and early-twentieth centuries.

The first theme of the course is the growing involvement of the United States in the affairs of the Middle East, a consequence of America's increasing global power. In the first four decades of the twentieth century, U.S. interests in the Middle East were almost entirely missionary, philanthropic, educational, and commercial. A brief exception to this rule was the flurry of activity immediately following World War I, when President Woodrow Wilson did become involved in the postwar political settlement in the Middle East. Wilson's vision was quickly rejected by the American body politic, and in the 1920s and 1930s, the United States reverted to a position of political aloofness from the affairs of most foreign countries, including those of the Middle East.

All this started to change with America's entry into World War II, which caused U.S. officials, for the first time, to see the geopolitical orientation of the Middle East as vital to American national security. During the war, U.S. military forces occupied large portions of the Middle East, turning Iran into a corridor for supplying the Soviet Union, and North Africa into a staging area for invading fascist Italy. After 1945, the Middle East remained vital to U.S. security, both as a staging area for a possible war against the Soviet Union, America's new adversary, and as a source of oil for Western Europe and Japan, America's new Cold War allies.

The United States did not, however, begin the postwar period as the preeminent Western power in the Middle East; that distinction belonged to Great Britain, which had long been an imperial power in the region. For the first decade of the Cold War era, the United States generally supported Britain's position as the Western standard-bearer in the Middle East. But following the Suez crisis of 1956—which demonstrated that Britain was no longer up to the job—Washington stepped in to take London's place.

A far more hostile contender for Middle Eastern influence (at least as far as the United States was concerned) was the Soviet Union, whose territory was adjacent to that of several Middle Eastern states. For another couple decades following the Suez crisis, the United States and the Soviet Union vied for political and strategic advantage in the Middle East. In the mid-1970s, however, the Soviet position in the region began to decline, foreshadowing, and in a small way contributing to, the demise of the Soviet system in the early 1990s. With the end of the Cold War, the United States has emerged as the sole remaining superpower, wielding unparalleled power and influence over Middle Eastern affairs.

The second theme of the course is Middle Easterners' ongoing quest for political independence and self-mastery. In the early decades of the twentieth century, Turks, Arabs, Jews, Iranians, and Kurds sought to gain political control over portions of the region, often in opposition to the imperial agendas of European powers. By mid-century, most of these groups, with some important exceptions, had succeeded in establishing formal national independence, but Middle Easterners remained preoccupied with combating external domination, real and perceived.

After 1945, as the United States grew more involved in the region's affairs, it increasingly became the object of indigenous resentment. In Iran and the Arab world in the 1950s and 1960s, secular nationalists resisted American pressure to side with the West against the Soviet Union, insisting on their right to enjoy profitable relations with both Cold War blocs. Arab nationalists, in particular, tried to defeat or contain Israel, which they saw as an instrument of Western power. By the 1970s, secular nationalism was a declining force in Arab and Iranian affairs, increasingly giving way to political Islam, whose rejection of Western influence was far more profound. In the decades since, Islamists have been generally unsuccessful at seizing state power (the Iranian revolution is the major exception to this rule), but they have posed a formidable challenge both to the United States and to existing regimes in the region.

Of all the Middle Eastern nations, Israel and Turkey have enjoyed the closest relations with the United States. Israel has long had a special relationship with the United States, a friendship borne of sentiment, cultural affinity, domestic politics, and strategic calculation. Turkey is the only Middle Eastern member of NATO, an alliance it joined in the early 1950s. Yet these countries, too, have sometimes chafed under Washington's restraints on their freedom of action. Israel's military operations against neighboring Arab countries, and its occupation of Arab lands taken in the Six-Day War of 1967, have frequently aroused Washington's ire, though such criticism has grown milder in recent years. Turkey's attempts to put down internal Kurdish rebellions, or to limit the activities of Kurds in neighboring countries like Iraq, have also elicited occasional American criticism.

The third theme is the difficulty the United States has experienced in balancing among diverse, and sometimes conflicting, interests and objectives in the Middle East. During World War I, Woodrow Wilson championed the principle of national self-determination, showing little sympathy for Britain's and France's imperial ambitions in the Middle East. Once the war ended, however, Wilson found that he needed British and French cooperation on other matters, so he allowed those two countries to continue to dominate the Middle East under the guise of League of Nations mandates. During World War II, U.S. officials had genuine sympathy for the nationalist aspirations of colonial peoples throughout the world. But in the Middle East, as elsewhere, Washington invariably suppressed that sympathy when it conflicted with the successful prosecution of the war.

After 1945, America's primary objectives in the region were securing Western access to Middle Eastern oil, preventing the Soviet Union from reaping political or strategic advantage in the area, and ensuring Israel's security. Pursuing the last of these objectives often complicated the pursuit of the other two. Washington's close relations with Israel generated anti-American sentiment in the Arab world, providing the Soviet Union with opportunities to increase its political influence in the region. A similar conflict of objectives occurred during the Arab-Israeli War of 1973, when President Richard M. Nixon airlifted military supplies to Israel to keep it from suffering a military defeat at the hands of Syria and Egypt. Nixon's airlift deeply angered the Arab world, and a number of oil-producing Arab states retaliated by imposing an embargo on oil shipments to the United States, causing major dislocations in the global economy.

As the Cold War drew to an end, the imperative of containing the Soviet Union gave way to two new objectives: combating international terrorism and preventing "rogue" states—like Libya, Iran, and Iraq—from challenging U.S. policies in the region. Both of these objectives acquired fresh urgency following the terrorist attacks of September 11, 2001, but Americans disagreed over whether the two goals could, or should, be pursued simultaneously. While President George W. Bush argued that the necessity of disarming Iraq (and perhaps overthrowing its government as well) could not be separated from the effort to defeat Osama bin Laden's al-Qa'ida network, others insisted that Bush's preoccupation with Iraq was diverting precious energy and resources from the war against al-Qa'ida. As in previous decades, Washington could find no easy formulas for pursuing its diverse objectives in the Middle East.

The fourth and final theme is the ever-growing antagonism between Americans and Middle Easterners, one of the most striking—and tragic—transformations to have occurred in U.S.-Middle East relations over the last century. In the first four decades of the twentieth century, the United States had a relatively benign reputation among Middle Easterners, who appreciated that the United States had no imperial ambitions in the Middle East, and who were grateful for the educational, philanthropic, and humanitarian services Americans provided in the region.

At mid-century, however, as the United States emerged as a global superpower, much of that goodwill began turning into resentment. The United States played a key role in bringing the state of Israel into being, a development that infuriated the Arab world, especially as it resulted in the uprooting of an existing Palestinian Arab society. America never regained the Arab goodwill it had enjoyed prior to Israel's creation. In more recent decades, as Washington has enclosed Israel in an ever tighter embrace—essentially underwriting its continuing occupation of Arab lands—Arab anger has turned increasingly bitter, occasionally finding outlet in terrorist violence. Further to the east, U.S. support for the authoritarian Shah of Iran antagonized two generations of Iranians, fueling an anti-Western and anti-American revolution that would challenge and complicate U.S. policy for decades.

The attacks of September 11 served as a wake-up call, of course, first by alerting ordinary Americans to the existence of a shadowy network of terrorists—transnational, but largely emanating from the Middle East—committed to the destruction of the United States and its allies, and second by calling attention to a dramatic rise in anti-American sentiment throughout the Arab and Muslim worlds, as documented by numerous public opinion surveys conducted in those regions in the months following 9/11. In explaining their negative views of the United States, respondents cited America's alliance with

Israel, its support for authoritarian regimes in the Middle East, and its increasing willingness to use military force in the region.

On the American side, one can also detect a rising tide of suspicion and anger directed at the dominant cultures of the Middle East. Orientalist stereotypes of Arabs and Muslims have long proliferated in American culture, but in the early years of the twentieth century those images were often benign, romanticizing Middle Easterners and their way of life as often as they vilified them. It was only in later years, as the substance of U.S.-Middle Eastern relations grew angrier and more violent, that popular images of Middle Easterners became uniformly threatening. For a quarter century prior to September 11, the figure of the Arab or Muslim terrorist—bent on attacking American society at its most vulnerable points—was a stock character in American popular culture. One of the many secondary tragedies of September 11 was that the attacks so vividly confirmed this frightening image, making it harder for Americans to see Middle Easterners in anything but the most threatening light.

There are, of course, some important exceptions to the general rule of growing mutual antagonism between Americans and Middle Easterners. The state of Israel has always been popular with Americans, not just with American Jews, who see Israel as a haven and homeland for their co-religionists the world over, but with many non-Jews as well, who see in the founding of the Jewish state a heroic reenactment of America's own pioneer origins. It's also true that Washington enjoys close and cooperative relations with numerous other Middle Eastern governments, though increasingly, in many cases, that cooperation has flown in the face of popular opinion in the region.

There are numerous other ways, of course, in which Americans and Middle Easterners have moved closer to each other, achieving a level of mutual understanding that would have been impossible a few decades earlier. Tens of thousands of Americans have lived and worked in the Middle East, and hundreds of thousands of Middle Easterners have immigrated to the United States, altering the texture of American cultural life. Islam has become one of the major religions in the United States, and is routinely recognized as such in official functions and ceremonies. In Middle Eastern countries, meanwhile, American popular culture is widely consumed, admired, and emulated.

So perhaps it would be more accurate to say that Americans and Middle Easterners have drawn ever closer to each other in recent years, and that their increasing proximity has led to simultaneous increases in both conflict and cooperation, in both enmity and understanding. Yet it's hard to avoid the conclusion that, in the aftermath of September 11, the negative impressions significantly outweigh the positive ones.

Those are the main themes that will be recurring throughout the lectures of this course. By way of further background, let me now make some brief remarks on the historical background of U.S. involvement in the Middle East after 1914.

In the late-nineteenth and early-twentieth centuries, two simultaneous developments—the accelerating decline of the Ottoman Empire and the emergence of the United States as a world power—created conditions for increased U.S. involvement in the Middle East. For several centuries, almost all of the societies of the Middle East—and some societies in southeastern Europe as well—were under the control of the Ottoman Empire, based in Turkey. For the last two or three centuries, the power of the Ottoman Empire had begun to decline relative to that of the European powers, and in the nineteenth century, a number of those powers, especially Britain and France, had started to encroach on portions of the empire, even though in many cases Ottoman authority remained formally intact.

Much of North Africa came under French domination, and France's cultural influence spread into Syria and Lebanon. Britain placed Egypt under military occupation and turned a number of sheikdoms on the Arabian Peninsula into military protectorates. Also in the nineteenth century, a handful of nations in southeast Europe—like Greece, Bulgaria, and Serbia—won their independence from the weakening Empire. Further to the east, the ancient nation of Persia, or Iran, enjoyed nominal independence but was heavily dominated by two European empires, Russia and Britain.

As I indicated, at the start of the twentieth century, the U.S. government had no real interest in the politics of the Middle East. The government did, however, have an obligation to protect the lives and property of American citizens who traveled or lived in that region—be they tourists, businessmen, philanthropists, or missionaries. Of these Americans, Protestant missionaries comprised the largest and most prominent single group; they lived and worked throughout the lands of the Ottoman Empire and, to a lesser extent, in Iran. From the mid-nineteenth century till the early-twentieth century, most of the attention the U.S. government devoted to the Middle East was aimed at ensuring that local governments did not trample on the rights of these American missionaries.

Sometimes, much to the irritation of U.S. officials, missionaries would get into serious trouble, forcing their government to intervene. In the mid-1890s, for example, the Ottoman government sponsored a series of pogroms against Turkey's Armenian population, a smaller-scale version of the anti-Armenian massacres that were to occur during World War I. Many fleeing Armenians took refuge in the homes and schools of American missionaries, and in the course of the rampages, some missionary property was destroyed. The missionaries were outraged, and they began pressuring the U.S. government to force the Turkish government to pay them compensation for their damaged property. The U.S. government obliged and got the Turks to agree to pay the missionaries $100,000 indemnity. But then the Turkish government, already in debt to a number of European countries, began dragging its feet, using its labyrinthine bureaucracy to frustrate the missionaries in their attempt to collect.

Once again, the missionaries descended on their own government, demanding that it force the Turkish government to pay the indemnity. Washington would have liked to forget the whole matter, but the missionaries were incredibly persistent and refused to let the matter die. Finally, in 1900, five years after the initial destruction of missionary property, the U.S. government succumbed to the pressure and sent a U.S. naval vessel to the port of Smyrna, on Turkey's Western coast. Officially, the ship was paying a friendly visit, but its presence in Turkish waters was meant to be vaguely threatening, a polite form of gunboat diplomacy, if you will. The Turks got the message and finally coughed up $100,000.

Another missionary imbroglio occurred in Iran in 1904, when an American missionary was murdered by Kurdish tribesmen, some of whom fled across the border into Turkey. The missionary community was incensed by the killing and demanded that the American consul in Iran take action. The consul convinced the Iranian government to send an expeditionary force into Turkey to capture the culprits; indeed, the consul was so zealous that he accompanied the search party himself. The Turkish government responded to the Iranian invasion by launching a counter-invasion of Iran.

Now the Iranian government complained to the U.S. government, saying, in effect, "This is all your fault. If the American consul hadn't pressured us to go after the Kurdish tribesmen, Turkey never would have attacked us." The Iranians demanded that the Americans pay them $100,000 in compensation, which the Americans refused to do. Eventually the crisis died down, but it was an indication of how burdensome the missionary community could be on the U.S. government.

In these episodes, and in numerous other ones, the U.S. government became embroiled in Middle Eastern controversies, but it did so solely to protect American citizens, not because it had any interest in Middle Eastern politics. This aloofness started to diminish in the early years of the twentieth century, as the U.S. government began to involve itself in political questions in the Mediterranean region.

In the Spanish-American War of 1898, the United States had made its debut as a major power on the world stage, stripping Spain of its imperial holdings in the Caribbean and the Philippines. The United States grew even more assertive during the administration of Theodore Roosevelt, who served from 1901 to 1909. Roosevelt asserted American power in ways that would have been unimaginable just a few years earlier.

A case in point was the Moroccan crisis of 1905-1906. Morocco had been under French domination since the mid-nineteenth century. In 1905, Kaiser William II of Germany tried to encroach on France's position in Morocco by pledging to support the Moroccan sultan in his struggle against the French. France condemned Germany's move, and Europe was thrown into an uproar. In early 1906, Roosevelt convened an international conference in Algeciras, Spain. The conference resulted in a general affirmation of France's dominant position in Morocco. For Roosevelt, however, the substance of the dispute was far less important than the opportunity for the United States to signal its growing willingness to take part in great-power deliberations, even in an area as peripheral to American concerns as the Mediterranean region.

In the following decade, the United States would thrust itself into great-power diplomacy over the Middle East itself. The occasion for this involvement would be the political disruptions from the First World War. To a considerable degree, World War I has its origins in the Near East—in particular, in the political crises resulting from the decline of the Ottoman Empire. You've probably heard it said that World War I was sparked by a crisis in the Balkans. This is certainly true, and that Balkan crisis was intimately connected to the simultaneous unraveling of two major empires, the Ottoman Empire and the Austro-Hungarian Empire.

For centuries, the Balkan countries had been under Ottoman domination. As Ottoman control began loosening in the late-nineteenth century, the subject peoples of the Balkans began agitating for political independence. This posed a serious problem for Austria-Hungary, because many of its own subject peoples were Slavs who wanted to gain independence from the Austro-Hungarian Empire and unite with the Slavic peoples of the Balkans. Austria-Hungary was unwilling to grant independence to the Slavs for fear of encouraging other subject peoples in the empire to begin demanding independence as well.

It was the combination of this growing instability in the Balkans with the existence of a rigid European alliance system that eventually sparked the First World War. For Serbia, which had gained its independence from the Ottoman Empire in the late-nineteenth century, had an alliance with Russia, which in turn had alliances with France and Britain; Austria-Hungary, Serbia's enemy, had an alliance with Germany. Whenever Serbia and Austria came into conflict with each other, a frequent occurrence in the early years of the twentieth century, they risked drawing in the major powers of Europe.

That's exactly what happened in the summer of 1914. After the Austrian Archduke Francis Ferdinand and his wife were assassinated in Sarajevo by a Serbian militant with informal links to the Serbian government, Austria declared war on Serbia. Russia came to Serbia's aid and began mobilizing for war against Austria, prompting Germany, Austria's ally, to declare war on Russia. When France showed signs of supporting Russia, Germany declared war on France, and shortly thereafter Britain declared war on Germany. Now all of Europe was at war.

In late 1914, Turkey, which had developed close ties to Germany, joined the war on the side of Germany and Austria, causing the conflagration to spread to the Middle East. World War I would have a devastating effect on Middle Eastern societies, less from the battlefield carnage itself than from the immense demographic and economic dislocations brought about by the war. Hundreds of thousands of people were uprooted from their homes, forced into exile, or—in the case of the Armenians of Turkey—subject to mass murder. Millions more fell victim to poverty, famine, and disease because the war disrupted trade, transportation, and sanitation systems throughout the Ottoman Empire, a situation exacerbated by the economic blockade that the Allies imposed on the empire.

These dislocations would, by war's end, contribute to the collapse of the Ottoman Empire as a whole. As we'll see in the next lecture, that collapse, in turn, would bring Washington into the center of great-power deliberations over the political fate of the Middle East.

Lecture Two
Wilson and the Breakup of the Ottoman Empire

Scope:

In this lecture, we discuss President Woodrow Wilson's actions in the Middle East during and immediately following World War I. We begin with U.S. policy toward the Middle East during the war, paying special attention to three major issues: the Armenian crisis, Zionism, and European imperialism. We then proceed to the immediate postwar period, in which the same three issues continue to define Washington's approach to the Middle East. In examining both wartime and postwar American policy, we see how Wilson's attachment to the principle of national self-determination, and the ethnocentrism with which he defined the concept, drove his efforts to shape the postwar settlement in the Middle East. The lecture ends with the U.S. Senate's rejection of Wilson's internationalist vision and with America's withdrawal from active involvement in world politics.

Outline

I. Generally speaking, it was not until World War II that the United States began following systematic and sustained "policies" toward the Middle East. There was, however, one important exception to this rule: the American experience during and immediately following World War I.

   A. In the late 1910s, President Wilson did become deeply interested in the political disposition of the countries of the Middle East.

   B. He made a brief but intensive effort to influence the postwar settlement that the victorious powers of Europe imposed on the region.

   C. Wilson's effort failed, however, when key segments of the American body politic rejected his ambitious agenda.

II. Throughout World War I, the U.S. government saw events in the Middle East as a sideshow to the main action in Europe. But there were three main issues that forced the United States to pay close attention to the Middle East: the Armenian question, Zionism, and European imperialism.

A. The first issue surrounded the Turkish government's crushing of an Armenian uprising in 1915, which resulted in the death or displacement of hundreds of thousands of Turkish Armenians. American missionaries played a key role in addressing this humanitarian catastrophe.

    1. The Armenians were a Christian people whose ancient homeland had been swallowed up by Turkey and Russia. The Turkish government attack on its Armenian population was, at least at first, a byproduct of warfare on the Turkish-Russian front in World War I.

    2. In Turkey, American missionaries established temporary hospitals and shelters and distributed food among the starving refugees.

    3. In the United States, missionary organizations and other sympathetic groups conducted a massive campaign to call attention to the Armenians' plight and solicit donations for their relief.

B. The second issue that drew the United States into Middle Eastern affairs was Zionism.

    1. In 1917, Zionist leaders convinced the British government to issue a statement, known as the Balfour Declaration, proclaiming Britain's support for "the establishment in Palestine of a national home for the Jewish people."

    2. The U.S. government played a role, albeit a passive one, in the issuing of this declaration.

    3. At the urging of Supreme Court Justice Louis Brandeis, Wilson told the British he supported the proposed declaration, emboldening them to issue it.

    4. In endorsing the Balfour Declaration, Wilson apparently gave little consideration to the possibility that establishing a "national home for the Jewish people in Palestine" might conflict with the concept of national self-determination—a principle that Wilson would soon present to the world as an indispensable ingredient in a just and stable world order.

C. The third issue that drew the Wilson administration into Middle Eastern affairs was that of European imperialism.

    1. The Bolsheviks denounced World War I as an imperialist conflict and, to prove their claim, published a document discovered in the Czech archives detailing a secret 1916 agreement between Britain and France, the Sykes-Picot Agreement, a postwar plan whereby Britain and France would carve up the territory of the Ottoman Empire and add it to their own empires.

2. On entering the war, Wilson was eager to demonstrate that the conflict was not simply a squabble over imperial spoils. In 1918, he issued his famous Fourteen Points, partly to answer the Bolshevik critique.

3. Point Twelve of the Fourteen Points called for the breakup of the Ottoman Empire.

4. Wilson said that Turkey proper should remain a sovereign state, but that the empire's non-Turkish components should be assured "an absolutely unmolested opportunity of autonomous development."

III. Immediately after the war, U.S. policy toward the Middle East continued to be defined by the same three issues, European imperialism, Zionism, and the Armenian question. Each of these issues revealed both the power and the limitations of Wilson's conception of national self-determination.

A. The issues of European imperialism and Zionism arose simultaneously in 1919, when Wilson sent a special commission to the Middle East, known as the King-Crane Commission, to ascertain the political aspirations of the native inhabitants. The King-Crane Commission reached two major conclusions:

1. It found that the people of Syria were implacably opposed to the establishment of a French mandate over Syria. The Syrians' first choice was immediate Syrian independence; failing that, they preferred an American mandate over Syria, with a British mandate coming in as a distant third choice.

2. The commission also concluded that the Zionist program could not be implemented without resulting in the "complete dispossession of the present non-Jewish inhabitants of Palestine." This would be a "gross violation" of the principle of national self-determination.

B. Despite the findings of the King-Crane Commission, the Wilson administration endorsed the following League of

Nations decisions, suggesting the limitations of Wilson's commitment to national self-determination.

1. France would be awarded a single mandate over Syria and Lebanon.
2. Britain would receive separate mandates over Iraq, Transjordan, and Palestine.
3. Britain would implement the Balfour Declaration in Palestine.
4. Of all the Arab nations east of Egypt, only Saudi Arabia was to receive immediate independence.

C. The Armenian issue resurfaced in 1919–1920, when Britain and France urged the United State to assume two mandates on Turkish territory.

1. The first mandate would be over Constantinople and the Turkish straits.
2. The second mandate would be over a separate Armenian republic to the east, carved out of eastern Turkey.

D. Wilson steered clear of Constantinople and the straits, but he did request U.S. Senate approval for an Armenian mandate. The U.S. Senate rejected this proposal, along with Wilson's more general vision of active American involvement in world affairs.

E. With the United States refusing to assume the Turkish mandates, the burden reverted to Britain and France.

F. Neither country, however, was interested in occupying Turkey, and the proposed Turkish mandates were abandoned altogether.

G. The 1923 Treaty of Lausanne freed Turkey of allied occupation. Turkey, now under the leadership of Mustafa Kamal (later Ataturk), regained control over Armenia and the straits.

H. The postwar settlement that emerged in 1922 is of crucial importance because it established territorial boundaries that, with few exceptions, would become permanent frontiers.

I. By this time, the United States had all but forsworn political involvement in the Middle East, a position it would maintain for the next two decades.

Suggested Reading:

DeNovo, John A. *American Interests and Policies in the Middle East, 1900–1939*. Minneapolis: University of Minnesota Press, 1963.

Fromkin, David. *A Peace to End All Peace: Creating the Modern Middle East, 1914–1922*. New York: H. Holt, 1989.

Questions to Consider:

1. What three issues forced Americans to pay closer attention to Middle Eastern affairs during World War I?
2. How faithfully did Woodrow Wilson adhere to the principle of national self-determination in the Middle East?

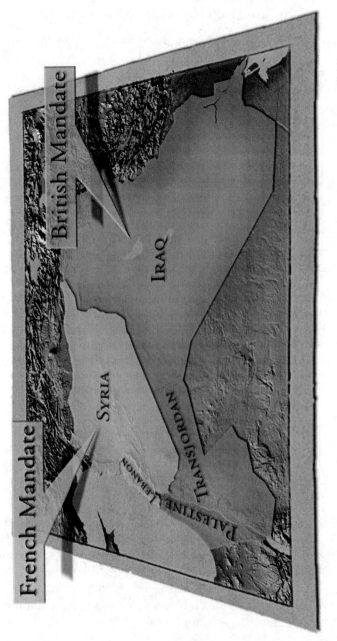

Outcome of San Remo Conference, 1920

French Mandate

British Mandate

SYRIA

LEBANON

PALESTINE

TRANSJORDAN

IRAQ

27

Lecture Two—Transcript
Wilson and the Breakup of the Ottoman Empire

In this lecture, we'll examine American policy toward the Middle East in the late 1910s. Generally speaking, it was not until World War II that the United States began following systematic and sustained "policies" toward the Middle East. There was an important exception to this rule: the American experience during and immediately following World War I.

In the late 1910s, President Wilson did become deeply interested in the political disposition of the countries of the Middle East, and he made a brief but intensive effort to influence the postwar settlement that the victorious powers of Europe imposed on the region. Unfortunately for Wilson, key segments of the American body politic rejected his ambitious agenda, and by the early 1920s the United States had all but forsworn political involvement in the Middle East, a position it would maintain for the next two decades.

The United States did not enter World War I until 1917. Even then it confined itself to declarations of war against Germany and Austria; it never declared war against Turkey. This decision was partly a response to lobbying efforts by American Protestant missionaries, who feared that war with Turkey would bring an end to their activities within the Ottoman Empire, and perhaps even endanger the lives of American missionaries. The absence of formal war between the United States and Turkey did make it easier for American missionaries to function inside the empire, and throughout the war they provided invaluable relief services to thousands of Middle Easterners afflicted by the war and its effects. Occasionally, American missionaries were granted privileges denied to citizens of countries with which Turkey was at war.

When the Turkish government banned all use of the English language—because this was the language of Turkey's enemy Great Britain—the U.S. ambassador intervened, pointing out that banning English would also affect citizens of the United States, with which Turkey was not at war. The Turkish government issued a special edict saying that, while the ban on English remained in effect, use of the "American language" was still permissible. From Washington's perspective, events in the Middle East were a sideshow to the main action in Europe. But there were three main issues that forced the

United States to pay close attention to the region. These were the Armenian issue, the Zionist issue, and the issue of European imperialism. Each of these three issues would occupy the United States in the immediate postwar period as well.

Let's look at the Armenian question first. The Armenians were a Christian people whose ancient homeland had been swallowed up by Turkey and Russia. In 1914, about two million Armenians lived in Turkey, mostly in the east. The Turkish government's attack on its Armenian population was, at least at first, a by-product of warfare on the Turkish-Russian front. After entering the war in late 1914, Turkey attempted to invade the Russian-controlled Caucasus. The offensive was a fiasco: the Russians not only repelled the advance but launched an invasion of their own into eastern Turkey. The Russian counteroffensive was aided by some of the Armenians living in eastern Turkey.

The Turkish government responded to this last development by launching a brutal campaign against the Armenians. In the areas of eastern Turkey still under government control, Turkish authorities rounded up all the Armenians they could find and forced them to march into the interior, where they could no longer assist the Russian invaders. In numerous instances, Turkish soldiers and police summarily executed all Armenian males over fifteen years of age; women and girls were raped and sometimes murdered as well. Many others perished on the month-long trek into the interior, falling victim to disease, starvation, exposure, or attacks by roaming bandits. Reliable figures are elusive, but apparently over one million Armenians died as a result of Turkey's anti-Armenian campaign.

American missionaries in Turkey played a key role in addressing this humanitarian catastrophe, establishing temporary hospitals and shelters and distributing food among the starving refugees. In the United States, missionary organizations conducted a massive campaign to call attention to the Armenians' plight and solicit donations for their relief. From 1915 to 1919, the campaign raised over $30 million, a huge sum in those days.

For the most part, missionaries focused on the plight of the suffering Armenians, rather than on the depravity of their Turkish tormentors. Inevitably, however, the Armenian issue stirred up deep anti-Turkish and anti-Muslim hostility in the United States, perpetuating long-standing stereotypes about "oriental despotism." All too often Americans viewed the situation as a simple case of Muslim persecution of Christians, ignoring the political dimensions of the Armenian crisis, as well as the fact that the war had made victims of many Ottoman Muslims as well.

The second issue that drew the United States into Middle Eastern affairs was Zionism. Since the late-nineteenth century, European Jews had been settling in Palestine, pursuing the Zionist dream of building a homeland for the scattered Jews of the world. Zionism was fueled by the bitter experiences of European Jews, who for centuries had endured brutal persecution, especially in Russia and Eastern Europe. At this time, most Jews in Europe hoped to assimilate into the larger societies in which they found themselves, but a determined minority believed that anti-Semitism was so pervasive that true assimilation was impossible. Jews could never be secure, they argued, until they had acquired a homeland of their own. Although some early Zionists favored establishing a Jewish state in Uganda, which was then a British colony, most Zionists wished to establish their state in Palestine, the site of the ancient kingdom of Israel and the spiritual and cultural homeland for much of the Jewish Diaspora.

Starting in the late-nineteenth century, European Jews began immigrating to Palestine, buying up land and laying the basis for an exclusively Jewish society. These efforts were strongly opposed by Palestinian Arabs, who feared that the creation of such a society would result in their own dispossession. They protested to the Ottoman authorities, who placed intermittent and largely ineffectual restrictions on Jewish land purchases in Palestine. This was where things stood before the First World War began in 1914.

Turkey's entry into the war presented political opportunities to both Arabs and Zionists. In their effort to defeat the Ottoman Empire, the British forged an alliance with Hussein, the Sharif (or governor) of Mecca, in western Arabia. Britain urged Hussein to lead an Arab uprising against the Ottoman Empire. In return, Britain pledged to support the creation of an independent Arab state encompassing much of present-day Saudi Arabia, Iraq, Jordan, and Syria. Hussein accepted the deal and in 1916 launched an Arab revolt against the Ottoman Empire. Hussein's uprising was a minor development, but it did succeed in tying down Turkish troops, making it easier for

Britain to defeat the Ottoman forces and occupy key positions in Palestine and Iraq.

After the war, a dispute would arise over precisely what the British had promised Hussein. Hussein insisted that Palestine was definitely to be included in the promised Arab state; the British maintained that a close reading of the correspondence that they had with Hussein indicated that Palestine was to be excluded. One reason the British took this position after the war was because they had, in the interim, made a separate pledge to the Zionist movement. Throughout 1917, a Zionist leader named Chaim Weizmann lobbied the British government to make a public statement supporting the Zionist project in Palestine. Such a statement, Weizmann said, could greatly aid the British war effort. Not only would it give German Jews an incentive to abandon their support for the German government, it might cause Russian Jews to pressure the Russian government (which seemed in danger of making a separate peace with Germany) to stay in the war on the side of Britain and France.

The British government accepted Weizmann's argument that supporting the Zionist program would aid the allied war effort. The British also calculated that sponsoring a Jewish homeland would serve their strategic interests in the postwar period. A friendly Jewish state would provide the British with a foothold in the Middle East, helping them gain control over the communication and transportation lines between British-occupied Egypt and British-occupied India.

Accordingly, in November 1917, British Foreign Secretary Arthur Balfour issued a public statement declaring that the British government viewed with favor "the establishment in Palestine of a national home for the Jewish people." This so-called Balfour Declaration did not give the Zionists everything they wanted. Instead of a Jewish state, it called for a "national home," and precisely what that meant was unclear. The declaration also indicated that this national home would be *in* Palestine, rather than comprising the whole of it. Still, getting a power of Britain's stature to issue such a statement was a major achievement, and the Zionists were overjoyed.

The U.S. government played a small role in the issuing of the Balfour Declaration. America entered the First World War in the spring of 1917, just about the time that Chaim Weizmann started lobbying the British government to issue a pro-Zionist statement.

Now that the United States was a belligerent, Weizmann wanted an American endorsement of Zionism as well. He enlisted the help of the American lawyer Louis Brandeis, a past president of the Zionist Organization of America who had recently become the first Jewish justice to sit on the U.S. Supreme Court. Brandeis, a friend and advisor to Woodrow Wilson, lobbied the president to give his support to the pro-Zionist statement that Balfour was preparing to deliver.

Wilson had plenty of other matters on his plate at the time, and he never gave the fate of Palestine a great deal of attention. To the extent that Wilson did pay attention to Palestine, he was favorably inclined toward the Zionist cause. Wilson was a devout Christian who saw the Jews' return to ancient Israel as an essential part of biblical prophecy. In October 1917, Wilson gave his blessing to the declaration, which Balfour issued the following month.

In endorsing the Balfour Declaration, Wilson apparently gave little consideration to the possibility that establishing a "national home for the Jewish people in Palestine" might conflict with the concept of national self-determination, the principle that Wilson would soon present to the world as an indispensable ingredient in a just and stable world order. At that time, Jews accounted for only about 10 percent of the population of Palestine, and if the non-Jewish majority were given the right to determine their political future, they would presumably opt for something other than a Jewish national home. How could the United States support self-determination and Zionism simultaneously? This dilemma would resurface in the immediate aftermath of the war.

The third issue that drew the Wilson administration into Middle Eastern affairs was that of European imperialism. In the very same month that Balfour issued his declaration, November 1917, the Bolsheviks seized power in Moscow. Upon taking power, the Bolsheviks called for unconditional negotiations to bring an end to the war, which they denounced as an imperialist conflict. They also proceeded to raid the Czarist archives and publish a large number of secret documents that supported their characterization of the war. One of the most notorious of these documents was a secret 1916 agreement between Britain and France (to which the Czarist government had been privy) known as the Sykes-Picot Agreement, named after the British and French diplomats who had negotiated it.

According to this agreement, after the war, Britain and France would carve up the territory of the Ottoman Empire and add it to their own empires.

The revelation of Sykes-Picot posed a problem for Wilson, who, since taking America into the war, had been trying to portray the conflict as a struggle for democracy. In January 1918, Wilson made a speech to Congress in which he outlined his own terms for ending the war. These terms were known collectively as the Fourteen Points. Wilson unveiled the Fourteen Points partly to answer the Bolshevik critique; he hoped to convince the nations and peoples of the world that the war was about something other than imperialist spoils and had a higher political and moral purpose.

In the Fourteen Points, Wilson presented a vision of a postwar order characterized by open trading systems, national self-determination, and the settlement of international disputes through transparent diplomacy, not secret treaties and aggression. Of particular concern to us is Point Twelve, which called for the breakup of the Ottoman Empire. Turkey proper should remain a sovereign state, Wilson said, but the empire's non-Turkish components should be assured "an absolutely unmolested opportunity of autonomous development." In this way, Wilson served notice on the allies that he would not support the carving up of Ottoman lands by victorious imperial powers. He also sought to reassure the Ottoman Empire's Arab subjects that the Sykes-Picot Treaty was not the last word on the empire's postwar disposition. If the Arabs kept fighting alongside Britain, Wilson implied, they would still be rewarded by something approaching political independence.

By the fall of 1918, Germany, Austria-Hungary, and Ottoman Turkey were defeated. Indeed, the strain of war had been so great that the Ottoman Empire, like the Austro-Hungarian Empire, disintegrated. Turkey survived as an individual nation, but its subject nations were stripped away from it and placed under the control of the victorious allies. What should become of those subject nations was one of the major questions that Wilson had to consider as he sailed off to Europe in December 1918 to take part in the postwar conference that the victorious powers held in Paris. The issues Wilson now faced were the essentially the same ones that had confronted him during the war itself—European imperialism, Zionism, and the Armenian question.

The powers that gathered in Paris were confronted with a welter of conflicting claims with respect to the Middle East. Britain and France still hoped to divide up the Ottoman Empire's Arab lands on the basis of the Sykes-Picot agreement. Sharif Hussein and his supporters demanded that those lands become an independent Arab state. The Zionists insisted that Britain fulfill its pledges in the Balfour Declaration and facilitate the establishment of a Jewish homeland in Palestine. The Armenians were calling for an independent state on portions of Turkish and Russian territory.

Initially, Wilson hoped to arrive at a Middle Eastern settlement that honored the principle of autonomy outlined in Point Twelve of his Fourteen Points, but it was difficult to reconcile this hope with Britain's and France's imperialist ambitions. Eventually, the powers reached a compromise: instead of being granted autonomy, the Ottoman Empire's non-Turkish areas would be temporarily administered by the victorious powers until they were ready for independence. Precisely who would administer which area would take a couple years to work out. By then, the United States had withdrawn from active participation in world affairs and had little involvement in the resulting arrangements.

Throughout much of 1919, however, Wilson still expected the United States to be an important player in the Middle East settlement. In the spring of that year he sent an American commission—headed by Henry C. King, the president of Oberlin College, and Charles R. Crane, a businessman and philanthropist—to travel to the region to ascertain the wishes of its native inhabitants. Theoretically, the findings of the King-Crane Commission would help determine what sort of mandate system would be placed over the region. Things didn't quite work out that way.

The King-Crane commission spent several weeks in the Middle East, mostly in Syria and Palestine, meeting with representatives of the various ethnic, religious, and national communities. By the summer of 1919, the commission had arrived at two fundamental conclusions. The first conclusion concerned Syria, which just about everyone assumed would be placed under a French mandate. The King-Crane commission discovered that the Syrians hated the French and were totally opposed to a French mandate over Syria. Over the last several decades, despite the fact that Syria had remained under Ottoman political administration, French cultural and religious institutions had proliferated in Syria, and the Syrians had chafed under this influence. The King-Crane commission reported that while the Syrians' first choice was immediate independence, if there had to be a mandate the Syrians would want it to be an American one, with a British mandate coming in as a distant third choice. A French mandate, however, was out of the question.

The commission's second finding concerned the fate of Palestine. The commission concluded that the Zionist program could not be implemented without causing the "complete dispossession of the present non-Jewish inhabitants of Palestine." This would be a "gross violation" of the principle of national self-determination, which President Wilson had publicly embraced. The commission urged that the Zionist program be abandoned and that Palestine (along with Transjordan, a large swath of territory east of the Jordan River) be joined to the Syrian mandate.

The findings of the King-Crane commission, which were submitted to the U.S. government in August 1919, had no influence on U.S. policy, and thus no impact on the deliberations over the Middle East mandates. The report itself was buried in the State Department archives, not to be made public until 1922, by which time the mandates had already been assigned. For years thereafter, historians sympathetic to the Arab cause would look back with great wistfulness on the King-Crane commission, and especially on its findings concerning Palestine. If only those findings had been implemented, they would say, just think how much bloodshed and violence could have been avoided. Zionist scholars countered that King and Crane, far from being disinterested and open-minded observers, were committed opponents of the Zionist movement, and that Crane in particular was a notorious anti-Semite, which was true.

In one sense, however, the whole question is moot, since the recommendations of the King-Crane commission had no real chance of being implemented. By the time King and Crane submitted their report in August 1919, Wilson's whole program of active involvement in Old World affairs had come under severe attack at home. Wilson's opponents in the U.S. Senate were threatening to reject ratification of the Treaty of Versailles, which had resulted from the Paris Peace Conference. American acceptance of the Treaty of Versailles was the foundation on which the entire edifice of Wilson's foreign policy rested. With much more urgent concerns on his plate, Wilson had little time for Middle Eastern affairs, and he probably never even read the King-Crane Report.

A month after the report was submitted, Wilson suffered a massive stroke that paralyzed half his body, and for the remainder of his presidency he holed up in the White House virtually incommunicado, with his wife, Edith, serving as the sole conduit of information between him and the outside world. Wilson was ill-equipped, to say the least, to exert his personal influence on behalf of the King-Crane Report.

Even if Wilson had remained healthy, it is extremely doubtful that he would have pressured the allies to implement a policy that not only denied the French a mandate in the Middle East, but repudiated a public commitment that the British government had made, and that Wilson himself had endorsed, to support the establishment of a Jewish homeland in Palestine. Indeed, once the U.S. Senate rejected the Treaty of Versailles in the fall of 1919, the United States was in a poor position to exert its influence in any direction. The United States did not even formally participate in the conference at which the final allocations of the mandates were made, the San Remo Conference, held in Italy in the spring of 1920.

At San Remo, the victorious European powers decided to give France a single mandate over Syria and Lebanon and to give Britain separate mandates over Iraq, Transjordan, and Palestine. Included in the British mandate was the obligation to implement the Balfour Declaration. These mandates would operate under the auspices of the League of Nations, the international organization created by the Treaty of Versailles. Of all the Arab nations lying east of Egypt, only Saudi Arabia was to receive immediate independence.

The decisions made at San Remo caused shock and dismay throughout the Arab Middle East. To most politically conscious Arabs, San Remo represented a disgraceful reneging on previous Western pledges of support for Arab independence, be they Britain's promises to Sharif Hussein, or Woodrow Wilson's soaring rhetoric of national self-determination. The Palestinians and the Syrians had clearly communicated their opposition to the Balfour Declaration and to a French mandate over Syria, and yet both projects were being imposed on them anyway. Not for the last time, the Western powers were accused of thwarting the basic political aspirations of the Arab people.

Syria was not the only area over which the United States had been urged to acquire a mandate. Shortly after the mandate system was first proposed, Britain and France began pressuring the United State to assume two mandates in Turkish territory, the first over Constantinople and the Turkish straits, which served as a passageway from the Black Sea to the Mediterranean, the second over a separate Armenian republic to the east, which had declared its independence during the war. Both Britain and France were afraid that Russia, now under Bolshevik leadership, might take advantage of Turkey's weakened state and start encroaching on the Middle East; allied control over Armenia and the straits would help prevent such expansion. But Britain and France were also deeply suspicious of each other. Neither country wanted to permit the other an opportunity to expand its power and influence in the Middle East. Giving the mandates to the United States, which was assumed to be free of imperial ambition in this region, seemed to be the best way around the problem.

Once the Senate rejected the Versailles Treaty in late 1919, it was clear that the United States could not assume responsibility for the Turkish straits, but the idea of establishing a U.S. mandate over Armenia persisted, largely because American missionary groups strongly supported the proposal. In May 1920, an ailing Wilson acceded to missionary pressure and asked the Senate to approve a mandate over Armenia. The Senate promptly rejected the idea.

With the United States refusing to assume the Turkish mandates, the burden reverted to Britain and France. Yet neither Britain nor France had the stomach for the task, which could not be accomplished without an indefinite and draining commitment of forces. For although Turkey had accepted the loss of its empire, it was determined at all costs to resist any encroachments on Turkey proper. The allies abandoned the proposed Turkish mandates and, in late 1920, quietly stood by as Turkey defeated the forces of the Armenian republic, whose territory was absorbed by Turkey and the Soviet Union.

Britain and France continued to occupy Constantinople and the Turkish straits for another couple years, but their presence was strongly resisted by an uprising within the Turkish military led by a dynamic young officer named Mustafa Kemal. In 1923, the allies signed a new treaty with Turkey, the Treaty of Lausanne, which finally freed Turkey of allied occupation. By now, Mustafa Kemal had become Turkey's de facto leader. In late 1922, a national assembly loyal to Kemal convened and formally abolished the Ottoman Sultanate and declared Turkey a republic. Kemal later became president of Turkey, a position he would hold until his death in 1938.

Also in 1922, the British and French mandates were formally established in the Middle East, under the auspices of the newly created League of Nations. As previously agreed, Britain got mandates over Iraq, Palestine, and Transjordan, while France was entrusted with Syria and Lebanon. In Palestine, the British began preparing the ground for an eventual Jewish homeland, facilitating the creation of Zionist state-building institutions and allowing a regular influx of European Jews to immigrate to the country. The postwar settlement that emerged in 1922 is of crucial importance since it established territorial boundaries that, with few exceptions, would become permanent frontiers. The European imperial powers would eventually relinquish their control over the Middle East, but the lines they drew remain with us today.

In all of these developments, the U.S. government had no official involvement, and not even much interest. For, by the start of the 1920s, the American body politic had rejected Wilson's vision of active U.S. involvement in international politics, returning to a posture of political aloofness. But, as we shall see in the next lecture, this isolationist stance extended only to political matters. In an economic sense—and, to some extent, a cultural one—Americans would find themselves bound up as never before in the affairs of the Middle East.

Lecture Three
The Interwar Period

Scope:

Because official U.S. involvement in the Middle East was minimal during the interwar years, this lecture focuses on nonofficial ties between Americans and the Middle East. We begin with the "Arabesque" craze that swept American popular culture in the 1920s, partly a result of the belated publicity surrounding Col. T. E. Lawrence ("Lawrence of Arabia") and his wartime exploits. We learn how films, such as *The Sheik*; songs, such as "The Sheik of Araby"; and dances, such as the "hootchie-cootchie," were aimed at satisfying the Jazz Age appetite for all things Arabian. As we proceed to the 1930s, our focus shifts to the activities of private oil prospectors in Saudi Arabia and to the growing activism of American Zionists in response to Hitler's persecution of German Jews.

Outline

I. Because official U.S. involvement in the Middle East was minimal during the interwar years, this lecture focuses on nonofficial ties between Americans and the Middle East. These ties took the form of popular infatuation with Middle Eastern culture (or at least a stereotyped conception of it) and involvement by private individuals and organizations in Middle Eastern affairs.

   A. World War I had radically changed the face of the Middle East by bringing about the collapse of the Ottoman Empire.

      1. The empire's non-Turkish holdings were stripped away from it and Turkey emerged as a modern republic under the leadership of Mustafa Kemal.

      2. In the 1920s and 1930s, Kemal, who was called Ataturk ("father of the Turks"), launched an ambitious campaign to recast Turkey as a modern, Westernized nation.

   B. The Arab nations that were newly freed from Ottoman control found themselves under the authority of the League of Nations mandates.

      1. France got a single mandate over Syria and Lebanon that remained in place until World War II.

2. Britain received separate mandates over Iraq, Transjordan, and Palestine. Iraq was granted formal independence in 1932, though Britain continued to exercise de facto control over Iraqi decision-making. Transjordan received a similar sort of "independence" in 1946. In Palestine, Britain set about implementing the Balfour Declaration.

3. Egypt was not placed under a formal mandate but remained subject to military occupation by Britain.

C. On the other side of the former Ottoman Empire, Iran came under the rule of an army officer, Reza Khan, who took the name of Reza Shah Pahlavi and sought to implement a program to modernize, Westernize, and secularize Iranian society.

II. The Republican administrations of the 1920s understood that the American public had a low tolerance for international activism.

A. Washington refrained from launching bold initiatives in its own right and, instead, used the private sector, especially American banks, as an instrument of policy.

B. Congress, too, reflected the public's isolationist mood by passing the National Origins Act of 1924, which limited or prohibited immigration into the United States from places other than Northern and Western Europe.

III. In the areas of technology and mass culture, however, Americans were becoming more, not less, connected to the outside world.

A. Radio, cinema, aviation, and cheaper ocean travel afforded Americans greater exposure to foreign lands and cultures.

B. Another reason for the growing cosmopolitanism of American culture was the recent experience of the world war.

1. For a brief but vivid period, hundreds of thousands of Americans had traveled abroad for the first time.

2. American newspapers had been full of lively dispatches about battles, peace conferences, revolutions, epidemics, and famines in faraway lands.

IV. One part of the world that World War I opened up to ordinary Americans was the Middle East.

A. During the war, a number of Arab tribes had mounted an uprising against the Ottoman Empire. A British army intelligence officer named T. E. Lawrence had helped train and advise the Arab tribes.

B. In the latter stages of the war, Lawrence was "discovered" by an American publicist named Lowell Thomas, who traveled to Arabia and spent a few months in Lawrence's company.

C. After the war, Thomas put together a multimedia presentation about Lawrence's exploits that was shown in theaters and lecture halls throughout the English-speaking world.

D. In the United States, the celebrity of "Lawrence of Arabia" helped launch an Arabian craze in the 1920s.

    1. Hip young Americans affected Arab-style dress, crooned Arabesque love ballads, and gyrated to the hootchie-cootchie, a sexually suggestive dance meant to approximate Middle Eastern belly-dancing.

    2. Americans also flocked to "sun and sand" movies, in which swashbuckling heroes rode, fought, and romanced their way across the deserts of Arabia and North Africa.

    3. The biggest star of this genre was an Italian-American actor named Rudolph Valentino, whose elegant gestures and smoldering good looks generated a huge, devoted following, consisting mainly of teenaged girls and young women.

V. To be sure, during the interwar years, America's engagement with Middle Eastern themes was not entirely frivolous.

A. In the 1930s, some of the concerns that would define the post-World War II period began forcing Americans to take a serious look at Middle Eastern events.

B. Two of those issues were Zionism and oil.

VI. During World War I, the Zionist movement had grown rapidly in the United States. After the war, however, American Zionism declined.

A. The improvement of living conditions for Middle Eastern Jews following the end of the war, combined with the issuing of the Balfour Declaration in 1917, convinced many American Zionists that their work was done.

B. The onset of the Great Depression in the early 1930s brought about a further decline in American Zionism. Few American Jews had the resources to devote to Zionist activities.

VII. All this started to change in 1933, when Hitler came to power and began persecuting German Jews.

A. Between 1933 and 1939, roughly one-third of Germany's Jewish population fled the country.

B. Because of the U.S. State Department's strict interpretation of the National Origins Act, however, only about 8500 German Jews were admitted into the United States each year, on average.

C. Other Western countries, too, severely restricted Jewish immigration. They feared that an influx of impoverished and jobless refugees would strain their resources.

VIII. The difficulty of settling German Jews in Western nations brought about a revival of Zionism among American Jews.

A. Like their counterparts in Europe and Palestine, American Zionists pressured Britain to increase the number of European Jews it allowed to enter Palestine each year.

B. Initially, Britain responded favorably to this pressure.

C. In the late 1930s, however, just as the plight of German Jews was becoming truly desperate, Britain began to rethink the wisdom of creating a Jewish state in Palestine, on account of Palestinian Arabs' strenuous opposition to the project.

1. The British government's White Paper of 1939 placed strict limits on Jewish immigration to Palestine

2. The White Paper also announced that such emigration would end in a few years' time.

D. Thus, on the eve of World War II, the Zionist movement appeared to have suffered a crippling blow.

IX. The second major issue that drew Americans into Middle Eastern affairs was oil.

A. The growing importance of the automobile dramatically increased America's reliance on foreign oil. By the 1920s,

American oil companies were launched on an intensive search for reliable overseas reserves.

   1. In 1928, a consortium of American oil companies signed an agreement with three other oil companies—one British, one French, and one Dutch—whereby all four parties pledged to cooperate with one another in exploring for oil in the lands of the former Ottoman Empire.

   2. This *Red Line Agreement* made it possible for American oil companies to extract oil from Iraq, at that time, the only country in the former Ottoman Empire with large, proven oil reserves.

B. In the early 1930s, King Ibn Saud of Saudi Arabia permitted a team of American geologists to conduct a survey of his kingdom.

   1. On the basis of this survey, an American oil company, Standard Oil of California (SOCAL), put in a bid with the Saudi government for an oil concession, which was granted in 1933.

   2. In 1938, geologists working for SOCAL, which had since merged with a number of other American companies, struck oil in Saudi Arabia.

   3. These American oil companies were to enjoy a virtual monopoly on Saudi oil.

   4. Given the magnitude of Saudi reserves, and their implication for American economic and strategic security, it was only a matter of time before the U.S. government stepped in to protect the American oil companies' concession.

   5. This involvement would start to become significant during World War II.

Suggested Reading:

Berman, Aaron. *Nazism, the Jews, and American Zionism*. Detroit: Wayne State University Press, 1990.

Christison, Kathleen. *Perceptions of Palestine: Their Influence on U.S.-Middle East Policy*. Berkeley: University of California Press, 1999 (2000).

Hodson, Joel C. *Lawrence of Arabia and American Culture: The Making of a Transatlantic Legend.* Westport, CT: Greenwood Press, 1995.

Questions to Consider:

1. Why did Middle Eastern culture, or at least a stereotyped version of it, have such wide appeal in American popular culture in the 1920s?

2. How did international events affect the strength and prominence of American Zionism during the interwar period?

Lecture Three—Transcript
The Interwar Period

Today I'm going to talk about the two decades separating World War I and World War II, a period in which official U.S. involvement in the Middle East was minimal, but in which images and ideas about the Middle East were widely circulated in American popular culture. I won't have a great deal to say about events in the Middle East itself, but rather will focus on what was going on within the United States.

Before I talk about that, let me briefly sketch in the political situation in each of the major areas of the Middle East during the interwar period. As we saw law last time, World War I brought about the collapse of the Ottoman Empire. The empire's non-Turkish holdings were stripped away from it, and Turkey emerged as a modern republic under the leadership of Mustafa Kemal, who served as president until his death in 1938. Some years after taking office, Kemal was given the surname Ataturk, which means "father of the Turks." In the 1920s and 1930s, Mustafa Kemal Ataturk launched a remarkably ambitious campaign to recast Turkey as a modern, Westernized nation. He undertook social and educational programs aimed at de-emphasizing Turkey's Middle Eastern and Islamic heritage, in favor of secularism and Turkish nationalism.

As for the Arab nations, newly freed from Ottoman control, they now found themselves under the authority of the League of Nations mandates. France got a single mandate over Syria and Lebanon, while Britain got separate mandates over Iraq, Transjordan, and Palestine. The French mandates remained in place until World War II. Of the British mandates, Iraq was granted formal independence in 1932, but only after it signed a defense treaty with Britain allowing Britain to maintain air bases in the country and to enjoy de facto control over Iraqi decision-making. A similar sort of "independence" would be arranged for Transjordan, though that wouldn't come to pass until 1946, a year after World War II ended. In Palestine, Britain set about the task of implementing the Balfour Declaration, assisting with the establishment of Jewish state-building institutions and permitting a regular flow of European Jews to enter the country.

Egypt had not been placed under a formal mandate, but it remained subject to military occupation by Britain. The British officially recognized Egypt as an independent nation but continued to exert de facto control over its government.

On the other side of the former Ottoman Empire lay Iran, which was formally independent, but had long been dominated by Russia and Britain. In the early 1920s, an army officer named Reza Khan took power in a coup and shortly thereafter crowned himself the monarch of Iran, taking the name Reza Shah Pahlavi. Reza Shah convinced Britain and Russia to withdraw the troops they had stationed in Iran during the war, and throughout the interwar period he was able to play the two powers off against each other such that Iran enjoyed a modicum of genuine independence. Somewhat like Ataturk, though on a less ambitious scale, Reza Shah sought to modernize, Westernize, and secularize Iranian society. With that background out of the way, let's look at the United States during the interwar period, and how events and images from the Middle East helped shape American society and culture.

As we saw last time, in the immediate aftermath of World War I, the U.S. Senate defeated Woodrow Wilson's internationalist agenda; it refused to ratify the Treaty of Versailles and kept America from joining the newly formed League of Nations. In the 1920 presidential election, the American people voted for Warren Harding, an amiable but unimaginative politician who promised the country a "return to normalcy." He meant to say "normality," but language was never Harding's strong point. Harding's election ushered in a dozen years of Republican control of the White House (the next two presidents, Calvin Coolidge and Herbert Hoover, were also Republicans), a period in which the U.S. government kept a low profile in world affairs.

The Republican administrations of the 1920s were hardly unconcerned about international matters, but they understood that the American public had a low tolerance for international activism. Washington refrained from taking bold actions in its own right and instead used the private sector as an instrument of policy. If, for example, the U.S. government decided that a particular country was in need of financial aid, it would encourage American bankers to extend loans to that country, rather than asking Congress to appropriate foreign aid.

Another way in which official policy reflected the public's isolationist mood was in immigration law. In 1924, Congress passed the National Origins Act, which imposed restrictions on future immigration to the United States based on nationality. Each nationality was given a quota based on its percentage of the U.S. population back in 1890. Obviously, this strongly favored those ethnic groups that already comprised the largest percentage of the population, northern European Protestants, while discriminating against those of eastern or southern European origin. The National Origins Act was even harder on people from East Asia, who were barred from entering the country altogether. These restrictive immigration policies would remain substantially in place until the mid-1960s.

For the purposes of the National Origins Act, Middle Easterners were officially regarded as white, so they were not excluded outright in the same way that East Asians were. If you look at the Arab-American press of the 1920s, you'll find that leaders of that community were extremely eager to maintain Arabs' status as whites, since the consequences of losing that status could be socially, legally, and economically devastating. This anxiety was especially pronounced in the American south, where racial discrimination was more formal and pervasive, and where darker skinned Arabs were sometimes mistaken for blacks.

Official whiteness did not, of course, spare Middle Easterners from the quota system, and because people of Middle Eastern origin represented such a small percentage of the U.S. population in 1890, immigration from that region was locked in at a very low level. Not until after the immigration reforms of the mid-1960s would the United States experience the massive influx of Middle Eastern immigrants that has done so much to alter the texture of American life.

For all the political insularity of America in the 1920s, it was impossible to turn back the clock when it came to technology and mass culture, and in these areas, Americans were becoming more, not less, connected to the outside world. Radio and cinema made sounds and images from faraway lands accessible to Americans everywhere, even in the smallest rural communities. Ocean travel was becoming faster, cheaper, and more comfortable, bringing overseas travel, once the preserve of the very rich, within reach of the middle class. By the end of the decade, the pioneers of aviation were conducting transoceanic flights, cutting the traveling distance between the continents to a matter of hours. It would be a few more decades before transoceanic flights became readily accessible to commercial travelers, but the exploits of Charles Lindbergh and other aviators were avidly followed by millions of Americans, expanding their geographical and cultural horizons.

Contributing to Americans' growing cosmopolitanism was the recent experience in the world war. For a brief but vivid period, hundreds of thousands of Americans—soldiers, sailors, engineers, diplomats, relief officials, reporters—had traveled abroad for the first time, and American newspapers had been full of lively dispatches about battles, peace conferences, revolutions, epidemics, and famines in faraway lands. To be sure, the war and its aftermath caused millions of Americans to turn away in disgust, to want nothing to do with such a dangerous and messy world, but it also created a new awareness of international events that could not be wiped away.

One part of the world that World War I opened up to ordinary Americans was the Middle East, especially the Arab world. As we saw in the previous lecture, the allied struggle against the Ottoman Empire had been an important, though secondary, aspect of the overall war effort. An Arab force, under the leadership of Sharif Hussein of Mecca, had mounted an uprising against the Turks, mainly in the deserts of present-day Syria, Jordan, and northern Saudi Arabia. Out of this uprising grew the romantic myth of Lawrence of Arabia. Colonel T.E. Lawrence was a British army intelligence officer sent by his government to the Arabian Desert to help train and advise the Arab tribes taking part in the revolt. Lawrence did make a real contribution to the allied war effort, mainly by helping the Arab tribesmen dynamite Turkish railway lines, but in the grand scheme of things, his role was fairly minor.

Lawrence's relative insignificance did not, however, prevent him from being transformed into a romantic hero. Toward the end of the war, Lawrence was "discovered" by an American publicist named Lowell Thomas. In 1917, the Wilson administration had sent Thomas to Europe to find dramatic stories that would generate public support for the war back home. Thomas spent a few months covering the trench warfare of Europe but, not surprisingly, was unable to come up with any appealing stories. He moved on to the Middle East, where Britain's attempts to capture the Holy Land from the Turks seemed to promise better copy.

In the Middle East, Lowell Thomas learned about Colonel Lawrence and the desert uprising against the Turks. He moved out to the Arabian Desert, spent a few months with Lawrence, and compiled some colorful stories about his exploits. The war ended before the U.S. government could make propaganda use of Thomas's material, but in the early postwar years, Thomas returned to the United States and struck out on his own, putting together a multimedia presentation about Lawrence that was shown in theaters and concert halls across America, and eventually throughout the English-speaking world. Combining lecture, film, music, and slides, Thomas's presentation depicted Lawrence as a dashing hero who had championed the cause of Arab independence and had almost single-handedly defeated the Ottoman armies.

Lawrence of Arabia became a huge celebrity in the United States, his fame rivaling that of Charles Lindbergh. Lawrence's celebrity was partly responsible for launching an Arabian craze in the 1920s, which had hip young Americans affecting Arab-style dress, crooning love ballads like "The Sheik of Araby," and gyrating to the "hootchie-cootchie," a sexually suggestive dance meant to approximate Middle Eastern belly-dancing. Perhaps the most prominent manifestation of the Arabian craze was the spate of "sun and sand" movies, in which swashbuckling heroes rode, fought, and romanced their way across the deserts of Arabia or North Africa. In the 1920s, nearly 90 movies with Arabian themes were produced in the United States, a considerable number given the relative infancy of the medium. The biggest star of this genre was an Italian-American actor named Rudolph Valentino, whose elegant gestures and smoldering good looks generated a huge, devoted following, consisting mainly of teenaged girls and young women.

Valentino's Arabian adventure movies, the most famous of which were *The Sheik* and *Son of the Sheik*, were pretty formulaic. They typically featured a young European or American woman who, while traveling in the Arabian Desert, was abducted by wicked and lust-filled Arab bandits, only to be rescued in the end by the dashing nomadic hero, with whom she had already fallen in love. What made these love stories palatable was the fact that the hero, though living the life of a nomadic Arab, was never actually of Arab blood himself, but was rather a European who, as an infant, had been separated from his true family and raised in the desert. Essentially, what you had were two Western protagonists celebrating their love against an exotic background.

To be sure, during the interwar years America's engagement with Middle Eastern themes was not entirely frivolous; it had its serious side as well. This was especially true in the 1930s, when some of the concerns that would define the post-World War II period began forcing Americans, once again, to pay attention to overseas events. As we'll see in future lectures, after World War II, U.S. policy toward the Middle East would often center on three major issues: Zionism, oil, and the Cold War. Two of those issues, Zionism and oil, began to impose themselves on American consciousness in the 1930s, prompting a reengagement with international affairs. Let's look at Zionism first.

During World War I, the Zionist movement had grown rapidly in the United States. The main Zionist group in the United States, the Zionist Organization of America, acquired 200,000 members. After the war, however, American Zionism went into decline. One of the main reasons for the movement's growth during the war, the wartime suffering of Jewish communities within the Ottoman Empire, was no longer so pressing, as life for Jews in the former empire improved in peacetime. Moreover, following the issuing of the Balfour Declaration in 1917, many American Zionists assumed that their work was done. Now that Britain had given its blessing to a Jewish "national home" in Palestine, they believed, it was up to European Jews to emigrate to Palestine and build such a homeland. Few American Jews wished to settle in Palestine themselves.

The onset of the Great Depression in the early 1930s brought about a further decline in American Zionism. The economic crisis was so severe that most American Jews, like Americans generally, were obliged to turn their attention inward and concentrate on the more pressing task of making ends meet. Few Jews had the time, energy, or resources to devote to Zionist activities at this time.

All this started to change with Hitler's coming to power in Germany in 1933. Hitler's anti-Semitic campaign forced American Jews to recommit themselves to bettering the lot of their co-religionists in Europe. Initially, Hitler seems not to have intended to exterminate the Jews outright. His main objective in the 1930s was to make life for German Jews so miserable that they would flee the country en masse, leaving their money and property behind. To accomplish this goal, the Nazi regime not only passed discriminatory laws, but launched a series of public campaigns to harass, intimidate, and physically attack German Jews. The culmination of this initial phase of Nazi anti-Semitism was an event in 1938 known as Kristallnacht, or the Night of the Broken Glass, when Nazi goons went on a violent rampage, looting Jewish shops, burning down synagogues, assaulting Jews, and engaging in other forms of violence.

As intended, Hitler's anti-Jewish campaign caused a major exodus of Jews out of Germany. Between 1933 and 1939, about 225,000 Jews, or roughly one third of Germany's Jewish population, fled the country. In retrospect, of course, that number was tragically small, since the vast majority of those left behind eventually ended up in the Nazi death camps. One reason that more Jews did not succeed in leaving Germany was the unwillingness of other countries to take them in. For the Great Depression was a global phenomenon, and just about every country to which German Jews might have fled was unwilling to put further strain on its own resources by permitting an influx of impoverished and jobless refugees.

The United States was no exception to this rule, and throughout the 1930s the number of German Jews admitted into this country was pitifully inadequate, given the magnitude of the problem. As I mentioned, in 1924 Congress had passed the National Origins Act, which imposed strict limits on the number of immigrants allowed into the country. According to the Act, total immigration into the United States could not exceed about 150,000 people per year, with each nationality allotted a share of that total based on its percentage of the population back in 1890.

Relative to most other nations, Germany had a fairly generous allotment, due to the large number of Germans who were already in the United States by 1890; under the terms of the National Origins Act, about 25,000 Germans could enter the country each year. But relative to the number of German Jews who needed a place of refuge, that allotment was hardly sufficient. Worse still, for many years in the 1930s, the German immigration quota was not even filled, because the Act contained a further provision authorizing the U.S. State Department to deny an entry visa to any prospective immigrant who did not have the means to support himself in the United States and was thus, in the words of the legislation, "likely to become a public charge." Since most of the Jewish refugees were required to leave their assets in Germany, many were denied entry on this account.

Franklin Roosevelt, the U.S. president at this time, sympathized with German Jews but did little to ease their plight. Roosevelt could have asked Congress to raise the quotas on immigration to allow more Jews to enter the country, but he declined to do so because he assumed that Congress would never grant such a request. This assumption was almost certainly correct. In the 1930s, anti-Semitism remained a potent force in the United States. It was still legal to refuse to sell your home to a Jew or to deny employment to Jews on account of religion. Moreover, in the desperate climate of the Great Depression, most Americans were strongly opposed to relaxing immigration restrictions for fear of attracting an influx of foreigners who would take away scarce jobs from struggling Americans. Roosevelt figured there was no point in even trying to change immigration laws. Between 1933 and 1941, the United States admitted only about 8,500 Jews into the country per year, on average.

The difficulty of settling German Jews in Western nations brought about a revival of Zionism among American Jews. The Zionist Organization of American underwent a major expansion in the mid- to late 1930s, increasing its membership by several-fold. American Zionists, like their counterparts in Europe and Palestine, began pressuring Britain to increase the numbers of European Jews it allowed to enter Palestine each year. Initially, Britain responded favorably to this pressure, significantly increasing the annual quota of European immigrants into Palestine. Then, just as the plight of German Jews was becoming truly desperate, following the Kristallnacht attacks of 1938, Britain began to rethink the wisdom of creating a Jewish state in Palestine. A major factor in Britain's reassessment was the attitude of Palestinian Arabs, whose opposition to the Zionist project was far stronger than the British had anticipated.

Over the last couple decades, Britain's pro-Zionist immigration policy had wrought a profound demographic change in Palestine. In 1920, only 10 percent of Palestine's population had been Jewish; by 1939 Jews accounted for 31 percent of the population. Palestinian Arabs were deeply alarmed by this transformation; their country was slipping away from them before their very eyes. In 1936, the

Palestinians mounted a major uprising against the British in Palestine. Although by 1939 the British had managed to suppress the revolt, the experience convinced them that the full Zionist program was unworkable. Establishing a Jewish state would require forcibly dispossessing the Palestinians; this in turn could alienate the whole Arab world from Britain, the last thing Britain needed as it prepared for another war with Germany, which by now appeared increasingly likely.

In 1939, Britain issued a new policy statement known as the White Paper. The White Paper placed strict limits on the number of Jews admitted into Palestine each year and announced that Jewish immigration would end entirely in a few years' time. It also called for the regulation of land sales to Zionist institutions and individuals. Thus, just as the world was about to plunge into another world war, the Zionist movement appeared to have suffered a crippling blow. During the ensuing war, even as it supported Britain in the struggle against the Nazis, the Zionist movement, whether in Palestine, Britain, or America, would bitterly oppose Britain's stance on Palestine. As David Ben-Gurion, the leader of the Zionist movement in Palestine and later the first prime minister of Israel, put it at the time, Zionists would "fight the war as if there were no White Paper, and fight the White Paper as if there were no war."

The second major issue that pushed Americans back into the hurly-burly of international affairs was oil. One of the most striking transformations in American life in the 1920s was the growing reliance on the automobile. At the start of the decade, 25 percent of American households owned a car; by decade's end the figure was 60 percent. This phenomenon, in addition to transforming American social and cultural life, dramatically increased America's reliance on foreign oil. To be sure, the vast majority of America's petroleum needs were met by domestic oil drilling; not until the late 1960s would the United States start getting most of its oil from overseas. But by the 1920s, the foreign share was growing at a rate that alarmed U.S. government officials and oil company executives, who began an intensive search for reliable overseas sources of oil.

Two countries known to have extensive oil deposits were Iran and Iraq. The British already had an unbreakable lock on the oil concessions of Iran, but American oil companies had better luck breaking into the oil business of Iraq. In 1928, after several years of intensive negotiation, a consortium of American oil companies signed an agreement with three other oil companies—one British, one French, and one Dutch—whereby all four parties pledged to cooperate with each other in exploring for oil in the lands of the former Ottoman Empire. The deal was known as the "Red Line Agreement" because, according to legend, one of the negotiators took out a red pencil, drew a line around the former Ottoman Empire, and proposed that that be the area covered by the agreement. The Red Line Agreement enabled American oil companies to extract oil from Iraq, at that time the only country in the former Ottoman Empire with large proven oil reserves.

That was soon to change, for a neighboring country, Saudi Arabia, would be shown to contain even larger reserves. In the early 1930s, Charles Crane, whom we met last time as a member of the King-Crane commission, got permission from Ibn Saud, the King of Saudi Arabia, to sponsor a geological survey of Saudi Arabia. The survey concluded that the country probably contained considerable reserves, and an American oil company, Standard Oil of California, or SOCAL, put in a bid with the Saudi government for an oil concession. Under the terms of the Red Line Agreement, the other oil companies that were party to the agreement had to be given the opportunity to place bids of their own. But none of the other governments had much faith that Saudi Arabia contained extensive oil reserves, and they declined to place serious bids, so in 1933, SOCAL was awarded the concession. The gamble paid off in 1938, when geologists working for SOCAL, which had since merged with a number of other American companies, struck oil in Saudi Arabia.

Once oil was discovered in Saudi Arabia, other parties rushed in to get their own concessions. These parties included not just the other companies that had signed the Red Line Agreement, now belatedly realizing their mistake, but the governments of Germany, Italy, and Japan, the nations that would shortly become the Axis powers in World War II. The American oil companies had the favored position and were able to enjoy a virtual monopoly on Saudi oil. Given the magnitude of Saudi reserves and their significance for American economic and strategic security, it was only a matter of time before the U.S. government stepped in to actively protect the American oil companies' concession. This would start to happen in a significant way during World War II.

So, on the eve of the second great war of the twentieth century, two of the major issues that would define postwar American policy toward the Middle East—Zionism and oil—had already started to come to the fore. In our next lecture, we'll look at the events of World War II, which catapulted the United States into superpower status, with profound and lasting implications for U.S. relations with the Middle East.

Lecture Four
The United States and the
Middle East During World War II

Scope:

In this lecture, we see how the entry of the United States into World War II fundamentally altered Americans' conception of the Middle East. For the first time, U.S. officials saw the geopolitical orientation of the Middle East as vital to American national security—a view of the region that persists to this day. We start by examining U.S. wartime strategy in the Middle East, noting that during the war, U.S. military forces occupied large portions of the Middle East, turning Iran into a corridor for supplying the Soviet Union and North Africa into a staging area for invading fascist Italy. We then consider U.S. responses to the nationalist aspirations of Middle Easterners struggling to free themselves from European imperial domination. Tradition and economic interest predisposed Americans to look favorably on such aspirations, but the imperative of defeating the Axis powers usually trumped Washington's anticolonialist impulses.

Outline

I.   The entry of the United States into World War II fundamentally altered Americans' conception of the Middle East. For the first time, U.S. officials saw the geopolitical orientation of that region as vital to American national security.

    A. Upon entering the war, the U.S. government deemed it essential that the Middle East not fall under the control of Nazi Germany and its allies.

        1. Should that happen, Germany and Japan might be able to link up with each other along Asia's southern rim, cutting off Russia's supply line to the Persian Gulf.

        2. The Axis powers would also gain control of the region's enormous oil reserves.

    B. To make the most of America's industrial potential in the war, Roosevelt devised a policy known as *Lend-Lease*, whereby the United States loaned its wartime allies military equipment without worrying too much about the timing or manner of repayment.

        1. The biggest recipient of Lend-Lease aid was Britain.

2. The Soviet Union also received a huge amount of aid, about $11 billion worth over the course of the war.

II. To ensure that the territory and resources of the Middle East would remain available to the United States and its allies, Washington took part in several wartime initiatives.

A. It occupied Iran and used it as a corridor—the so-called *Persian Corridor*—for transporting war materiel from the Persian Gulf to the Soviet Union.

  1. A huge American military establishment was created in Iran, employing tens of thousands of U.S. troops and Iranian civilians.

  2. The main functions of this operation were to offload cargoes at the docks, assemble trucks and planes in specially designed plants, then ship the materiel to the Soviet Union on trains operated by the U.S. Army.

  3. Russia received millions of tons of American equipment in this way, enough to sustain 60 Soviet combat divisions on the eastern front against Germany.

  4. At the same time, there were occasional social and cultural tensions between the American servicemen stationed in Iran and the local population.

  5. Iran was important to the United States not only for its strategic location but also for its considerable oil reserves, which were crucial to the American war effort.

B. To ensure that Saudi Arabia's vast oil reserves would be available for the allied war effort (and beyond), the U.S. government established diplomatic relations with Saudi Arabia and extended economic aid to it.

  1. These overtures caused friction with the British, who suspected the United States of seeking to monopolize Saudi oil opportunities.

  2. Toward the end of the war, however, the British and American governments worked out an agreement whereby each country pledged to respect the other's existing oil concessions.

C. The United States and Britain used economic incentives and pressures to preserve Turkey's neutrality in the war.

  1. Except for a brief period in 1943, the Allies did not want Turkey to enter the war on their side. If Turkey joined the Allied side and was attacked by Nazi Germany, the Allies would have the burden of defending Turkey.

2. On the other hand, it would be disastrous if Turkey joined the war on the side of Germany, because then it would close the Turkish straits and cut Russia off from the Mediterranean Sea.

3. The best arrangement, from the Allies' perspective, was for Turkey to remain neutral. The Americans and the British spent much of the war bribing and pressuring Turkey not to go over to the other side.

D. The United States and Britain used North Africa as a staging area for an invasion of fascist Italy.

1. In the fall of 1942, the Americans and the British landed troops on the shores of Morocco and Algeria and began moving eastward to confront German forces in Tunisia.

2. In 1943, the Allies took German-held Tunisia and used it as a launching pad for invading Sicily.

3. From there, they proceeded to the Italian peninsula and knocked Italy out of the war.

4. The Allies then advanced up the peninsula into Central Europe, an operation that contributed significantly to Germany's ultimate defeat.

III. Though primarily preoccupied with winning the war, the U.S. government also had to concern itself with the nationalist aspirations of Middle Easterners struggling to free themselves from European imperial domination.

A. The default position of the United States was to look favorably on such aspirations.

1. This was in keeping with Wilson's principle of national self-determination and with America's tradition of anticolonialism, stemming from its own fight for independence from a colonial power.

2. America also stood to benefit by decolonization, which would remove the tariff barriers the European powers had erected around their imperial holdings and dissolve their monopolies of industries in the countries they dominated.

3. The United States wanted to differentiate itself starkly from the Nazi doctrine of racial supremacy and could do

so by distancing itself from the legacy of European imperialism, which had itself so often relied on supremacist doctrines.

B. The imperative of defeating the Axis powers, however, usually trumped Washington's anticolonial impulses. A case in point was a political crisis that occurred in Egypt in 1942.

    1. When Egypt's King Farouk tried to install a new, pro-German cabinet, British tanks surrounded the royal palace and forced the king to name a pro-British cabinet instead.

    2. The U.S. government supported this violation of Egyptian self-determination, reasoning that Egypt was too strategically valuable to be permitted to fall into Axis hands.

Suggested Reading:

Bryson, Thomas A. *Seeds of Mideast Crisis: The United States Diplomatic Role in the Middle East during World War II*. Jefferson, NC: McFarland & Company, 1981.

Lytle, Mark. *The Origins of the Iranian-American Alliance, 1941–1953*. New York: Holmes & Meier, 1987.

Rubin, Barry. *The Great Powers in the Middle East, 1941–1947*. London: Frank Cass, 1980.

Questions to Consider:

1. In what ways did the entry of the United States into World War II fundamentally alter Americans' conception of the Middle East?

2. How did the U.S. government attempt to reconcile its war aims with the nationalist aspirations of Middle Easterners struggling to free themselves from European imperial domination?

Lecture Four—Transcript
The United States and the
Middle East During World War II

In this lecture we're going to look at American involvement in the Middle East during the Second World War. It was during that conflict that the pattern we still witness today—whereby the United States is vitally concerned about the political character and geopolitical orientation of Middle Eastern states, and devises deliberate and elaborate policies accordingly—was first established.

In the decades leading up to the war, American interests in the region had been almost entirely missionary, philanthropic, educational, and commercial. The main concern of the U.S. government was making sure that the individuals and institutions engaging in such activities were not obstructed or endangered, and that they received reasonable compensation for their efforts. Apart from the brief flurry of Wilsonian activity in the aftermath of World War I, the United States had not concerned itself with the political character or geopolitical orientation of the countries of the Middle East. As long as the various American interests in the region were allowed to function and prosper, Washington was satisfied.

Once it entered World War II, however, the U.S. government could no longer ignore the geopolitical orientation of Middle Eastern countries. It was essential for the war effort that the Middle East not fall under the control of Nazi Germany and its allies. Should that happen, Germany and Japan might be able to link up with each other along Asia's southern rim, making it impossible for the United States to send war supplies to Russia, its wartime ally. Should the Axis powers take over the Middle East, they would also, of course, gain control of the region's enormous oil reserves.

Further to the West, North Africa assumed vital importance as a staging area for the United States and Britain to launch their invasion of fascist Italy, from which they hoped to move northward to attack German positions in Central Europe. In these ways, it became—for the first time—essential to the overall security of the United States that the countries of the Middle East be under the control of friendly forces, whether indigenous or European. Formal U.S. involvement in World War II began, of course, with Japan's attack on Pearl Harbor in December 1941, to which Washington responded by declaring war on Japan. A few days later, Nazi Germany declared war on the United States, bringing America into the European theater of the war as well.

One of the principal advantages the United States enjoyed in waging World War II was its enormous industrial capacity. This capacity, combined with the fact that the United States was the only major combatant to escape physical devastation, allowed America to serve as "the great arsenal of democracy," in the words of President Franklin D. Roosevelt. To make the most of America's industrial potential in the war, Roosevelt devised a policy known as *Lend-Lease*, whereby the United States loaned its wartime allies military equipment—planes, ships, weapons, ammunition, and so on—without worrying too much about the timing or manner of repayment. For the duration of the war, the Allies would not have to compensate the United States for any equipment they received. Once the war was over, they could either give the equipment back or compensate the United States in some other way.

The biggest recipient of Lend-Lease aid was Britain, but the Soviet Union also received a huge amount of aid, about $11 billion worth over the course of the war. One of the most important routes by which the United States supplied Russia with aid was the so-called *Persian Corridor*; material would be shipped through the Persian Gulf to Iran and then transported northward over Iranian territory. The great advantage of the Persian Corridor was that it could be operated at all times of year, due to the relatively warm climate. Most of the other corridors for supplying Russia were frozen over during the winter months. For the Persian Corridor to remain open, of course, it was essential that Iran remain in Allied hands.

To accomplish this, in early 1942 the United States sent its troops to occupy Iran, which was already under joint Anglo-Soviet occupation. Some months earlier, in August 1941, Britain and the Soviet Union had forced Reza Shah, the ruler of Iran, to abdicate his throne, on the grounds that he was too sympathetic to Germany. Reza Shah was replaced by his son, Mohammed Shah Pahlavi, who was then in his early twenties and was much more malleable than his father. Mohammed Shah permitted Britain, the Soviet Union, and, later, the United States to occupy Iran for the duration of the war.

A huge American establishment, employing tens of thousands of U.S. troops and Iranian employees, was built up in Iran. The main functions of this operation were to offload cargoes at the docks, assemble trucks and planes in specially designed plants, and then ship the materiel to the Soviet Union on trains operated by the U.S. army. Russia received millions of tons of American equipment in this way, enough to sustain 60 Soviet combat divisions on the eastern front against Germany. Iran itself became a recipient of Lend-Lease assistance, although most of the aid it received consisted of grain and other foodstuffs that had become scarce during the war, rather than military equipment. U.S. military personnel also assisted the Iranian government in organizing and training its internal police forces. It was the start of an extremely intimate relationship between the U.S. and Iranian governments that would continue right up until the Iranian revolution of the late 1970s.

If governmental relations between the two countries were close, social relations between the two peoples were not without tension. The sudden appearance in Iran of tens of thousands of American troops made a certain amount of friction inevitable. One of the most serious problems was the large number of traffic accidents involving military personnel driving through the narrow streets of Iranian towns. On hundreds of occasions, Iranian civilians were injured or killed by American drivers, causing the Iranian government to file protests with the U.S. diplomatic mission in Tehran. Unfortunately, American diplomats were not always as sensitive about the issue as they could have been. In a cable to Washington, the U.S. minister to Iran offered the following explanation for why Iranians kept getting hit by American cars: "The reflexes of the Iranian, to whom the automobile is still a comparatively recent innovation, are relatively slow, and by the time the pedestrian endeavors to get out of danger it is apt to be too late."

Iran was important to the United States, not only for its strategic location, but for its considerable oil reserves as well. Access to cheap and readily available oil was crucial to the American war effort, especially since the United States was exporting oil to many of its wartime allies. Moreover, in the early 1940s it was mistakenly assumed that domestic American oil reserves were nearly exhausted and that any additional oil required by the United States would have to come from overseas.

Of the three countries that occupied Iran during World War II, only Britain had been granted the right to extract and market Iranian oil. The Soviet Union and the United States were eager to gain oil concessions of their own, and both countries pressured the Iranian government to grant such concessions. Many Iranian politicians resented this pressure, and in 1944 the Iranian parliament passed a law forbidding the cabinet from granting any additional oil concessions without the parliament's permission. At least for the time being, Britain was able to retain its monopolistic position in Iran.

Another Middle Eastern country of crucial interest to the United States was Saudi Arabia. As we saw in the previous lecture, in the 1930s American oil companies had acquired an oil concession in Saudi Arabia. For the reasons I just mentioned—the importance of oil to the war effort and the belief that the United States was about to run out of oil—Saudi oil assumed much greater significance after the United States entered World War II.

To ensure that Saudi oil would remain available to the United States, during the war Roosevelt forged closer relations with the Saudi Kingdom. He established a diplomatic mission in Saudi Arabia and declared the kingdom eligible for Lend-Lease aid. U.S. aid was welcome news to the King of Saudi Arabia, Ibn Saud, whose country's economy had been hard hit by the war. Ordinarily, the Saudi royal family derived a good deal of its revenues from the annual pilgrimage to Mecca, but the war had interrupted the pilgrim traffic. U.S. aid at this crucial moment cemented Ibn Saud's relationship with the United States.

America's growing involvement in Saudi Arabia caused considerable friction with the British, who suspected the United States of seeking to monopolize Saudi oil opportunities. This perception, combined with America's simultaneous attempts to acquire oil drilling rights in Iran, caused the British to fear that their whole position in the Middle East was in danger of being undermined. The Americans, for their part, suspected the British of trying to take over the American oil concession in Saudi Arabia, and they reacted with paranoia to every move the British government made in that country. When Britain sent a team of pest control experts to help Saudi Arabia deal with an influx of locusts, American oil men were convinced it was really a team of oil prospectors in disguise.

Another cause of misunderstanding was the fact that much of the materiel the United States sent to Saudi Arabia via the Lend Lease program was processed through a British-run supply center in Cairo. Some of that materiel arrived in Saudi Arabia inscribed with British markings, convincing U.S. officials that the Brits were trying to take credit for American generosity. Toward the end of the war, the British and American governments came to the conclusion that their rivalry in Saudi Arabia was doing neither of them any good, and they worked out an agreement whereby each country pledged to respect the other's existing oil concessions. Although the U.S. Senate never ratified the agreement, it did allow for a more cooperative relationship between the two countries.

As for U.S.-Saudi relations, they continued to grow closer as the war drew to an end, and seemed destined to grow closer still in the postwar era. In February 1945, on his way home from the Yalta conference in the Soviet Crimea, Roosevelt briefly stopped at the Suez Canal Zone in Egypt, where, on the deck of an American naval vessel, he hosted a visit by King Ibn Saud of Saudi Arabia. The two leaders got on famously. Out of deference to Ibn Saud's religious sensibilities, Roosevelt refrained from smoking in the king's presence, a considerable sacrifice for the nicotine-addicted president. During the lunch break, however, Roosevelt wheeled himself into the ship's elevator, pushed the emergency button and chain-smoked two cigarettes before rejoining his guest at the table.

At another point in the meeting, Ibn Saud said he could identify with the disabled Roosevelt since he, Ibn Saud, also had difficulty walking, on account of old war wounds to his legs. To this Roosevelt said, "You are luckier than I because you can still walk on your legs and I have to be wheeled wherever I go."

"No, my friend," replied Ibn Saud, "you are more fortunate. Your chair will take you wherever you want to go and you know you will get there. My legs are less reliable and are getting weaker every day." So then, much to Ibn Saud's delight, Roosevelt got out a spare wheelchair he had brought along for the trip and presented it as a gift to the old Saudi king.

Another country of crucial interest to the United States and its allies was Turkey. Turkey remained neutral for most of the war, and the Allies expended considerable effort to keep things that way. Except for a brief period in 1943, the Allies did not want Turkey to enter the war on their side. This may seem like an odd position, but there were sound reasons for it. The Allies realized that if Turkey joined the war on their side, it would be attacked by Nazi Germany, and then the Allies would have the burden of coming to Turkey's defense. On the other hand, it would be disastrous if Turkey joined the war on the side of Germany, because then it would close the Turkish straits and cut Russia off from the Mediterranean Sea. The best arrangement, from the Allies' perspective, was for Turkey to remain neutral, and the Americans and the British spent much of the war bribing and pressuring Turkey not to go over to the other side.

Turkey, for its part, skillfully maneuvered between the Axis and Allied pacts, balancing a non-aggression pact with Germany against a defensive alliance with Britain and a Lend-Lease agreement with the United States. Periodically, Turkey would threaten to move closer to Germany as a way of extracting more aid from the Allies. For most of the war the United States and Britain tolerated this behavior, since Turkey's neutrality was so prized. The Allies were angered, however, by Turkey's insistence on supplying Germany with chrome, a material necessary for the production of armament steel. In 1944, the United States and Britain began playing hardball. They cut off aid to Turkey and threatened to blockade the country unless it stopped sending chrome to Germany. Turkey succumbed to the pressure. In August 1944, after the D-Day invasion of France made it clear that Germany would lose the war, Turkey severed diplomatic relations with Germany. In February 1945, Turkey declared war on Germany, assuring itself a seat at the victors' table.

Still another area of crucial interest to the U.S. war effort was North Africa, which played a key role in the basic strategy that Britain and the United States devised for winning the war against Nazi Germany. In late December 1941, just a couple weeks after Pearl Harbor, British Prime Minister Winston Churchill came to Washington to meet with Roosevelt and coordinate allied war strategy. Churchill was quite literally Roosevelt's guest, for he stayed in the residential quarters of the White House.

A number of personal anecdotes have arisen out of Churchill's stay in the White House. According to one of them, which is probably too good to be true, Roosevelt is being wheeled down the hallway past Churchill's bedroom, when the bedroom door opens and Churchill steps out, stark naked, with a towel over his shoulder, heading for the shower. Roosevelt does a double take and says, "I'm sorry Winston, I didn't realize you weren't decent." Churchill sticks out his chest and says, "Not at all—the Prime Minister of Great Britain has nothing to conceal from the President of the United States."

In their substantive discussions, Roosevelt and Churchill agreed that the struggle against Hitler should take priority over the effort to defeat Japan, but they differed over how to achieve the defeat of Nazi Germany. The Americans wanted to launch a frontal assault on German forces in Western Europe, probably by mounting an invasion of France across the English Channel, and to do this as soon as possible. Churchill, however, was opposed to opening a western front anytime soon. He was haunted by the memory of World War I, in which whole armies had been massacred while launching frontal assaults against entrenched positions. Churchill wanted to postpone any invasion until Germany had first been weakened by a combination of naval blockade, aerial bombardment, and attacks on other fronts.

Yet both countries agreed that some sort of offensive had to be mounted soon. With some reluctance, the Americans accepted Churchill's suggestion that the Allies invade Europe by way of North Africa. Specifically, the idea was to land forces in Morocco and Algeria, move east to seize the German airfield in Tunisia, and then use the airfield as a launching pad for an invasion of Sicily. Sicily, in turn, would serve as a stepping stone to the Italian peninsula, from which the Allies would then move up into Nazi-occupied central Europe.

One major obstacle to this plan was the fact that both Morocco and Algeria were under the control of Vichy France. When Germany defeated France in 1940, the country was split into two parts. The northern part of France came under direct German occupation. The southern part was not occupied, but it was placed under a new government that, while nominally independent, was clearly subservient to Nazi Germany. Still, the fact that Vichy France, as this country was called, was not completely under Germany's control created an opportunity for the Allies, especially when it came to France's far-flung colonies. Although the French officials governing these colonies now worked for the Vichy government, they were not uniformly committed to advancing Germany's war aims. In some cases, colonial officials were willing to permit Allied forces to operate within the areas they controlled. The question now facing the Allies was whether, and to what extent, Vichy officials would allow Allied forces to operate in North Africa.

In the fall of 1942, the Americans and the British landed their forces on the shores of Morocco and Algeria, meeting only scattered Vichy resistance. The Allies were worried, however, that they would encounter stiffer Vichy opposition as they proceeded eastward toward Tunisia. The Allied commander of the North African operation—an American army general named Dwight D. Eisenhower—cut a deal with a Vichy French admiral named Jean Darlan, promising to make him High Commission in North Africa if Darlan ensured that local Vichy officials cooperated with the Allies.

The specter of an American general cutting a deal with a Vichy official (especially Darlan, who was known to have fascist sympathies) was extremely controversial in the United States. Indeed, the public outcry was so intense that Eisenhower's career almost ended then and there. But President Roosevelt defended the Darlan Deal as a temporary expedient and kept Eisenhower on. The bottom line, after all, was that Allied forces had gotten a foothold in North Africa and were now in a position to push on to Tunisia. In 1943, the Allies defeated the German forces in Tunisia, seized the German-run airfield, and used it as a launching pad for invading Sicily, proceeding from there to the Italian peninsula. Fascist Italy was knocked out of the war, and the Allies advanced up the peninsula into Central Europe, an operation that contributed significantly to Germany's ultimate defeat.

Throughout the first half of the 1940s, U.S. diplomacy toward the Middle East was overwhelmingly geared toward defeating the Axis powers. Virtually every major decision American leaders made in that region was determined on the basis of how it would aid the war effort. But the progress of the war was not necessarily the overriding concern of the political leaders and peoples of the Middle East, who were primarily interested in gaining or enhancing the political independence of their own countries. The more the United States became politically involved with region, the more it had to concern itself with these nationalist aspirations.

The default position of the United States was to be sympathetic to the desire of colonized peoples or emerging nations to achieve full national sovereignty after the war. This was in keeping not just with the Wilsonian principle of national self-determination but with an even older American tradition of anti-colonialism, stemming from the fact that United States itself had gained its independence by staging a revolt against a colonial power.

Another, more pragmatic reason to favor independence for subject peoples was that in many cases the United States stood to benefit by such support. The European powers had erected high tariff barriers around their imperial holdings, and had monopolized the industries inside the countries they dominated. Americans believed that the removal of such protections would benefit American exporters and investors, who, given the enormous strength of the U.S. economy, were bound to perform well on a level playing field.

The third reason was the nature of America's enemies in the war. On the one hand, the United States found itself opposing Nazi Germany, which was committed to the doctrine of racial supremacy. It was natural for the United States to try to differentiate itself from that doctrine as starkly as possible, and one way to do that was to distance itself from the legacy of European imperialism, which had itself so often relied on supremacist doctrines.

On the other hand, the United States was in a mortal struggle against Japan, which was explicitly appealing to the nonwhite and colonized peoples of the world. Roosevelt feared that these peoples might indeed rally to Japan's side. The best way to prevent that, he believed, was to demonstrate that the United States was not committed to white supremacy or imperialism, but was instead well-disposed toward emerging peoples and nations.

Paradoxically, both of these conflicts—against white supremacist Germany and against anti-white supremacist Japan—pushed the United States to take a stronger anti-imperialist position than it might have otherwise. This, at least, was the default position that the United States espoused during the war. In the Middle East, U.S. officials often found that the requirements of waging the war made it necessary for them to modify, downplay, or altogether ignore their professed devotion to national self-determination. When the demands of Middle Eastern nationalists were seen as conflicting with the war effort, Washington invariably sided with the war effort.

A case in point was a political crisis that occurred in Egypt in 1942. By this time, Egypt was nominally independent, but it was under de facto control of Britain, whose troops occupied the country. Nationalist and anti-British sentiment ran high in Egypt, and some Egyptian politicians wanted to join the war on the side of Nazi Germany to rid the country of British rule. Egypt's King Farouk was responsive to this mood, and in February 1942 he tried to install a new, pro-German cabinet. To prevent this from happening, British tanks surrounded the royal palace and the British ambassador flatly ordered Farouk to name a pro-British cabinet. Farouk had no choice but to comply.

Here was a clear case of an imperial power trampling on the right of self-determination, and, in the U.S. State Department, some mid-level officials recommended that the U.S. government file a protest with the British. But top U.S. officials refused to criticize the British action, believing it was justified by wartime necessity. Not only was Egypt strategically located as the land bridge between Africa and the Middle East, it contained the Suez Canal, which provided a maritime link between the Mediterranean Sea and the Red Sea. It was utterly essential that Egypt remain in Allied hands. Moreover, at the very time Farouk was attempting to install a pro-German cabinet, German forces in Libya, Egypt's neighbor to the west, were trying to push their way into British-held Egypt. The loss of Egypt to the Axis powers would have opened the way for a Nazi invasion of the Middle East. Under the circumstances, denying the right of self-determination seemed to be the lesser evil.

The Allied victories of 1945—over Germany in the spring and over Japan the following summer—put an end to the Axis menace and catapulted the United States into the role of a superpower. Shortly thereafter, disagreements between the capitalist and communist elements of the anti-Axis alliance, which had been submerged during the war, reasserted themselves in the guise of an all-encompassing Cold War. These circumstances, combined with the inauguration of the nuclear age following America's use of atomic bombs against Japan, constituted a fundamental transformation in the entire international order.

When it came to U.S. attitudes toward the Middle East, however, there would be important elements of continuity. In the new postwar era, as in World War II, the United States would continue to believe that its own security depended on keeping the Middle East in friendly hands. The global enemy would be different, but the geostrategic importance of the Middle East would be remarkably similar in American eyes. In this sense, we can identify World War II as the real turning point in American attitudes toward the Middle East, as the event that caused American policy makers, for the first time, to be vitally concerned about the political character and geopolitical orientation of Middle Eastern states, and to devise deliberate and elaborate policies to protect their interests in that region.

Lecture Five
Origins of the Cold War in the Middle East

Scope:

This lecture deals with the rise of Cold War tensions in the Middle East in the late 1940s. After establishing the strategic importance of the Middle East to Washington's efforts to contain the Soviet Union, we examine Harry S. Truman's responses to three Cold War Crises that erupted in the region: the Turkish straits crisis of 1945–1946, the Iran crisis of 1946, and the crisis stemming from Britain's financial abandonment of Greece and Turkey in 1947. This last crisis, we learn, resulted in the issuing of the Truman Doctrine—a crystallization of American thinking that would guide Cold War policies for a generation. Finally, we examine the evolution of U.S.-Saudi relations in the late 1940s, culminating in Truman's formal pledge in 1950 to defend the oil-rich kingdom from possible Soviet attack.

Outline

I.   Soon after the defeat of the Axis powers in 1945, the Soviet Union emerged as America's new global adversary. In this new Cold War era, the United States continued to believe that its own security depended on keeping the Middle East in friendly hands.

    A. The United States was not itself dependent on Middle Eastern oil, but Western Europe and Japan were, and Washington needed those areas to be prosperous and stable.

    B. Because the Middle East was adjacent to the Soviet Union, its territory could be used as a staging area for land and air attacks on the Soviet Union in the event that the Cold War turned hot.

II. For all of America's growing political involvement in the Middle East, Britain continued to be the dominant Western power in the region.

    A. As of 1945, Britain still had League of Nations mandates in Palestine and Jordan.

    B. It had military bases in Egypt, Libya, Jordan, Iraq, and Yemen.

    C. It had several protectorates on the Arabian Peninsula.

D. It had major oil concessions in Kuwait and Iran.

E. One major problem with continued British domination of the Middle East was that it ran counter to the nationalist aspirations of most of the region's inhabitants.

III. At least for the time being, the United States was happy to see Britain retain its position of dominance in the Middle East. Soon after the war, however, the Soviets began probing at the edges of the Middle East, prompting the United States to increase its own involvement in the region.

A. In 1945–1946, the Soviet Union demanded that Turkey grant it a base in the Turkish straits.

    1. Turkey appealed for British and U.S. support in resisting the Soviet demand.

    2. A tough Anglo-American diplomatic note, combined with less direct signals of Western resolve, prompted Moscow to back down.

B. In 1946, the Soviet Union refused to withdraw its troops from Iran, as Britain and the United States had already done. The ensuing crisis coincided almost exactly with two of the most iconic moments of the early Cold War.

    1. Just one day after Stalin informed the Iranian government that his troops would not be withdrawing from Iranian territory as originally promised, U.S. foreign service officer George Kennan sent an 8,000-word cable, later known as the *Long Telegram*, detailing Soviet aggressiveness and advocating a strategy of "containment" whereby the United States and its allies could prevent the Soviets from achieving world domination.

    2. Three days after the deadline for Soviet withdrawal from Iran came and went—without any withdrawal—former British Prime Minister Winston Churchill gave a speech in Fulton, Missouri, warning that "an iron curtain" had descended across the continent of Europe.

    3. Following an official protest from Washington, Moscow removed its troops.

    4. In this case, however, the Soviet withdrawal appears to have had more to do with shrewd Iranian diplomacy than with American toughness.

C. In 1947, Britain granted independence to the Indian subcontinent and informed the United States that it could no longer take financial responsibility for Greece and Turkey. President Harry S. Truman and his advisors agreed that the United States should assume Britain's burden.

   1. To convince Congress to appropriate the necessary funds, Truman delivered a speech in which he presented an alarming picture of the threat posed by international communism.

   2. Truman was able to obtain Congress's support was by stressing the regional implications of a rebel victory in Greece.

   3. Truman's statement, "It must be the policy of the United States to support free peoples who are resisting attempted subjugation by armed minorities or by outside pressures," became known as the *Truman Doctrine* and would guide American Cold War policy for the next generation.

   4. To ensure availability of Middle Eastern oil, the Truman administration constructed a pipeline across Jordanian, Syrian, and Lebanese territory, gaining Syria's approval only by quietly encouraging a bloodless coup that deposed Syrian president Shukri Quwatli.

IV. As the Cold War intensified in the late 1940s, the United States drew closer to oil-rich Saudi Arabia. In 1950, the Truman administration took two steps to solidify U.S.-Saudi friendship.

   A. President Truman formally pledged that if Saudi Arabia were attacked by the Soviet Union, the United States would come to its defense.

   B. The U.S. Treasury Department issued tax regulations—which became known as the *Golden Gimmick*—that made it less costly for American oil companies to share their profits with the Saudi government.

Suggested Reading:

Bill, James A. *The Eagle and the Lion: The Tragedy of American-Iranian Relations*. New Haven: Yale University Press, 1988.

Goode, James F. *The United States and Iran, 1946–51: The Diplomacy of Neglect*. New York: St. Martin's Press, 1989.

Kuniholm, Bruce R. *The Origins of the Cold War in the Near East: Great Power Conflict and Diplomacy in Iran, Turkey, and Greece*. Princeton: Princeton University Press, 1980.

Questions to Consider:

1. In the early postwar years, what role did the U.S. policymakers envision for the Middle East in the new struggle against Soviet communism?

2. What attitudes did U.S. policymakers take toward continuing British domination of the Middle East?

Lecture Five—Transcript
Origins of the Cold War in the Middle East

In this lecture we're going to look at U.S. actions in the Middle East during the early Cold War years, from 1945 to 1950. As we saw in the previous lecture, America's entry into World War II fundamentally altered the way in which the U.S. government thought of the Middle East. For the first time, U.S. officials became convinced that American security depended on the political character and geopolitical orientation of Middle Eastern countries. Accordingly, Washington began devising and implementing comprehensive and deliberate policies toward the region, something it had never bothered to do in the past except during that brief period of Wilsonian activism in the immediate aftermath of World War I.

Once World War II ended, the United States continued to be concerned with the geopolitical orientation of the Middle East. Although the Axis powers had been vanquished, the United States faced a new rival in the form of international communism. In this struggle, too, the U.S. government was determined to ensure that the Middle East's resources and strategic positions remained accessible to America and its allies, a position Washington maintains to this day.

The American president confronting this new postwar world was, of course, Harry S. Truman of Missouri, who had been suddenly thrust into the presidency following the death of Franklin Roosevelt in April 1945, just prior to Nazi Germany's surrender in World War II. Truman had been vice president for only a few months before Roosevelt's death, and even as vice president he had been kept largely in the dark about developments in foreign policy, knowing little more about foreign affairs than what he could read in the newspapers. Roosevelt had neglected to tell him, for example, that the United States was developing an atom bomb. Truman would have to learn on the job during one of the most complex periods in the history of American policy making, in which numerous institutions, alliances, procedures, and norms had to be established for the first time and made to work in a new and unfamiliar international environment.

On the other hand, the United States emerged from World War II in an extremely advantageous position. Unlike most other industrialized nations, which had been weakened and, in some cases, devastated by the war, the United States had become much more powerful and prosperous, capable of setting the postwar agenda in the United Nations and in other international bodies. The United States was also the sole possessor of the atom bomb, a monopoly it would retain until 1949.

As I mentioned a moment ago, in the dawning Cold War era, U.S. officials continued to believe that American security depended on keeping the Middle East in friendly hands. The region's vast oil reserves were, of course, one of the principal causes of this perception. The United States was not itself dependent on Middle Eastern oil; most of the oil Americans consumed came from the Western hemisphere. But Western Europe, which the United States was trying to revive economically, got about 75 percent of its oil from the Middle East. Japan, another nation the Untied States was trying to rebuild, was also overwhelmingly dependent on Middle Eastern oil.

The economic revival of Europe, and to a lesser extent of Japan, was a fundamental objective of the U.S. government for two main reasons: one reason was economic and the other geopolitical. From an economic standpoint, U.S. officials understood that American prosperity depended on the existence of prosperous societies abroad, which could provide markets for American products and investment opportunities for American capital. Geopolitically, the U.S. government wanted to prevent communist parties from making political inroads into Western Europe; the best way to do that was to ensure that Western Europe was prosperous. Indeed, the U.S. government was so eager to achieve European prosperity that in 1947 it launched the Marshall Plan, which pumped billions of dollars from the U.S. treasury into the economies of Western Europe. Essential to the success of the Marshall Plan was the easy availability of Middle Eastern oil.

The United States also saw the Middle East as possessing great geostrategic value. Because the Middle East was adjacent to the Soviet Union, its territory could be used as a staging area for land and air attacks on the Soviet Union in the event the Cold War turned hot. Intercontinental ballistic missiles (or ICBMs) had not yet been developed, and U.S. war plans relied heavily on the ability to conduct short- and medium-range bombing raids against enemy targets.

As of 1945, Britain was still the dominant power in the Middle East. It had mandates in Palestine and Jordan, military bases in Egypt, Libya, Jordan, Iraq, and Yemen, several protectorates on the Arabian Peninsula, and major oil concessions in Kuwait and Iran. France continued to dominate much of North Africa, but its position in the Middle East had been seriously weakened during the war, as both Britain and the United States had essentially ganged up on France and forced it to give up its mandates in Syria and Lebanon, both of which emerged from the war as fully independent nations. At least for the time being, the United States was happy to see Britain retain its position of dominance in the Middle East.

One reason for this was that U.S. officials tended to defer to Britain's longer experience in Middle Eastern political affairs. Britain, after all, had been a major player in the international politics of the Middle East since the early-nineteenth century, whereas the United States was a relative newcomer to the game. Britain also had a long tradition of scholarly study of Islam and of Middle Eastern culture. This, too, impressed U.S. officials, though they sometimes tweaked the Brits for being a little pedantic.

To be sure, there was some economic rivalry between the United States and Britain, especially over the oil riches of Saudi Arabia and Iran, but overall the Americans highly valued Britain's involvement in the Middle East and wanted it to continue for as long as possible. A more serious problem, of course, was that continued British domination of the Middle East ran counter to the nationalist aspirations of most of the region's inhabitants. America's anti-colonial heritage, as well as ordinary caution, made U.S. officials wary of giving too much support to Britain's position in the Middle East.

On the other hand, most Middle Eastern countries were governed by monarchs or authoritarian leaders who believed their interests lay in maintaining close ties to the West. Even though public opinion in the region was becoming increasingly antagonistic toward Western Europe, these views did not necessarily affect the positions taken by Middle Eastern governments, though in some cases, when public sentiment was simply too strong to ignore, it did have an impact on government behavior. As long as regional governments remained basically pro-Western, and as long as they had the means to stifle most forms of dissent, the United States could afford to be relatively unconcerned about the political consequences of following Britain's lead in the Middle East.

The crux of the Cold War lay in Europe, as the United States and the Soviet Union tangled first over the fate of Eastern Europe and then over the postwar role of Germany. The importance of the Middle East, in American eyes, lay primarily in its ability to provide economic and physical security to America's Western European allies. Even so, the first major Cold War crises actually erupted in the Middle East, as the Soviet Union began probing at the edges of the region, prompting the United States to increase its own involvement there. It was these Middle Eastern crises, in fact, that convinced President Truman that the Soviet Union was not inclined to cooperate with the United States and Britain, and that vigorous efforts to counter Soviet ambitions would be necessary.

The first Cold War crisis to hit the Middle East took place in Turkey in 1945 and 1946. Russia had long wanted guaranteed access to the Dardanelles and the Bosporus, the Turkish straits that served as an outlet from the Black Sea to the Mediterranean. During the war, Winston Churchill had expressed some sympathy for the Soviet position, leading Joseph Stalin, the Soviet dictator, to believe that Britain would support, or acquiesce in, Russia's claims regarding the straits. In the summer of 1945, the Soviets presented a note to the Turks requesting that Turkey allow for joint Turkish-Soviet control of the straits. Although the note was phrased in polite terms, it was accompanied by Soviet troop concentrations on the border with Turkey and by harsh anti-Turkish propaganda in the Soviet media, so the overall impression was quite menacing from Turkey's perspective. The Turkish government appealed to the United States and Britain for diplomatic support.

The crisis over the straits occurred against a backdrop of growing U.S. suspicion of Moscow's motives, and Truman was inclined to interpret the Soviet demand in extremely ominous terms. "There isn't a doubt in my mind," he privately wrote in January 1946, "that Russia intends an invasion of Turkey and the seizure of the Black Sea Straits to the Mediterranean. Unless Russia is faced with an iron fist and strong language, another war is in the making. Only one language they understand: 'How many divisions have you?'"

Even so, Truman reacted modestly at first, relying on indirect signals rather than direct threats. One such signal was issued in the spring of 1946, when the U.S. government sent the body of the Turkish ambassador to the United States, who had died in Washington during the war, back to Turkey for burial. The body was sent home on board the U.S. battleship *Missouri*, a conspicuous symbol of American solidarity with Turkey.

The Soviets continued to put pressure on Turkey, renewing their demand for joint control of the Turkish straits. So in the summer of 1946, the Truman administration joined the British government in sending a tough note to the Soviet government, forcefully rejecting the Soviet position. As Truman privately remarked upon approving the note, "We might as well find out whether the Russians are bent on world conquest now as in five or ten years." This time, the Soviets backed down.

The second Cold War crisis to occur in the Middle East took place in Iran. During the war, as we saw, the United States, Britain, and Russia had occupied Iran for the purpose of maintaining a supply route from the Persian Gulf to the Soviet Union. In early 1946, the Americans and the British withdrew their troops from Iran, but the Russians refused to withdraw their own troops, at least refused to do so immediately. The Soviets hoped to use their presence in northern Iran to pressure the Iranian government to grant them oil-drilling rights in the country.

To increase the pressure on the Iranian government, the Soviets had allied themselves with local communists in Azerbaijan, a province in northern Iran. In late 1945, these communists had proclaimed a separatist government in Azerbaijan, backed by occupying Soviet troops. Indeed, far from withdrawing their troops from Iran, in early 1946 the Soviets began sending additional forces into Azerbaijan, including over 200 tanks. Like the Turkish crisis of 1945–46, the Iranian crisis unfolded against a background of growing East-West tension. In this case, the background was especially relevant, since the Iranian crisis occurred in February and March 1946 and thus coincided almost exactly with two of the most iconic moments in early Cold War history.

On February 22, 1946, just one day after Stalin informed the Iranian government that his troops would not be withdrawing from Iranian territory in early March as originally promised, an American foreign service officer named George Kennan, then serving as chargé d'affaires at the U.S. embassy in Moscow, sent an 8,000-word cable to Washington outlining his thoughts on the emerging rivalry with the Soviet Union. Kennan's message, which became known as the *Long Telegram*, presented an alarming picture of Soviet aggressiveness and outlined a strategy—later dubbed "containment"—by which the United States and its allies could prevent the Soviets from achieving world domination. Kennan's Long Telegram caused a sensation in official Washington. Its appeal lay in the fact that it offered both a plausible analysis of the Soviet phenomenon and an apparently realistic approach for dealing with it.

Then, on March 5, 1946, three days after the deadline for the Soviet withdrawal from Iran came and went without any Soviet withdrawal, former British Prime Minister Winston Churchill gave a graduation speech at Westminster College in Fulton, Missouri. With President Truman sitting behind him on the stage, Churchill warned that "an iron curtain" had descended across the continent of Europe, and that all the areas to the east of that curtain were now subject to increasing levels of Soviet control.

In other words, Moscow issued its challenge in Iran just as the full dimensions of the world crisis were becoming clear both to U.S. officials and to the American public. In this case, too, the U.S. government reacted with alarm, speculating that the Soviet moves in Azerbaijan were part of a larger attempt to take over the rest of Iran and perhaps the whole Persian Gulf. After receiving a briefing on the Soviets' troop buildup in Azerbaijan, Secretary of State James F. Byrnes smacked his fist into his palm and said, "Now we'll give it to them with both barrels." Byrnes then sent a note of protest to the Soviet government, and shortly thereafter the Soviets withdrew their forces from Iran.

Although it appeared at the time as if Moscow had backed down under U.S. threats, what really happened was that the Soviets were outmaneuvered by the Iranian government, especially the prime minister, a shrewd operator named Ahmad Qavam. In the interim between Byrnes's note of protest and the Soviet withdrawal, Qavam met with Soviet officials and promised to grant the Soviets oil drilling rights in Iran, subject to approval by the Iranian parliament, if they withdrew their troops from the country, and the Soviets agreed.

Once the Soviets withdrew, the Iranian government crushed the separatist movement in Azerbaijan. Soon thereafter, the oil concession for the Soviets was presented to the Iranian parliament, which overwhelmingly rejected it. The Soviets had apparently assumed—mistakenly—that the Iranian parliament was a rubber stamp for all cabinet decisions. Having already withdrawn their troops from northern Iran, and having seen their Azerbaijani allies go down to defeat, the Soviets were in a poor position to reoccupy the country, and they let the matter drop.

The third crisis in the region occurred in 1947, and it led to a crystallization of U.S. Cold War policy. World War II had been financially devastating to Britain, and in the immediate postwar years the British were forced to drastically scale back their overseas commitments. In 1947, Britain granted independence to the Indian subcontinent, which split up into the separate states of India and Pakistan. Early that same year, Britain announced that it would be abandoning its mandate in Palestine, a subject we'll discuss in our next lecture. Also in early 1947, Britain warned the United States that it could no longer keep giving financial aid to Turkey and Greece.

The Truman administration was extremely worried about Turkey and Greece. Turkey, as we've just seen, was subject to Soviet diplomatic pressure, and Greece was in a state of civil war, with a leftist insurgency, including local communists, trying to overthrow a right-wing government. The Truman administration was strongly inclined to assume Britain's role as the financial backer of Turkey and Greece, and it decided to ask Congress to appropriate $400 million for this purpose. The challenge was getting Congress, now under the control of tight-fisted Republicans, to agree to such an expenditure.

One way to try securing congressional support would be to warn that if the United didn't bail out Turkey and Greece, both countries would be taken over by the Soviet Union. Such a claim was debatable at best in the case of Turkey and quite implausible in the case of Greece. During the war, Stalin had promised Churchill that Britain could have a free hand in Greece, and after the war Stalin kept his word. Although the leftist rebels appealed for Soviet aid, Stalin refused to give them any. The rebels did get aid and support from Yugoslavia, which had a communist government, but Yugoslavia was an independent communist state, in no sense a satellite of Russia.

Truman's solution to this dilemma was to use language that was simultaneously alarmist and vague. In his request for the $400 million, which he made in person in a major speech before the Congress, Truman divided the world into two camps, one based on freedom and the other on tyranny. He warned that if the United States failed to help Greece and Turkey, both countries would succumb to tyranny. It sounded as if Truman was referring to the Soviet Union, but technically he wasn't. He was able to scare Congress into appropriating the money without actually accusing the Soviet Union of anything.

Another way Truman was able to obtain Congress's support was by stressing the regional implications of a rebel victory in Greece. "It is necessary only to glance at the map," Truman said in his speech to Congress, "to realize that the survival and integrity of the Greek nation are of grave importance in a much wider situation. If Greece should fall under the control of an armed minority, the effect upon its neighbor, Turkey, would be immediate and serious. Confusion and disorder might well spread throughout the entire Middle East." Truman did not have to mention how important the resources and strategic positions of this region were to the United States and its allies.

Over the next three years, the United States supported the Greek government in its civil war against the leftist rebels. The Greek government was extremely brutal and authoritarian, jailing and torturing political activists accused of supporting the leftist rebels. The U.S.-supported war against the rebels was aided by the fact that in 1948, the government of Yugoslavia, which had been backing the rebels, publicly broke with the Soviet Union, resulting in a major diplomatic crisis. Worried about possible Soviet retaliation, Yugoslavia no longer had time to help out the Greek rebels, whom the Greek government finally defeated in 1950.

Truman's 1947 speech to Congress had an impact that transcended the crises in Greece and Turkey or even in the broader Middle East. For Truman had couched his request for aid in extremely general terms. "It must be the policy of the United States," he said, "to support free peoples who are resisting attempted subjugation by armed minorities or by outside pressures." This statement, which became known as the *Truman Doctrine*, was a totally open-ended commitment. Wherever and whenever "free peoples" were threatened by Soviet-style revolution or tyranny, the United would now have a self-proclaimed obligation to help them. To be sure, the United States would not always fulfill this obligation, but the obligation now existed, and it added to the growing sense of crisis between the superpowers. To a considerable degree, it was the general sense of mission fostered by the Truman Doctrine that eventually propelled the United States into the disastrous military intervention in Vietnam.

As I mentioned earlier, the success of the Marshall Plan depended on the easy availability of Middle Eastern oil. To ensure such availability, the Truman administration worked closely with American oil companies operating in the region, especially in Saudi Arabia, where U.S. companies enjoyed a favored position. In the early postwar years, the Truman administration waived the antitrust laws, permitting American oil companies in Saudi Arabia to share information and pool resources, the better to coordinate the delivery of oil to Europe. Washington also used its diplomatic clout to pave the way for the construction of a pipeline that could carry crude oil from Saudi Arabia to the Mediterranean coast, from which it could then be shipped to Europe.

The most feasible route for such a pipeline was across Jordanian, Syrian, and Lebanese territory. The U.S. government had little difficulty getting the Lebanese and Jordanian governments to agree to the construction of the pipeline across their territory, especially as each government was guaranteed transit fees. But Syria's permission was harder to obtain, since Shukri Quwatli, the Syrian president, was a strident Arab nationalist who was unwilling to be bought off by a few paltry dollars. In 1949, the Truman administration quietly encouraged Husni Zaim, the Syrian army chief of staff, to depose Quwatli in a coup. The coup went off smoothly and bloodlessly, and shortly thereafter President Zaim signed an agreement granting permission for the transit of oil across Syrian territory.

As the Cold War intensified in the late 1940s, the United States drew closer to the Saudi government, whose territory was not simply oil-rich, but strategically located as well within striking distance of the Soviet Union. In 1949, the two countries concluded an agreement whereby the Saudis, in exchange for economic and military aid from the United States, allowed the U.S. Air Force to use an air base in Saudi Arabia. In 1950, President Truman sent a letter to King Ibn Saud pledging that, if Saudi Arabia was ever attacked by the Soviet Union, the United States would come to its defense.

In that same year, 1950, American oil companies reached a historic agreement with the Saudi government over the sharing of oil profits. Interestingly enough, this agreement had its origins in Venezuela, another oil-rich country in which American oil companies were active. In the late 1940s, Venezuela's nationalist government began threatening to nationalize the country's oil facilities. To head off nationalization, the American oil companies agreed to share their profits with the Venezuelan government on a 50-50 basis. The Saudis soon got wind of this arrangement and began demanding similar treatment; they, too, threatened to nationalize the oil facilities if their demand wasn't satisfied. The American oil companies realized that Saudi Arabia would probably have to get a 50-50 deal as well, but they were extremely reluctant make such a significant financial sacrifice, so they turned to the U.S. government for relief.

In 1950, in a controversial decision, the U.S. Treasury Department told the oil companies that, if they went ahead and made a 50-50 deal with the Saudi government, they could deduct the amount of money they turned over to the Saudis from the taxes they paid to the U.S. government. This arrangement benefited almost everyone: the Saudis got a substantially larger share of the oil profits; the oil companies were able to head off nationalization; and the U.S. government could rest assured that Saudi oil would remain available for economic recovery in Europe and in Japan. The big loser in the deal was, of course, the U.S. taxpayer, whose burden would have to be increased to make up for the taxes that American oil companies would no longer be sending to Washington. This clever arrangement came to be called the *Golden Gimmick*.

So in the second half of the 1940s, the Middle East became thoroughly integrated into America's strategy for waging the Cold War. The Middle East was essential not only because its oil was needed to ensure the economic revival of Western Europe, on which America's own geopolitical security was staked, but because its bases could be used in a possible war with Soviet Union. But there were other reasons for U.S. officials to pay close attention to the Middle East in the late 1940s. For it was in those years that the Zionist movement made its bid to establish a Jewish state in Palestine, an endeavor from which Americans could not hope to remain aloof. We'll examine U.S. policy toward the creation of Israel in our next lecture.

Lecture Six
Truman and the Creation of Israel

Scope:

In this lecture, we consider Truman's role in the creation of the state of Israel in the period 1945–1949. We learn that Truman, against the recommendations of most of his foreign policy advisors, gave crucial support to the establishment of a Jewish state in Palestine, first by endorsing the 1947 United Nations partition plan, then by extending immediate recognition to Israel when it declared its independence in 1948. As we recount these events, we consider competing explanations for Truman's support for Zionism: To what extent was Truman motivated by humanitarian considerations, by domestic political concerns, or by Cold War strategizing? We then examine some of the consequences of Israel's creation, in particular, the dispossession of the Palestinian people and the resulting decline in America's reputation in the Arab world.

Outline

I.   In the years 1945–1949, President Harry Truman played a key role in bringing Israel into being and securing its existence. It is safe to say that no other single American action has done more to embitter the Arab world against the United States.

II. Since the early 1920s, Britain had governed Palestine as a League of Nations mandate. On the question of Palestine's future political status, Britain had followed an inconsistent policy.

   A. In the 1920s and 1930s, Britain had worked to implement the Balfour Declaration, permitting a massive influx of European Jewish immigration into Palestine. This development deeply alarmed Palestinian Arabs, who feared that the Zionist movement would result in their dispossession.

   B. In 1939, Britain reversed course and placed severe restrictions on Jewish immigration into Palestine. These restrictions were imposed just as the plight of German Jews was becoming truly desperate, arousing bitter conflict between the Zionist movement and British forces in Palestine.

III. World War II profoundly transformed the Palestine issue.

A. The Nazi Holocaust gave enormous impetus to the Zionist movement, convincing Jews throughout the Western world that they could never be fully secure without a state of their own.

B. The Nazi conquest of Europe, combined with the Zionists' alienation from Britain, caused the center gravity of the Zionist movement to shift to the United States.

C. The issue had been exacerbated by the problem of "displaced persons" (DPs), hundreds of thousands of Europeans—refugees, concentration camp survivors, former prisoners of war, and others—who were being housed in American military camps in Europe.

    1. The U.S. State Department favored returning DPs to their countries of origin; for Jewish DPs, however, this would mean going back to live among the very societies that had victimized them.

    2. Immigrating to Britain or the United States was another conceivable option, but both countries had placed strict limits on the number of Jewish immigrants they would accept.

D. In the immediate aftermath of the war, the Zionists intensified their demands that Britain allow increased Jewish immigration into Palestine.

    1. Britain, which was suffering severe postwar shortages of basic commodities, was reluctant to take any action that might destabilize the Middle East and jeopardize the flow of oil.

    2. A special Anglo-American commission studied the Palestine problem and recommended a solution, the Morrison-Grady Plan, which called for the division of Palestine into semiautonomous Arab and Jewish cantons, loosely linked to each other in a binational federal state. Further Jewish immigration into Palestine was to be subject to approval by both Arabs and Jews.

    3. Zionists rejected the plan because it fell short of their objective: unlimited Jewish immigration into Palestine, resulting in the establishment of an exclusively Jewish state in all or most of that territory.

4. Arabs rejected the plan because they viewed Palestine as an integral part of the Arab world; it should either become an independent Arab state or be attached to another independent Arab state. Asking Palestinians to share their lands with Jewish immigrants from Europe was asking them to pay the price for a tragedy for which they had not been responsible.

IV. The British resisted Zionist pressure, prompting the Zionists to step up their military operations against British forces in Palestine.

A. The Haganah, a military organization representing the Zionist mainstream in Palestine, smuggled thousands of Jews out of DP camps and shipped them illegally to Palestine, in defiance of British restrictions.

B. The Irgun, a right-wing Zionist group, launched commando and, occasionally, terrorist attacks against British targets in Palestine. The bombing of British military and diplomatic headquarters at Jerusalem's King David Hotel resulted in the deaths of 88 people, many of them civilians.

V. In early 1947, Britain gave up on trying to govern Palestine and turned the matter over to the United Nations. The UN formed a special Palestine commission, which recommended that Palestine be partitioned into a Jewish state and an Arab state.

A. The Zionists accepted the partition plan, albeit with some reluctance, because they wanted a larger share of the country than the UN allotted them.

B. The Arab countries, along with the Arabs of Palestine, flatly rejected the partition plan.

1. They objected that the partition plan would force them to share their country with people they regarded as interlopers from Europe.

2. They objected that the specific terms of the partition were unfair, granting more than half of Palestine's territory to a group representing only a third of Palestine's population.

3. The final Arab argument was that the partition plan could not be implemented without uprooting thousands of Palestinian Arabs from their ancestral homes, because

the area set aside for the Jewish state contained many Arab villages.

VI. Although the U.S. State Department opposed the partition plan, Truman instructed his UN ambassador to vote in favor of it. In November 1947, the UN General Assembly approved the partition plan.

   A. Historians have long debated Truman's reasons for supporting the partition plan.

      1. Some stress Truman's humanitarian interest in addressing the plight of Jewish Holocaust survivors.

      2. Others stress his desire to curry favor with American Jews before the 1948 presidential election.

      3. No doubt both motives were present, but there was a third factor in Truman's thinking that historians have too often ignored: the power of inertia. By the fall of 1947, partition seemed to be the least troublesome solution, the one that would get the whole Palestine mess off of Truman's desk at the soonest possible date.

   B. Once Truman decided in favor of partition, his White House advisors, Clark Clifford and David Niles, both committed Zionists, went to work to ensure its passage in the UN. Possibly without Truman's knowledge, they began meeting with the UN delegations of other nations and putting massive pressure on them to vote for partition.

      1. The Philippines, until 1946 an American colony, switched its position after Truman's advisors hinted that U.S. aid to the Philippines might be affected by a negative vote.

      2. It was likewise hinted to Latin American delegations that construction of the Pan-American Highway, on which the economies of many of these countries depended, might not go forward if they voted the wrong way on partition.

VII. Following UN approval of the partition plan by an extremely narrow margin, fighting broke out between Zionists and Palestinian Arabs. Although the Palestinians at first seemed to have the advantage, in early 1948, the tide of battle began turning in the Zionists' favor.

    A. As the Palestinian military position worsened, Palestinian civilians began fleeing from the area allotted to the Jewish state.

    B. As fighting intensified, the State Department convinced Truman to propose that the partition plan be suspended in favor of a UN trusteeship over Palestine, warning that the longer the violence continued, the angrier the Arab world would become at the United States.

    C. But there was insufficient support in the UN General Assembly to adopt this change of policy.

VIII. In May 1948, the Zionists declared the independent state of Israel. Against vigorous opposition from his secretary of state, George Marshall, Truman extended immediate recognition to the new state.

    A. Truman recognized Israel for much the same reasons that he supported the partition plan: humanitarianism, domestic politics, and inertia.

    B. An additional reason was Truman's desire to prevent the Soviet Union from recognizing Israel first and, thus, currying favor with the new state.

IX. Immediately following Israel's declaration of independence, the armies of the surrounding Arab states invaded Palestine in an effort to prevent Israel from coming into being. But the Israeli forces, better armed and better organized, won a decisive military victory over the Arab states.

    A. By the time armistices were concluded in early 1949, the Israelis not only had successfully held on to the area allotted to them by the UN but had managed to take over a large part of the projected Arab state.

    B. Meanwhile, about 750,000 Palestinian civilians had either fled or been driven from their homes in the territory now held by Israel.

X. Over the next few years, Israel and the Arab states generally abided by the armistice, but they were far from real peace.

    A. Israel refused to repatriate the Palestinian refugees or to relinquish any of the additional territory it had seized.

    B. The Arab states refused to make peace with Israel, or to extend it formal recognition, as long as Israel held to these positions.

XI. Truman himself was unhappy with Israel's postwar attitude, especially regarding Palestinian refugees. For the next two years, he tried to convince Israel to repatriate at least some of the refugees.

    A. But the Israelis adamantly opposed such a course, and Truman, preoccupied with other foreign crises, eventually gave up on trying to change Israel's position.

    B. Such passivity was in keeping with Truman's whole approach to the Palestine crisis.

XII. For all his passivity, however, the fact remained that Truman had played a key role in bringing Israel into being and displacing a preexisting Arab society. Consequently, America's reputation in the Arab world drastically declined.

Suggested Reading:

Christison, Kathleen. *Perceptions of Palestine: Their Influence on U.S.-Middle East Policy*. Berkeley: University of California Press, 1999 (2000).

Cohen, Michael J. *Truman and Israel*. Berkeley: University of California Press, 1990.

Smith, Charles D. *Palestine and the Arab-Israeli Conflict*. 4th ed. New York: St. Martin's Press, 2001.

Questions to Consider:

1. Were the aspirations of Zionists and Palestinian Arabs completely irreconcilable, or could some formula have been found that would have been acceptable to both peoples?

2. Even if the establishment of a Jewish state in Palestine was a foregone conclusion, could President Truman have helped to implement that decision in a way that minimized Arab resentment of the United States?

Borders of State of Israel at armistice 1949

JEWISH STATE

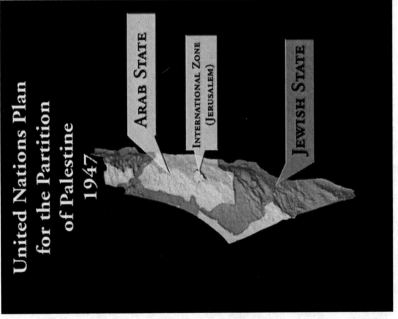

United Nations Plan for the Partition of Palestine 1947

ARAB STATE

INTERNATIONAL ZONE (JERUSALEM)

JEWISH STATE

Lecture Six—Transcript
Truman and the Creation of Israel

In this lecture we're going to look at the circumstances surrounding the creation of the state of Israel in 1948. Needless to say, this was a momentous event in Middle Eastern history, one that would influence virtually every aspect of subsequent U.S. policy in the region, down to the present day. The U.S. government, under President Harry Truman, played a key role in bringing Israel into being, and it's safe to say that no other single American action has done more to embitter the Arab world against the United States. Justified or not, that bitterness has become a basic fact of life in U.S.-Arab relations, one that American policy makers cannot afford to ignore.

Much of the historical background for the creation of Israel has already been sketched out in the previous lectures for this course. As you know, after World War I, the League of Nations awarded Britain a mandate over Palestine, and Britain took over that mandate determined to fulfill the Balfour Declaration of 1917, in which Britain had pledged to support the establishment in Palestine of "a national home for the Jewish people." In the 1920s and 1930s, with official British support, there was a massive influx of Jewish immigration into Palestine. Jewish immigration was especially high after Hitler came to power in 1933 and began persecuting German Jews, causing a growing number of them to flee the country. Between 1920 and 1939, Jews went from being about one-tenth of the population of Palestine to being nearly one-third.

Palestinian Arabs were deeply alarmed by this development. Their opposition to the Zionist program was so intense that Britain decided to reverse course by issuing the White Paper of 1939, which placed strict limits on the number of Jews admitted into Palestine each year, and which announced that Jewish immigration would end entirely in a few years' time. It also called for the regulation of land sales to Zionist institutions and individuals. The Zionists bitterly opposed the White Paper and began an uprising of their own against the British in Palestine. This uprising remained muted during World War II, mainly because the Zionists, for obvious reasons, supported the British war effort against Germany, but it would erupt in full fury in the immediate aftermath of the war.

World War II had a profoundly transforming effect on the Palestine issue. First and foremost, the Nazi holocaust of the 1940s gave an enormous impetus to the Zionist movement. Prior to Hitler's rise to power, most Jews in the West had been committed to the idea of assimilating into the larger societies in which they found themselves. But with the rise of Hitler and the subsequent holocaust, Jews became increasingly convinced that anti-Semitism was so powerful that true assimilation was impossible. Jews could never be truly secure, the argument went, until they had acquired a homeland of their own. So by 1945 many Jews who had previously opposed Zionism were taking a more serious look at the Zionist project in Palestine.

It was also during World War II that the center of gravity of the Zionist movement shifted from Europe to the United States. Not only was most of continental Europe now under Axis control, but Britain had alienated the Zionists by issuing the White Paper. Increasingly, therefore, Zionist activists began seeking the support of American Jews and the patronage of the American government. This shift in orientation was both symbolized and accelerated by the Biltmore Conference of 1942, named for the hotel in New York City where the main components of the international Zionist movement met to coordinate policy. At the Biltmore Conference the Zionist movement united behind a call for unlimited Jewish immigration into Palestine, leading to the establishment in that territory of a fully sovereign Jewish state.

These were the circumstances that Harry Truman confronted when he was suddenly thrust into the presidency in April 1945, following the death of Franklin Roosevelt. Initially, Truman approached the Palestine issue as an extension of the crisis surrounding "displaced persons," or DPs. In the immediate aftermath of World War II, hundreds of thousands of homeless Europeans—refugees, concentration camp survivors, former prisoners of war, and others— were being housed in American military camps in Europe. Among these DPs were tens of thousands of Jewish holocaust survivors. Conditions in the DP camps were often squalid, and in the first year after the war their inmates continued to die in the hundreds, succumbing to disease or to the cumulative effects of years of malnourishment.

What to do about the DPs was a pressing and delicate issue. The U.S. State Department favored returning them to their countries of origin. But for most Jewish DPs this was out of the question, since that would mean going back to live amid the very societies that had victimized them during the war, or had acquiesced in their victimization. Immigrating to Britain or the United States was another possibility, which many Jewish holocaust survivors would no doubt have welcomed, but both countries had placed strict limits on the number of Jewish immigrants they would accept. Palestine emerged as the logical alternative, and Jews throughout the Western world—in DP camps, in Britain, and in the United States—stepped up their demands that Britain ease its restrictions on Jewish immigration into Palestine.

Britain, however, was unwilling to increase its quotas on Jewish immigration into Palestine, which now admitted 15,000 people per year. In the early postwar months, Britain was suffering from severe shortages of basic commodities, including oil, and its government was extremely reluctant to take any action that might destabilize the Middle East and jeopardize the flow of the oil. Still, something had to be done about the DP camps, whose terrible conditions were becoming a public scandal in the United States.

In June 1945, President Truman, then only weeks in office, of course, asked Earl G. Harrison, dean of the University of Pennsylvania Law School, to go to Europe to investigate the condition of the camps. Harrison was shocked by what he found, and he wrote a report in which he recommended that Britain be pressured to allow 100,000 Jewish DPs to immigrate to Palestine immediately. Truman accepted this recommendation and officially conveyed it to the British government. The British were not thrilled by the request, and they put Truman off by proposing instead that a special Anglo-American commission be formed to study the Palestine problem and recommend a solution. Truman agreed.

The result of this inquiry was the Morrison-Grady Plan, named for its British and American authors, which was submitted in the spring of 1946. The Morrison-Grady Plan called for the division of Palestine into semi-autonomous Arab and Jewish cantons, which would be loosely linked to each other in a bi-national state. The plan also proposed that any further Jewish immigration into Palestine be subject to approval by both Arabs and Jews. The Morrison-Grady plan was immediately rejected by Zionists and Arabs alike.

The Zionists' position is easy enough to fathom, since Morrison-Grady fell far short of their objectives: unlimited Jewish immigration into Palestine, resulting in the establishment of an exclusively Jewish state in all or most of that territory. Morrison-Grady didn't satisfy those demands, so the Zionists rejected it. The Arab rejection of the plan may be little harder to fathom since, considering how things would turn out later, the Palestinians probably would have been better off had Morrison-Grady been adopted. To comprehend the Arabs' rejection, it is important to appreciate how things appeared from their perspective.

As the Arabs saw it, Palestine was an integral part of the Arab world and should either become an independent Arab state in its own right or be attached to some other independent Arab state. It should not have to be shared with an influx of immigrants from Europe. The only reason Jews now made up about a third of the whole population of Palestine was because Britain had taken over the country and opened it up to foreign immigration against the will of its Arab inhabitants. Most Arab leaders acknowledged that the Nazi holocaust had been an immense tragedy for the Jewish people, but they insisted that the Arabs should not be made to pay the price for it. After all, they were not the ones who had tried to exterminate the Jews. The Arabs, too, rejected Morrison-Grady.

With no solution to the DP problem on the immediate horizon, Zionist activists were increasingly taking matters into their own hands. The Haganah, the military organization representing the Zionist mainstream in Palestine, smuggled thousands of Jews out of the DP camps and shipped them illegally to Palestine, in defiance of British restrictions. Meanwhile, the Irgun, a right-wing Zionist group, launched commando, and occasionally terrorist, attacks against British targets in Palestine. The most notorious of these attacks occurred in 1946, when the Irgun set off a bomb in Jerusalem's King David Hotel, which was then serving as Britain's military and diplomatic headquarters. Eighty-eight people, many of them civilians, died in the blast.

By 1947, the British had had enough. Early that year, around the same time that they said that they could no longer take responsibility for Greece and Turkey, the British announced that they would be pulling out of Palestine and turning the whole mess over to the newly created United Nations. A special UN commission was formed to investigate the Palestine issue and propose a solution. In the late summer of 1947, the UN commission issued its report, which recommended that Palestine be partitioned into two states, one Arab and one Jewish. The Zionists accepted this proposal, albeit with some reluctance, since they had wanted a larger share of the country than the UN had allotted them.

The Arab countries, along with the Arabs of Palestine, flatly rejected the partition plan by a very narrow margin. They did so for much the same reason that they had rejected Morrison-Grady: In their view, Palestine was essentially an Arab country, and it should not have to be shared with European Jews, whether that sharing took the form of federation or partition. The Arabs also objected that, even if the partition plan could be justified in principle, its terms were unfair, since it allotted 56 percent of the land to a group that then represented only one-third of the population of historic Palestine. There were then about 600,000 Jews to 1.3 million Arabs. The final Arab argument was that the partition plan could not be implemented without uprooting thousands of Palestinian Arabs from their ancestral homes, since the area set aside for the Jewish state contained many Arab villages.

In the fall of 1947, the partition plan was voted on in the UN General Assembly, and President Truman had to decide how the United States would vote. The U.S. State Department strongly opposed the partition plan, warning that it would so enrage the Arab states that they might embargo oil shipments to the West or even align with the Soviet Union in the Cold War. But Truman overruled the State Department and decided to support partition.

Truman's motives in doing so have long been debated by historians. Some stress the moral angle, noting that Truman was deeply moved by the plight of Jewish holocaust survivors and saw Jewish statehood as a just measure to help rectify their situation. Other historians have emphasized domestic politics, arguing that Truman supported the Zionist program mostly to gain the support of American Jews—and supporters of Zionism generally—in the 1948 presidential election. Scholars making this argument point to the ceaseless activities of Truman's White House advisors, especially Clark Clifford, the special counsel to the president, and David Niles, the president's special advisor for minority affairs. Unlike the officials at the State Department, Clifford and Niles were deeply concerned with Truman's reelection prospects, as well as being committed Zionists in their own right, and they constantly reminded Truman of the domestic implications of his policy decisions on Palestine.

Undoubtedly, Truman acted out both of these motivations. He thought supporting the establishment of a Jewish state was morally right and politically wise. But there was a third factor at work that historians have all too often ignored: the power of inertia. By the fall of 1947, partition seemed to be the least problematic solution, the one that would cause Truman the fewest headaches, take up the smallest amount of his time, and get the whole Palestine mess off of his desk at the soonest possible date. The main alternative to partition, the Morrison-Grady Plan, had been rejected by both Zionists and Arabs, whereas partition had the support of at least one of the contending parties. Truman instructed the American delegation at the UN to vote in favor of partition.

Once Truman decided in favor of partition, Clifford and Niles went to work to ensure its passage in the UN. Without Truman's explicit approval, and possibly without his knowledge as well, they began meeting with the UN delegations of other nations and putting massive pressure on them to vote for partition. The government of the Philippines, which until 1946 had been an American colony, initially planned to vote against partition but changed its position when Truman's underlings hinted that U.S. aid to the Philippines might be affected by a negative vote. It was likewise hinted to Latin American delegations that construction of the Pan-American Highway, on which the economies of many Latin American countries depended, might not go forward if Latin American countries voted the wrong way on partition. In November 1947, the General Assembly approved the partition plan by a very narrow margin.

As soon as partition was approved by the UN, fighting broke out between Zionists and Palestinian Arabs. The conflict was extremely vicious, with close hand-to-hand combat and high civilian casualties on both sides. Although the Palestinians at first seemed to have the advantage, in early 1948 the tide of battle began turning in the Zionists' favor. As the Palestinians' military position worsened,

Palestinian civilians began fleeing from the area allotted to the Jewish state. At first, this exodus consisted primarily of wealthy and upper middle-class Palestinians, but soon peasants and poorer townspeople were fleeing as well.

As the situation in Palestine deteriorated, officials at the U.S. State Department began lobbying for reconsideration of the partition plan, arguing that the outbreak of violence had vindicated their opposition to partition. The longer that violence continued, they warned, the angrier the Arab world would become with the United States, with dire consequences for U.S. interests in that oil-rich and strategically located region. In January 1948, a State Department policy study warned that:

> As a result of U.S. sponsorship of UN action leading to the recommendation to partition Palestine, U.S. prestige in the Moslem world has suffered a severe blow and U.S. strategic interests in the Mediterranean and Near East have been seriously prejudiced. Our vital interests in those areas will continue to be adversely affected to the extent that we continue to support partition.

The State Department urged Truman to abandon the partition plan and adopt a new policy instead. The alternative approach the State Department favored was for Palestine to be placed under a UN trusteeship until a new political solution to the conflict could be found. This would calm down the situation and reduce the likelihood that the Arab world might be overtaken by anti-American feeling.

Truman's White House advisors, not surprisingly, strenuously opposed the idea of abandoning the partition plan in favor of trusteeship. Although domestic politics certainly played a role in their thinking, they defended their position on substantive grounds, arguing that the State Department was vastly overestimating the ability of the Arab states to punish America for supporting the Zionist movement. In March 1948, Clark Clifford complained to Truman that "the United States appears in the ridiculous role of trembling before threats of a few nomadic desert tribes…The Arabs need us more than we need them. They must have oil royalties or go bankrupt."

On this occasion, however, Truman sided with the State Department, authorizing the U.S. delegation to propose the trusteeship idea to the

United Nations. But trusteeship could not be adopted until two-thirds of the nations in the UN General Assembly voted in favor of it, and such a super-majority proved impossible to obtain. Although the outbreak of fighting in Palestine had caused many governments to reconsider the wisdom of partition, they found it difficult to justify switching over to trusteeship, which was opposed not just by the Zionists but by the Arabs as well, because it fell short of full self-determination for the Palestinians. Much to the Zionists' relief, the UN General Assembly failed to adopt the trusteeship proposal.

Meanwhile, back in Palestine, the Zionists continued to gain the upper hand, and in May 1948 they decided to declare an independent state of Israel. Now Truman had to decide whether to recognize the new state. Once again, the State Department advised against recognition, and once again Truman rejected the advice. In addition to the moral and political reasons I mentioned already, Truman now worried that if he failed to recognize Israel immediately, and if the Soviet Union recognized it first, then the new state might not be so favorably inclined toward the United States. For although the Soviets would later side with the Arabs, in 1948 they supported the creation of a Jewish state in Palestine, seeing it as a potential vehicle for the extension of Soviet influence in the Middle East. To beat Moscow to the punch, Truman recognized Israel just 11 minutes after it declared its independence.

Immediately following Israel's declaration of independence, the armies of the surrounding Arab states invaded Palestine in an effort to prevent Israel from coming into being. But the Israeli forces were better armed and better organized, and even had a numerical advantage over the combined Arab armies, a fact that is seldom acknowledged; in June 1948, there were about 36,000 Israeli soldiers to about 30,000 Arab ones. By summer, the disparity was even more heavily in Israel's favor. Consequently, Israel won a decisive military victory over the Arab states. By the time armistices was concluded in early 1949, the Israelis had not only successfully held on to the area allotted to them by the UN but managed to take over a large part of the projected Arab state as well.

The independent Arab state never came into being, since its territory was taken over by neighboring Arab states. Jordan annexed the West Bank and the eastern part of Jerusalem, while Egypt took over the Gaza Strip. Meanwhile, about 750,000 Palestinian civilians had either fled or been driven from their homes, and were now living in squalid refugee camps in neighboring Arab countries. The Arab states insisted that the refugees be allowed to return to their homes, but the Israelis refused on the grounds that this would alter the Jewish character of their newly enlarged state. Truman was not happy that the Israelis were taking this position, and for the next couple years he tried to convince them to repatriate at least some of the refugees. But the Israelis were adamantly opposed to such a course, and Truman, increasingly preoccupied with other foreign crises, especially the Korean War, which began in mid-1950, eventually gave up on trying to change Israel's position.

Such passivity was in keeping with Truman's whole approach to the Palestine crisis. While Truman's pro-Israel stance was motivated by both humanitarianism and domestic politics, inertia, too, played a large role in his attitude. Beyond supporting partition and extending recognition, Truman was not prepared to take concrete steps to bring a Jewish state into being. He refused, for example, to take part in any UN effort to enforce partition militarily, even though many of his advisors had warned that such an effort might be necessary. When fighting erupted between Zionists and Palestinians after the partition vote, and when a full-scale war broke out after Israel's declaration of independence, Truman essentially left the Zionists to fight their own battle. His administration's passivity and ineffectualness were nicely captured in a public statement made in 1948 by the U.S. ambassador to the United Nations, who implored the Zionists and the Arabs to end the fighting and to "settle this problem in a true Christian spirit."

Accordingly, when the Zionists eventually prevailed in the war, showing they could secure their political independence on their own, there was palpable relief in the White House over the fact that outside intervention had not been necessary. To be sure, Truman was not happy about Israel's postwar attitude, especially regarding Palestinian refugees, but getting Israel to compromise on such questions would have required far more energy and political capital than Truman was prepared to expend. He eventually abandoned the effort, leaving these contentious issues to his successors. But for all his passivity, the fact remains that Truman played a key role in bringing Israel into being, first by pushing through the partition plan, and then by extending recognition to the newly proclaimed Jewish state. As a consequence of these actions, America's image in the Arab world drastically declined.

Prior to 1947, the United States had enjoyed a benign reputation in the Arab countries, especially when compared with that of other major Western powers; American involvement in the region had been almost entirely missionary, philanthropic, educational, or commercial. Now, in the space of a few years, much of that goodwill turned to bitter resentment, an attitude that persists to this day. Although most Arab governments remained pro-American, Arab public opinion was deeply distressed by the plight of the Palestinian refugees and placed much of the blame for it on the United States. In the coming years, it would be harder for such governments to justify their close relations with the United States

The Arab countries' relations with Israel were, of course, even more embittered. In early 1949, as I mentioned, the Arabs and the Israelis had agreed to armistice agreements, but they were far from peace. Israel not only refused to repatriate the refugees, but refused to give up any of the additional territory it had seized. The Arabs refused to make peace with Israel, or extend formal recognition to it, as long as Israel took these positions.

It is often claimed that in the first few decades following Israel's creation, the Arab states were entirely opposed to its existence. This is not quite true. The official position of most Arab states was that there could be no peace with Israel until Israel gave up the territory exceeding its allotment in the 1947 partition plan, which most Arab governments now retroactively accepted, and until it allowed Palestinian refugees to return to their homes. The implication was that peace would be possible if those conditions were met. In their public statements, however, Arab governments seldom stated this position plainly; rather than coming out and saying that they were prepared to recognize Israel under certain conditions, they would simply insist on the implementation of all relevant UN resolutions, by which they meant the 1947 partition plan and subsequent resolutions calling for the repatriation of Palestinian refugees. They would say, "Implement all the resolutions" and leave it at that.

This coyness was mainly a response to public opinion in Arab countries, which remained outraged by what had happened to the Palestinians. It was very difficult, politically, for any Arab leader to speak publicly about making peace with Israel. Still, the official position of most Arab governments, conveyed in diplomatic documents, did leave the door open to a negotiated settlement. But publicly, as I said, the overwhelming mood in the Arab world was one of fierce resistance to Israel's existence, and deep resentment against the United States for having served as the midwife for Israel's birth.

As we'll see in the next lecture, in the 1950s, this mood would help fuel a powerful Arab nationalist movement, seriously challenging Washington's efforts to keep the nations of the Middle East oriented toward the West.

Lecture Seven
Eisenhower, the Cold War, and the Middle East

Scope:

In this lecture, we examine Dwight D. Eisenhower's response, in the years 1953–1956, to the challenges posed by indigenous Middle Eastern nationalists, who often resisted Eisenhower's efforts to enlist the countries of the Middle East in the Cold War. We first consider Iran, where in 1953, the Eisenhower administration colluded with the British government to achieve the overthrow of Muhammad Mossadeq's nationalist regime. We then move to the Arab world, where Washington faced a more formidable adversary in Egypt's Gamal Abdel Nasser, whom Eisenhower was reluctant to confront directly. We examine how the Eisenhower administration tried to win Nasser over by hastening the decolonization process and taking a more "even-handed" position on the Arab-Israeli conflict. But these measures failed to arrest Nasser's drift toward the Soviet orbit, prompting the administration to adopt a far less tolerant attitude toward the Egyptian leader in the spring of 1956.

Outline

I. During the Eisenhower years, the United States was confronted by the forces of indigenous Middle Eastern nationalism. These nationalist forces posed a serious challenge to Washington's efforts to enlist the countries of the Middle East in the Cold War.

   A. Eisenhower was regarded, especially by liberal intellectuals, as a doddering old geezer who was not really "on top of things" in governing the country. Eisenhower's strategy, however, was to let everyone think he was not really in charge so that, if any of his policies failed or were controversial, all the criticism would be directed at his advisors and cabinet members rather than at him.

   B. Eisenhower was also dismissed at the time because his extemporaneous speaking style was artless and convoluted.

II. In the Middle East, the Eisenhower administration's fundamental objectives were the same as the Truman administration's.

   A. Eisenhower wanted to maintain Western access to the region's oil reserves and strategic positions.

B. He also hoped to deny those assets to the Soviet Union.

III. Yet Eisenhower also thought that the previous administration had been excessively partial to Israel. He resolved to follow a more "even-handed" policy on the Arab-Israeli conflict.

A. In practice, this meant encouraging the Israelis to make modest territorial concessions in exchange for peace with the Arabs.

B. The Eisenhower administration did not, however, favor a return to the 1947 partition plan. Rather, it favored a territorial compromise between the partition plan and post-1949 status quo.

C. Nor did the administration favor the wholesale repatriation of Palestinian refugees. It preferred that most refugees be resettled in other Arab lands.

IV. The Eisenhower administration was ambivalent about the future role in the Middle East of its European allies.

A. On the one hand, the administration was committed in principle to full political independence for Middle Eastern countries.

B. On the other hand, it feared that too rapid a withdrawal of European power and influence would leave Middle Eastern states susceptible to Soviet influence.

V. U.S. actions in Iran in 1953 reveal the Eisenhower administration's determination to keep the region oriented toward the West.

A. For the last couple of decades, a British company, the Anglo-Iranian Oil Company (AIOC), had controlled the extraction, production, and marketing of Iranian oil.

B. In early 1951, the Iranian parliament voted to nationalize the facilities of the AIOC. Shortly thereafter, Mohammed Mossadeq, the main architect of Iran's nationalization policy, was elected prime minister.

1. Mossadeq was ridiculed in the West as a hypochondriac, given to crying fits in public.

2. In his own country, Mossadeq was revered as a charismatic figure whose defiant opposition to British domination, especially his nationalization of the AIOC, captured the imagination of the Iranian public.

C. Britain responded harshly to the nationalization of the AIOC's facilities.

   1. It imposed an embargo on Iranian oil in an attempt to wreck Iran's economy.

   2. It advocated a military takeover of the AIOC's oil refinery in Abadan, on the southern coast of Iran.

D. The Truman administration opposed military intervention, fearing that it might provoke a Soviet invasion in Iran.

E. Meanwhile, Britain's boycott was devastating Iran's economy.

   1. This, in turn, caused Mossadeq to lose popularity, compelling him to govern in an increasingly authoritarian manner.

   2. He also began challenging the pro-American Shah for supremacy in Iran.

F. Eisenhower took a harsher view of Mossadeq than Truman had done, seeing Mossadeq's radical policies as destabilizing the country and paving the way for an ultimate Soviet takeover.

G. In the summer of 1953, the CIA sent Kermit Roosevelt to Iran to recruit officers in the Iranian military to stage a coup against Mossadeq.

   1. Roosevelt hired local gangs to stage anti-government demonstrations in the streets of Tehran.

   2. With the city in chaos, the pro-U.S. Iranian army officers seized control of the government, replacing Mossadeq with a pro-Shah prime minister.

H. It was a crushing defeat for Mossadeq and Iranian nationalism.

   1. The nationalization of Iranian oil facilities remained formally intact. But a consortium of foreign oil companies was allowed to control and market Iran's oil, with the AIOC surrendering a large share of the operation to American oil companies.

   2. Iran became a major recipient of U.S. economic aid. The Shah himself was now deeply beholden to the United States.

3. At the time, U.S. officials thought they had won a splendid victory, but once the Shah was reinstalled in power, he governed much more repressively than before. Ordinary Iranians came to see him as a puppet of Washington; the ultimate consequences of these perceptions were later to become clear in the Iranian revolution of the late 1970s.

VI. Eisenhower faced a more potent challenge in Arab nationalism. Two issues made it extremely difficult, politically, for Arab leaders to align with the United States in the Cold War.

A. The first issue involved the lingering vestiges of British and French imperialism in the Arab world. The fact that the United States was formally allied with Britain and France aroused considerable popular resentment in the Arab world.

B. The second issue was Zionism. The fact that the United States had played a key role in the creation of Israel aroused even deeper Arab resentment.

C. As the 1950s began, the United States faced a basic dilemma regarding its approach to the Arab world because of its close alliances with Britain and France. It had to keep the Arab states favorably disposed toward the West and keep the region's oil reserves and strategic positions accessible to the United States while, at the same time, remaining committed to Israel's survival and security, a position that caused deep resentment in the Arab world.

D. Arab resistance to U.S. Cold War policy became especially potent after 1952, when a group of officers led by Gamal Abdel Nasser took power in Egypt. Over the next two decades, Nasser was to be an extremely forceful and charismatic advocate of radical Arab nationalism and of resistance to Western domination.

E. Initially, however, the Eisenhower administration hoped for a cooperative relationship with Nasser. Instead of pressuring Egypt to join an anti-Soviet pact, the administration sought to address Egypt's grievances against European imperialism and Zionism.

    1. It convinced Britain to agree to withdraw its troops from the Suez Canal Zone.

2. It began trying to broker a peace agreement between Egypt and Israel.
3. These measures, the administration hoped, would cause Egypt and other Arab countries to become favorably disposed toward the West.

F. Britain, however, did not fully cooperate with Eisenhower's soft-sell approach. In 1955, it formed a Middle Eastern defense organization, known as the *Baghdad Pact*, which Nasser regarded as threatening to Egypt.
1. Nasser reacted by publicly advocating a policy of nonalignment in the Cold War and vilifying Arab governments with close ties to the West.
2. Nasser also purchased arms from the Soviet bloc.

G. Still, the Eisenhower administration was not yet ready to give up on Nasser. In late 1955 and early 1956, it took two actions aimed at renewing Egypt's ties to the Western camp.
1. It agreed to finance the Aswan Dam project.
2. It pushed harder for an Arab-Israeli settlement.

H. In March 1956, however, Nasser indicated that he was not willing to take the lead in reaching a peace agreement with Israel. He feared that doing so would jeopardize his political standing in the Arab world.

I. The Eisenhower administration reacted by adopting a much tougher policy on Nasser.
1. It curtailed economic aid to Egypt.
2. It made it difficult for American charitable groups to function in Egypt.
3. It began dragging out the negotiations over Western financing of the Aswan Dam.
4. It increased economic aid to pro-U.S. Arab governments.
5. Although it did not increase U.S. military aid to Israel, it encouraged other Western countries, such as France and Canada, to sell military aircraft to Israel.

J. All these measures, the administration hoped, would leave Egypt so impoverished and isolated that it would have to rethink its defiant position.

Suggested Reading:

Hahn, Peter L. *The United States, Great Britain, and Egypt, 1945–1956*. Chapel Hill: University of North Carolina Press, 1991.

Heiss, Mary Ann. *Empire and Nationhood: The United States, Great Britain, and Iranian Oil, 1950–1954*. New York: Columbia University Press, 1997.

Questions to Consider:

1. In what ways did the forces of indigenous Middle Eastern nationalism pose a challenge to U.S. efforts to wage the Cold War?

2. What broad political strategy did the Eisenhower administration use to meet the challenge of Arab nationalism in particular?

Lecture Seven—Transcript
Eisenhower, the Cold War, and the Middle East

In this lecture, and in the next, we'll look at U.S. Middle East policy during the presidency of Dwight D. Eisenhower. In these years, the United States was confronted by the forces of indigenous Middle Eastern nationalism, first in Iran and then in the Arab world. These nationalist forces posed a serious challenge to Washington's efforts to enlist the Middle East in the Cold War.

During the whole time he served in the White House, Eisenhower was widely regarded, especially by liberal intellectuals, as a doddering old geezer who cared more about his golf game than about governing the country. But years later, when Eisenhower's presidential papers were opened to researchers, it became clear that he was much more on top of things than he seemed at the time. In fact, Eisenhower was so supremely self-confident, that he was perfectly happy to let everyone think he was not really in charge. That way, if any of his policies failed or were controversial, all the criticism would be directed at the relevant advisers and cabinet members, rather than at him.

Another reason Eisenhower was dismissed at the time was that his extemporaneous speaking style was incredibly artless and convoluted. His syntax was so tangled up, that it was often hard to tell what he was trying to say, strengthening the impression of a befuddled old man seriously out of his depth. Here, too, Eisenhower knew exactly what he was doing. Once, when the president was preparing for a press conference, his press secretary fretted over how to handle a particularly sensitive foreign policy issue. "Don't worry, Jim," Eisenhower said. "If that question comes up, I'll just confuse them."

In the Middle East, Eisenhower's fundamental objectives were much the same as Truman's had been: maintaining Western access to the region's oil reserves and strategic positions while denying them to the Soviet Union. Yet Eisenhower and John Foster Dulles, his secretary of state, also thought that the previous administration had been excessively partial to Israel, an attitude that had heightened the Arabs' sense of grievance against the West and given the Soviets an opportunity to increase their political influence in the area. While committed to Israel's survival and security, Eisenhower and Dulles resolved to follow a more "even-handed" policy.

The Eisenhower administration was ambivalent about the future role of its European allies in the area. While committed in principle to full political independence for Middle Eastern countries, it still hoped that the allies, France and especially Britain, would be able to hold the line in the Middle East and keep that area oriented toward the West. The administration feared that too rapid a withdrawal of European power and influence would leave Middle Eastern states susceptible to Soviet influence. Ideally, Britain and France themselves would work out an arrangement whereby the countries of the Middle East, in exchange for a gradual increase in independence, would voluntarily consent to the continuation of close ties to the West and allow those European countries to maintain their military bases and other interests in the area.

U.S. actions in Iran in 1953 reveal the Eisenhower administration's determination to keep the region oriented toward the West. Back in 1946, as we've seen, the Soviets had been reluctant to withdraw their troops from the country. Even after the Russians did withdraw, the Americans remained concerned about a possible Soviet takeover of Iran, if not by direct military means, then perhaps by political means, in particular by exploiting Iranian grievances against the West.

At the time, Iran was under heavy British domination, and a British company called the Anglo-Iranian Oil Company, or AIOC, enjoyed a monopoly over the drilling, refining, and marketing of Iranian oil. Only about 20 percent of the profits from that oil stayed in Iran. Although the AIOC hired thousands of Iranians, the managerial positions were occupied by British subjects, with Iranians confined to menial jobs. The company's facilities were strictly segregated and highly unequal; there were drinking fountains with signs saying, "Not for Iranians." The behavior of the AIOC was one Iranian grievance against the West; another was Britain's strong support for the young Shah of Iran, Mohammed Reza Shah Pahlevi, a reactionary ruler out of touch with his own people.

In the spring of 1951, when Truman was still president, the Iranian parliament voted to nationalize the facilities of AIOC. Shortly thereafter Mohammed Mossadeq, the main architect of Iran's nationalization policy, was elected prime minister. Mossadeq was easily ridiculed in the West. He liked to spend all day in his pajamas, even when giving speeches and receiving official visitors; he was given to crying fits in public; he was a hypochondriac, always pretending to be sicker than he really was. He would use this to his advantage in negotiations; if he was dealing with someone and the other person pushed him a bit too hard, he would go into a coughing fit that would cause the other person to worry that he might cause Mossadeq to keel over if he wasn't careful.

In his own country, however, Mossadeq was a revered and charismatic figure whose defiant opposition to British domination, and especially his nationalization of the AIOC, captured the imagination of the Iranian public. Britain retaliated for the nationalization decree by mounting a boycott against Iranian oil. As long as the nationalization remained in effect, Britain refused to extract, refine, or market any Iranian oil. The Truman administration, too, was disturbed by the nationalization of the AIOC, seeing it as a dangerous precedent for other oil-producing countries, and it supported the British boycott by discouraging American companies from distributing Iranian oil. Since oil exports accounted for two-thirds of Iran's foreign exchange, Britain's boycott was deeply damaging to the Iranian economy. But Mossadeq refused to rescind the nationalization, and for the time being, the Iranian public strongly backed him up.

Although the British and the Americans both opposed Iran's nationalization policy, they did not fully agree over how to respond to that challenge. The British wanted to force Mossadeq from power, and when the oil boycott failed to accomplish this objective, they began advocating a military takeover of the AIOC's oil refinery in Abadan, on the southern coast of Iran. The Abadan facility was the largest oil refinery in the world; by seizing it, Britain would regain a huge share of Iranian oil production. The Truman administration was opposed to this course; it warned that a British intervention in Abadan might provoke the Soviet Union, Iran's neighbor to the north, to launch a much larger intervention of its own, causing the whole country to fall under Soviet control. The Americans instead hoped that Mossadeq could be compelled, by the pressure of the boycott, to agree to a compromise with the British.

To facilitate such an outcome, Truman offered to mediate the dispute between Iran and Britain. In the fall of 1951 Mossadeq came to Washington to discuss the matter with U.S. officials. After weeks of intensive bargaining, Mossadeq and the Americans worked out the general outlines of a deal. The nationalization of Iranian oil fields themselves would remain in effect, but the AIOC would be permitted to set up a separate company to buy, ship, and market Iranian oil. The resulting profits would be shared by Iran and the AIOC on a 50-50 basis, the same deal American oil companies had recently made with Saudi Arabia. That was the deal worked out by U.S. and Iranian governments. The British rejected the U.S.-Iranian agreement, on the grounds that nationalization was unacceptable in and of itself, so the standoff continued.

Britain's boycott had a devastating effect on Iran's economy, and the longer it continued the harder life became for ordinary Iranians. Inflation ran rampant, law and order collapsed, and Mossadeq began losing popularity. To compensate for his loss of domestic support, Mossadeq governed in an increasingly authoritarian manner, dissolving parliament, imposing martial law, issuing decrees, and intimidating his opponents. Mossadeq even began challenging the Shah for supremacy in the country. The Shah, for his part, was extremely weak and indecisive, and seemed to have no idea of how to counter Mossadeq.

This was where things stood when Eisenhower became president in January 1953. Eisenhower's appearance on the scene was bad news for Mossadeq. The Truman administration had been exasperated by Mossadeq, but it did see him as a genuine nationalist who would serve as a barrier to Soviet domination of Iran. Eisenhower and his advisors took a much harsher view. Although they realized that Mossadeq himself was no communist, they thought his radical policies were destabilizing the country in such a way as to make it vulnerable to an ultimate Soviet takeover. So the Eisenhower administration joined with the British government in plotting Mossadeq's downfall.

In the summer of 1953, a CIA agent named Kermit Roosevelt—who happened to be the grandson of President Teddy Roosevelt—was secretly dispatched to Iran, where he began recruiting officers in the Iranian military to stage a coup against Mossadeq. In the early phase of the operation, the entire effort almost collapsed when Mossadeq learned of the plot and had one of the dissident officers arrested, causing the Shah to panic and flee the country, eventually ending up in Rome, but Roosevelt pushed ahead with the operation.

With CIA money, he recruited a motley collection of street thugs, off-duty policemen, soldiers out of uniform, and even muscle-men from a local circus and got them to stage anti-government demonstrations on the streets of Tehran, Iran's capital. With the city in chaos, the pro-U.S. Iranian army officers seized the parliament building and began rounding up Mossadeq's supporters. Mossadeq himself tried to escape by jumping over his garden wall, but he, too, was captured by the pro-U.S. officers. The Shah learned of Mossadeq's ouster over breakfast at the Excelsior Hotel in Rome. "I knew they loved me," he said to his wife, and then rushed back to Iran to resume his royal duties.

It was a crushing defeat for Mossadeq and Iranian nationalism. Although the nationalization of Iranian oil facilities formally remained in effect, the Iranian government, now administered by a pro-Shah prime minister, allowed a consortium of foreign oil companies to control and market Iran's oil, with the AIOC surrendering a large share of the operation to American oil companies. Iran became a major recipient of U.S. economic aid, and the Shah himself was now deeply beholden to the United States. The British weren't entirely happy about the result, but they accepted it as the price for America's support in ousting the hated Mossadeq.

At the time, U.S. officials thought they had won a splendid victory in Iran, and to a considerable degree they had. But success came at a heavy price. Once he was reinstalled in power, the Shah governed much more repressively than before, using his internal security forces to crush any potential dissent. Ordinary Iranians would come to loathe the Shah and to see him as a puppet of the United States. The ultimate consequences of these perceptions would become clear in the Iranian Revolution of the late 1970s.

If the full power of Iranian nationalism took a quarter century to assert itself, the power of Arab nationalism was readily apparent in the 1950s. The potency of Arab nationalism grew out of the particular circumstances of the Arab world, especially its experience with Western domination. By the time World War II ended in 1945, a large number of Arab countries, most of them lying to the east of the Suez Canal, had achieved or were about to achieve national independence. Still, there were two major issues that prevented the Arab nations from enjoying the full benefits of independence, and that caused their relations with the West to remain embittered—indeed, to become even more so.

The first issue was the lingering vestiges of European imperialism. Despite the general trend toward national independence, portions of the Arab world remained under direct European control. In North Africa, Morocco and Tunisia would not gain their independence from France until 1956, and Algeria would remain a French colony until 1962, gaining independence only after a long and bloody struggle. Britain would hold on to a number of protectorates on the Arabian Peninsula, not granting them independence until the late 1960s or early 1970s. In addition to these vestiges of formal imperial control, a number of other Arab countries, like Egypt, Jordan, and Iraq, remained under de facto British domination until the middle or late 1950s.

The second major issue impinging on the Arabs' sense of independence was the establishment of the state of Israel in 1948. In the view of most Arabs, Israel was a creation of Western imperialism, designed to re-enslave the Arab world just as it was on the verge of gaining true political liberty. This was, of course, a simplistic view, one that overlooked the central role that ordinary Jews themselves had played in building the Zionist movement, but there were some elements of truth to it. For most of the interwar period, Zionism had indeed been promoted by imperial Britain, and not long after the British stopped serving as a patron with the issuing of the White Paper of 1939, the United States stepped in to lend crucial support to the movement.

Both of these factors—the legacy of imperialism and the creation of Israel—greatly contributed to the Arabs' perception that they were being victimized by the West, including the United States. As the 1950s began, the United States faced a basic dilemma regarding its approach to the Arab world. On the one hand, it wanted to keep the Arab states favorably disposed toward the West so that the region's oil reserves and strategic positions would remain accessible to the United States and its allies. On the other hand, the United States had close alliances with Britain and France and was committed to Israel's survival and security, circumstances that caused deep resentment in the Arab world.

Washington's dilemma became more acute in the early 1950s. In 1952, the Egyptian monarchy was overthrown by a group of young army officers, who established a new, military government for Egypt. Leading the officers was a 34-year-old lieutenant colonel named Gamal Abdel Nasser. Initially, the new Egyptian regime was governed by a figurehead, a benign and fatherly general named Mohammed Naguib, but by 1954 Nasser had emerged as Egypt's formal leader, serving first as prime minister and then, from 1956 until his death in 1970, as president. Nasser was an extremely dynamic and charismatic figure. He was an electrifying public speaker who projected an aura of confidence and defiance, capturing the imagination of the Egyptian and later the Arab masses.

Initially, the Eisenhower administration was fairly optimistic about working with Nasser. He cracked down on Egyptian communists, outlawing the communist party and throwing its leaders in jail, and gave the impression that he wanted a close relationship with the United States. Nasser made it clear, however, that while his regime would be basically pro-Western it would not enter into a formal alliance with the West against the Soviet Union, nor would it be happy if other Arab countries joined such an alliance. The Eisenhower administration thought it could live with this condition. Instead of trying to bring Egypt or any other Arab states into an anti-Soviet pact, it encouraged those countries to make peace with Israel.

This may seem to have nothing to do with U.S. efforts to contain the Soviet Union, but in fact, there was an intimate connection between the Arab-Israeli conflict and the Cold War. U.S. officials were convinced that resolving the first conflict would make it easier then to prevail in the second. Here's how the logic worked. The creation of Israel had heightened the Arabs' sense of grievance against the West. As long as the conflict remained unresolved, the Soviet Union had an opportunity to exploit Arab grievances and increase its own political influence in the region. It is true that the Soviet Union had supported the creation of the state of Israel, but in the early 1950s the Soviets had started to take a pro-Arab stance in the Arab-Israeli conflict. Eisenhower and Dulles feared that the Arab states might eventually conclude that the Russians were their true friends and thus align with Moscow in the Cold War.

The best way to keep this from happening, Eisenhower and Dulles believed, was to encourage a resolution of the Arab-Israeli conflict. Starting in late 1954, the Eisenhower administration began a sustained diplomatic effort to convince Egypt and Israel to reach a preliminary peace settlement. The administration calculated that if Egypt, the most populous and influential of all the Arab states, could be induced to enter into a peace process with Israel, then other Arab states would be willing to do so as well.

Another way to diminish the Arabs' sense of grievance—and thus prevent them from turning against the West in the Cold War—would be to hasten the process by which the Arab states gained true independence. Again, the administration concentrated on Egypt, whose Suez Canal Zone had been occupied by British troops since 1882. If Britain could be convinced to end that occupation, then Egypt and, by extension, other Arab states might look upon the West in a more positive light. The Eisenhower administration did achieve a partial success in 1954. That year it facilitated an agreement between Egypt and Britain, whereby Britain pledged to withdraw its troops from the Suez Canal Zone by 1956, on the condition that Britain could reoccupy the zone in the event that Egypt, or any other Arab state, was attacked by the Soviet Union.

In other ways, however, Washington's Middle East strategy ran into serious difficulties. In the first place, the British did not fully cooperate with the American approach. In 1955, against the Eisenhower administration's advice, the British unilaterally established a Middle East pact consisting of Britain, Turkey, Iran, Pakistan, and Iraq. This alliance became known as the *Baghdad Pact*. The Eisenhower administration realized that the inclusion of an Arab country like Iraq in a pro-Western pact would infuriate Nasser. To minimize Nasser's anger, the administration declined to join the pact itself. Nasser was indeed infuriated by the pact, and he began vilifying the Iraqi government as a traitor to the Arab cause. More generally, the establishment of the Baghdad Pact led to a hardening of Nasser's international position.

Prior to the pact's formation, Nasser had made it clear that he opposed participation by any Arab government in an anti-Soviet pact sponsored by the West. Still, he had left open the possibility that the Arab states could, in a less formal way, be basically pro-Western in their political and economic orientation. The formation of the Baghdad Pact, however, convinced Nasser that the Western powers would never refrain from pressuring the Arabs, and that even an informal alliance with the West would be a bad idea. In 1955, Nasser took a big step away from the West and began publicly advocating a policy of nonalignment in the Cold War. He insisted that Egypt and the other Arab states should not align themselves with either the United States or the Soviet Union, but should position themselves to receive military and economic aid from both Cold War blocs.

Egypt was not the only country taking this stance. By the mid-1950s, several newly independent nations in what we now call the "Third World"—countries like India and Indonesia—had publicly declared themselves to be nonaligned, willing to do business with both Cold War camps. In practice, however, these nations tended to be more critical of Western nations than of the communist bloc, for the simple reason that most of them had recently been subjected to Western colonialism.

Nasser's emergence as a forceful advocate of nonalignment posed a serious challenge to the United States. It was bad enough, from Washington's perspective, that such a large and influential Arab country as Egypt had ruled out an alliance with the West. But Nasser didn't stop there; he insisted that the Arab world as a whole be neutral in the Cold War and began harshly criticizing Arab states that already did have close ties to the West, not just Iraq, but countries like Jordan and Lebanon as well.

Even more disturbing, from Washington's standpoint, was Nasser's decision to move closer to the Soviet bloc. The formation of the Baghdad Pact, along with the perceived threat posed by Israel, made Nasser extremely anxious to enhance Egypt's military capabilities. In the fall of 1955, he concluded a major agreement with Czechoslovakia, underwritten by the Soviet Union itself, whereby the Czechs gave Egypt about $80 million worth of sophisticated weapons in exchange for surplus Egyptian cotton. The Eisenhower administration was extremely upset by the arms deal, which gave the Soviets an excellent opportunity to increase their influence in the Middle East.

Still, the Eisenhower administration was not yet ready to give up on Nasser, and in late 1955 and early 1956, it took two actions aimed at wooing him back to the Western camp. The first was to show a more active interest in the so-called Aswan Dam project. This was an ambitious public works project, planned by the Egyptian government, designed to regulate the Nile's flow and thus increase agricultural yield and produce hydroelectric power, thereby raising the living standards of the Egyptian people, the vast majority of whom lived in grinding poverty. In late 1955, the United States and Britain offered to help Egypt finance the Aswan Dam project.

The second U.S. response was to push harder for an Arab-Israeli settlement. In January 1956, Eisenhower sent a special envoy named Robert B. Anderson on a secret mission to the Middle East. Anderson's task was to meet separately with Nasser and Israeli Prime Minister David Ben-Gurion to seek a workable formula for a peace settlement. Anderson spent several weeks in the Middle East, shuttling back and forth between Egypt and Israel. It was clear from the start that Nasser and Ben-Gurion were very far apart on both procedural and substantive grounds.

Procedurally, Nasser was opposed to direct negotiations with Israel, preferring to communicate through a mediator instead, whereas Ben-Gurion insisted on face-to-face talks. Substantively, Nasser demanded that Israel relinquish large portions of southern Israel to Egypt and Jordan; he also insisted that Israel give Palestinian refugees the choice of either returning to their former homes in Israel or receiving compensation if they settled elsewhere. Ben-Gurion rejected any territorial concessions and refused to take responsibility for the Palestinian refugees.

Despite these disagreements, Anderson believed there was an implicit understanding that, should Nasser and Ben-Gurion find a mutually acceptable formula, Nasser would recommend it to other Arab leaders, so there was that slim basis for hope. By early March, however, Nasser was backing away from this understanding. Even if Egypt and Israel could agree on an approach, Egypt would not be willing to sell it to other Arab states. Instead, Nasser insisted, some other party, like the United States or the United Nations, would have to present the proposal to each of the other Arab countries, and they in turn must be free to propose modifications. In other words, Nasser would not be putting his imprimatur on such an agreement.

Apparently, this was a significant retreat on Nasser's part. Apparently, Nasser feared that if he took the lead in advocating peace with Israel, his rivals in the Arab world, especially the Iraqi government, which was eager to retaliate for Nasser's own attacks on the Baghdad Pact, would vilify Nasser as a traitor to the Arab cause. As Anderson explained in a cable to Washington, Nasser "would like to see war avoided but...is not willing to assume aggressive leadership to avoid it, as doing so would endanger his prestige in the Arab world." Whatever its cause, Nasser's attitude brought an end to Anderson's peace mission.

Eisenhower and Dulles were furious with Nasser. They said to themselves, "Look, we've gone out of the way to address Nasser's political concerns. We got Britain to agree to withdraw its forces from the Suez Canal Zone; we refused to join the Baghdad Pact; we expressed interest in funding the Aswan Dam project; and we tried in good faith to settle the Arab-Israeli conflict. How has Nasser repaid us? By buying arms from the Soviet Bloc and refusing to make peace with Israel." In the spring of 1956, Eisenhower and Dulles decided to get tough with Nasser. Instead of trying to placate the Egyptian leader, as they had done up until now, they imposed a whole set of economic and diplomatic pressures on him. The purpose of these measures, Dulles outlined in a memo, was "to let Nasser realize that he cannot cooperate as he is doing with the Soviet Union and still enjoy most favored treatment from the United States."

Accordingly, Eisenhower and Dulles curtailed economic aid to Egypt, made it difficult for American charitable groups to function in Egypt, and began dragging out the negotiations over Western financing of the Aswan Dam. At the same time, they increased economic aid to other Arab countries, especially those with more pro-U.S. governments, and while they did not increase U.S. military aid to Israel, they encouraged other Western governments, like France and Canada, to sell military aircraft to Israel. All of these measures, Eisenhower and Dulles hoped, would leave Egypt so impoverished and isolated that it would have to rethink its defiant position.

So the stage was set for the Suez crisis of 1956, one of the most fascinating episodes of the Cold War period, and an event that clearly illustrates the American dilemma I mentioned earlier between accommodating Arab political sensibilities on the one hand, and accommodating the needs of Israel and the allies on the other. We'll look at the Suez crisis and its aftermath in our next lecture.

Lecture Eight
The Suez Crisis and Arab Nationalism

Scope:

In this lecture, we discuss the Eisenhower administration's responses to the Suez crisis of 1956 and to the subsequent surge in Nasser's regional popularity. We begin by describing the diplomatic maneuvers leading to Nasser's nationalization of the Suez Canal Company in July 1956. Then, after outlining the Eisenhower administration's initial reaction to Nasser's move, we examine Britain's, France's, and Israel's military invasion of Egypt and Eisenhower's surprisingly forceful—and successful—opposition to that operation. Next, we discuss Eisenhower's attempts to fill the perceived vacuum created by Britain's failure and to forge a coalition of pro-U.S. Arab regimes capable of countering Nasser's growing regional influence. We end with the U.S. intervention in Lebanon in 1958 and Eisenhower's subsequent decision to mend fences with Nasser.

Outline

I. The Suez crisis is a crucial turning point in world history, because it marks Britain's demise as the preeminent Western power in the Middle East and the assumption of that role by the United States—a role Washington continues to play to this day.

II. In the spring and early summer of 1956, Nasser continued to take actions that rankled the Eisenhower administration.

   A. He extended diplomatic recognition to communist China.

   B. He hinted that he might turn to the Soviet Union for funding of the Aswan Dam project if Western terms were unsatisfactory.

III. In July 1956, the administration withdrew its offer to finance the Aswan Dam project.

   A. Nasser responded by announcing that he was nationalizing the British-owned Suez Canal Company and would use toll revenues to finance the Aswan Dam.

   B. Britain regarded Nasser's action as intolerable and began advocating a military intervention to reverse it.

C. The United States strongly opposed military intervention, believing that a British attack on Egypt would enflame the entire Muslim world against the West. To avoid military action, the Eisenhower administration sponsored a series of international conferences aimed at finding a compromise solution to the crisis.

D. Although the British paid lip service to finding a diplomatic solution, they began secretly conspiring with the French and the Israelis to achieve the overthrow of Nasser. The French and the Israelis had reasons of their own for opposing Nasser.

    1. The French were angered by Nasser's support for a nationalist rebellion then taking place against French colonial rule in Algeria.

    2. The Israelis feared that Nasser was building up his army in preparation for war against them.

IV. In the fall of 1956, Britain, France, and Israel attacked Egypt.

    A. The U.S. government received no prior notice of the British-French-Israeli plan.

        1. According to the plan, Israel would attack Egypt in the Sinai Peninsula and begin advancing across the peninsula.

        2. Once Israel had seized most of the peninsula, Britain and France would demand that Israel and Egypt withdraw their forces from the canal area.

        3. If either party refused the ultimatum—as Egypt was sure to do because the canal lay within its own sovereign territory—British and French forces would seize the canal, ostensibly to protect it from damage in the fighting.

    B. Eisenhower strongly opposed the action.

        1. He publicly spoke out against the attack.

        2. He instructed his representatives to condemn the attack in the UN. The Soviets voted with the United States in the UN, an odd spectacle in those Cold War days.

        3. Following Nasser's closure of the Suez Canal, which disrupted oil shipments from the Middle East to Western Europe, Eisenhower refused to send oil from the

Western Hemisphere to Europe until the attack on Egypt ended.

    4. Eisenhower threatened to support UN economic sanctions against Israel unless it withdrew its forces from Egypt.

  C. These measures forced Britain, France, and Israel to end their attack on Egypt. Nasser's regime was saved.

V. The Suez crisis revealed that Britain could no longer be considered the primary Western power in the Middle East. This situation posed a serious problem for the United States.

  A. Although Eisenhower had strongly opposed Britain's attack on Egypt, he believed that the rapid erosion of British influence in the Middle East would enable the Soviet Union to increase its own influence in the region.

  B. To prevent this from happening, in early 1957, Eisenhower launched an initiative that became known as the *Eisenhower Doctrine*.

    1. Eisenhower got Congress to pass a resolution that authorized the executive branch to give more economic and military aid to Middle Eastern countries.

    2. The resolution also declared the intention of the United States to intervene militarily to protect any Middle Eastern country that was the victim of "overt armed aggression from any nation controlled by International Communism."

  C. Although Eisenhower did not really expect any Middle Eastern countries to be attacked by the Soviet bloc, he thought that by offering such protection, he could convince nations in the region to ally with the United States. This, in turn, would discredit Nasser's stance of nonalignment in the Cold War.

    1. On a material level, the United States would offer military and economic aid to those Arab countries that openly supported the United States and resisted Nasser's program of nonalignment.

    2. On a psychological level, the United States sought to reassure pro-U.S. regimes with a promise of U.S. aid in the event of a conflict. The United States also sought to isolate Egypt, Syria, and any other Arab country that refused to state, publicly and unequivocally, that it regarded international communism as a menace.

VI. The Eisenhower Doctrine was not a great success.

    A. Middle Eastern governments were generally eager to accept U.S. aid under the new program.

    B. But regional public opinion, especially Arab opinion, was hostile to the Eisenhower Doctrine, seeing it as an effort to impose Cold War thinking on the Arabs by pressuring them to join an anti-Soviet alliance.

    C. Consequently, few Arab governments publicly endorsed the Eisenhower Doctrine.

        1. The governments of Iraq and Lebanon endorsed the doctrine in defiance of domestic opinion, decisions that led to enormous turmoil in their countries.

        2. The governments of Jordan and Saudi Arabia declined to endorse the doctrine, though they convinced the United States to give them substantial aid anyway.

VII. Contrary to his own expectation, Eisenhower did end up having to intervene militarily in the Middle East.

    A. The Lebanese government had been one of the few Arab governments to endorse the Eisenhower Doctrine. But this decision was so controversial among the Lebanese people that it helped spark a civil war in the country.

    B. In July 1958, Iraq's pro-Western monarchy was overthrown, and fearing that his own regime would be next, Lebanon's president requested that the United States send troops to Lebanon to prevent his government from being overthrown. Eisenhower reluctantly complied by sending 14,000 Marines to land on the coast of Lebanon.

    C. By now, the Eisenhower administration was convinced that challenging Nasser was counterproductive.

        1. In late 1958, it quietly abandoned the Eisenhower Doctrine and decided to seek an accommodation with Nasser.

        2. This decision was facilitated by an unexpected deterioration in relations between Nasser and the Soviet Union.

3. The result was a modest U.S.-Egyptian rapprochement lasting for the rest of Eisenhower's term and into that of his successor.

VIII. It is important to distinguish between the Eisenhower Doctrine's ultimate objective and the strategy employed to achieve that objective.

   A. The objective was to prevent a Soviet takeover of the Middle East and, given that such a takeover never occurred, it has to be said that the objective was achieved.

   B. The strategy to achieve the objective—discrediting Arab figures deemed "soft on communism" by promoting other Arab figures who were conspicuously anticommunist—failed miserably.

IX. What was definitely accomplished under Eisenhower—more by default than strategy—was that the United States became the dominant power in the Middle East.

Suggested Reading:

Neff, Donald. *Warriors at Suez: Eisenhower Takes America into the Middle East*. New York: Simon & Schuster, 1981.

Ashton, Nigel John. *Eisenhower, Macmillan and the Problem of Nasser: Anglo-American Relations and Arab Nationalism, 1955–59*. London, Macmillan, 1996.

Questions to Consider:

1. Why was Eisenhower so strongly opposed to British, French, and Israeli actions during the Suez crisis of 1956?

2. How did Eisenhower react to the sharp decline in British influence in the Middle East in the aftermath of the Suez crisis?

Lecture Eight—Transcript
The Suez Crisis and Arab Nationalism

In this lecture we're going to continue looking at Middle East policy under President Eisenhower, and in particular we'll examine the Suez crisis of 1956 and its aftermath. The Suez crisis is a crucial turning point in world history, for it marks Britain's demise as the preeminent Western power in the Middle East and the assumption of that role by the United States, a role Washington continues to play to this day.

We left off last time in March 1956, with Eisenhower and John Foster Dulles, his secretary of state, adopting a much tougher line on Egyptian President Gamal Abdel Nasser than the one they had followed over the previous couple years. You will recall that one way Eisenhower and Dulles decided to get tough was by stalling on negotiations over Western funding for the Aswan Dam project. The idea was to "keep Nasser guessing" about the status of the funding, in the hopes of making him more deferential in his dealings with the United States. Over the next few months, a couple factors convinced Eisenhower and Dulles to withdraw funding for the project altogether.

First, Egypt established formal diplomatic relations with communist China, a huge no-no in American eyes. Second, Nasser hinted that he might turn to the Soviet Union for funding if the Western terms were unsatisfactory, a move that infuriated Eisenhower and Dulles. In July 1956, the Eisenhower administration formally withdrew its offer to help finance the dam, prompting Britain to follow suit. Nasser's response to the funding withdrawal was totally unexpected and quite ingenious. On July 26, 1956, addressing a huge audience in the Egyptian city of Alexandria, Nasser announced that Egypt was nationalizing the Suez Canal Company, which was mainly British owned, and would use the canal's toll revenues to finance the construction of the Aswan Dam. With this decision, Nasser said, "Arab nationalism has been set on fire from the Atlantic Ocean to the Persian Gulf." Nasser's declaration was wildly applauded throughout the Arab world.

The nationalization of the Suez Canal Company was legal in that Egypt pledged to compensate the company's shareholders at prevailing market rates. Britain, however, saw the act as politically, economically and strategically intolerable. Two-thirds of Western Europe's oil imports were shipped through the Suez Canal, and Britain saw itself as the guarantor of those oil shipments. For Britain to lose control of the canal meant that Britain could no longer be considered a global power. So, the British government began advocating a military intervention to reverse Nasser's action.

The Americans were strongly opposed to military intervention, believing that a British attack on Egypt would enflame the entire Arab world against the West and perhaps cause the Arab nations to align with the Soviet bloc. Instead, Eisenhower sponsored a series of diplomatic conferences aimed at finding a compromise solution to the crisis, one that respected Egypt's sovereignty but also placed some measure of international control over the canal.

The British, however, were not buying the Eisenhower administration's approach. Although they paid lip service to finding a diplomatic solution, they began secretly conspiring with the French and the Israelis to achieve the overthrow of Nasser. The French government was already angered by Nasser's support for a nationalist rebellion then taking place against French colonial rule in Algeria. As for Israel, it feared that Nasser was building up his army in preparation for war against Israel. The Israelis were especially determined to knock Egypt down to size before it had a chance to absorb the huge shipment of arms it had purchased from the Soviet bloc in 1955. All three of these countries—Britain, France, and Israel—believed their situations would vastly improve if Nasser vanished from the world scene.

So the British, French, and Israelis worked out a plan for attacking Egypt that may have seemed clever at the time, but was actually very stupid. According to that plan, Israel would attack Egypt in the Sinai Peninsula and begin advancing across the peninsula. Once Israel had seized most of the peninsula, Britain and France would demand that Israel and Egypt withdraw their forces from the canal area. If either party refused the ultimatum, as Egypt was sure to do since the canal lay within its own sovereign territory, British and French forces would seize the canal, ostensibly to protect it from damage in the fighting. The British, French, and Israelis also agreed that the U.S. government should receive no prior notice about the impending attack. The thinking seems to have been that, while the Americans would never approve such an operation in advance, they would probably accept it after the fact, given their own dislike of Nasser. This was, it turned out, a fatal miscalculation.

In late October 1956, Israeli forces crossed into the Sinai Peninsula as planned, overwhelming Egyptian border posts and quickly advancing toward the Suez Canal. The next day Britain and France issued their ultimatum, demanding that Israel and Egypt withdraw to within ten miles of either side of the Suez Canal and permit Anglo-French forces to occupy the canal zone. Israel predictably accepted the ultimatum, and Egypt, equally predictably, rejected it out of hand.

This is why I said the plan was so stupid. The Anglo-French ultimatum was so patently unfair that it became immediately obvious that the two countries were in collusion with Israel. It would be as if Canada had invaded the United States from the north, and the United Nations stepped in and said, "Stop! Cease fire! Both sides—the Americans and the Canadians—withdraw to within ten miles of either side of the Ohio River." The Americans would say, "What? The Ohio River? We get attacked, and the aggressor is allowed to keep his forces in Ohio, Indiana, and Michigan? That's outrageous!" That's about how it appeared to the Egyptians—and indeed to most fair-minded observers at the time—and nobody was surprised when Nasser immediately rejected the Anglo-French ultimatum.

But Britain and France ignored world opinion and pushed ahead with their ill-considered plan. They responded to Nasser's rejection by bombing Egyptian airfields near the canal zone; a few days later British and French paratroopers began landing in Egypt, and were soon followed by amphibious forces. Nasser was in a weak position to resist the attack, and his country was quickly occupied. But one thing Nasser was able to do was close the Suez Canal by clogging it up with old sunken ships. As I said, two-thirds of the oil Western Europe consumed passed through the canal. To get from the Persian Gulf to Europe, oil tankers now had to sail all the way around the Cape of Good Hope in southern Africa, imposing major shortages and delays on the countries of Western Europe.

The Eisenhower administration was shocked and outraged by the attack on Egypt and, like everybody else, immediately figured out that Britain and France had colluded with Israel. The notion that America's closest allies could plan such an operation behind its back was utterly infuriating to U.S. officials. Worse still, the attack on Egypt had thrown the Middle East into turmoil; it seemed possible that the entire Arab world might turn against the West, with disastrous consequences for the American position in the Cold War. Eisenhower realized that the only way to salvage the situation was to bring an immediate end to the war, and to make it clear that the United States was utterly opposed to it.

So Eisenhower publicly condemned the attack and had his UN representative sponsor resolutions in the UN opposing the intervention. The Soviets shared Eisenhower's outrage and voted with the United States in the UN, an odd spectacle indeed in those Cold War days. Eisenhower then placed extraordinary political and economic pressure on the attackers to cease their intervention and withdraw from Egypt. As we saw, Nasser's decision to block the Suez Canal caused a major oil shortage in Europe. Eisenhower refused to allow any oil from the Western Hemisphere to be sent to Western Europe until the British and French agreed to a cease-fire. He also saw to it that Britain was unable to borrow gold reserves from the International Monetary Fund, causing a sudden devaluation of the British pound. Finally, Eisenhower threatened to impose economic sanctions against Israel unless it, too, pulled out of Egypt.

In early November, Egypt's attackers reluctantly agreed to a cease-fire, and in late December, Britain and France withdrew their forces from the country. The Israelis continued to occupy the Sinai Peninsula and the Gaza Strip into early 1957, but they, too, were finally compelled to withdraw by the threat of economic sanctions by the United States and the UN. The Suez crisis revealed to all the world that Britain could no longer be considered the primary Western power in the Middle East. British power had been declining for years, but the events of late 1956 drastically accelerated that decline and made it irreversible. Britain would continue to dominate certain countries in the region, like Iraq, Kuwait, and the British protectorates on the Arabian Peninsula, but its ability to call the shots in a more general sense was severely diminished.

This situation posed a serious problem for the United States. Although Eisenhower had strongly opposed Britain's attack on Egypt, he was equally unhappy about the rapid erosion of British influence in the Middle East resulting from that attack. Such erosion, he believed, had created a political and strategic vacuum in the

Middle East that the Soviet Union would fill by giving more economic and military aid to Middle Eastern countries, unless the United States took action. The United States, in other words, would have to take Britain's place as the primary Western power in the Middle East.

The Eisenhower administration also believed that the Middle East represented a weak link in the chain of alliances that the United States and its allies had forged around the Sino-Soviet bloc. NATO had come into being in 1949, with Greece and Turkey joining the alliance in the early 1950s. In the mid-1950s, a similar Western pact had been established in Southeast Asia, for the purpose of containing communist China. The Baghdad Pact, which the British established in 1955, and which I mentioned last time, had been designed to fill the gap between the European and Southeast Asian pacts. The Baghdad Pact was extremely unpopular in Middle Eastern countries, especially after the British attack on Egypt, and the Eisenhower administration thought it would likely disintegrate. The administration believed that some new mechanism was needed to keep the nations of the Middle East oriented toward the West.

In early 1957, Eisenhower launched an initiative that became known as the *Eisenhower Doctrine*. He got Congress to pass a resolution that first authorized the executive branch to give more economic and military aid to Middle Eastern countries and, second, authorized the U.S. military to intervene to protect any Middle Eastern country that was the victim of "overt armed aggression from any nation controlled by International Communism." This phrase was puzzling not just to observers at the time but to historians ever since. What did Eisenhower mean by a "nation controlled by International Communism," and how likely was it that such a nation would attack a country in the Middle East? Certainly there seemed little prospect that the Soviet Union, or any Eastern European country, would commit "overt armed aggression" in the Middle East. So what was the point of the Eisenhower Doctrine?

Actually, the Eisenhower Doctrine did have a clear set of purposes, though it was difficult to glean them from the public statements. Essentially, what Eisenhower and Dulles wanted to do was weaken Nasserist Egypt and its ally Syria, and to strengthen Arab countries that had pro-American regimes, like Iraq, Saudi Arabia, Lebanon, and Jordan. This was to be done on both a material level and psychological level. The material dimension was pretty straightforward: the United States would offer military and economic aid to those Arab countries that openly supported the United States and resisted Nasser's program of nonalignment in the Cold War.

On a psychological level, the Eisenhower Doctrine had two purposes, one positive and the other negative. On the positive side, the Eisenhower administration wanted to reassure pro-U.S. regimes that if they stood with the United States, the United States would stand with them. No one really expected that any of these countries would come under direct Soviet attack. But they could conceivably get into a conflict with some other Arab state, like Egypt or Syria, that already had close ties to the Soviet bloc, in which case the United States could come to the aid of the pro-U.S. Arab governments. That was why the administration used the murky formulation "any nation controlled by International Communism," to be prepared for the possibility of inter-Arab conflict, not a Soviet bloc attack on a Middle Eastern country. If Arab governments with pro-U.S. leanings knew in advance that the United States was squarely on their side, they would, Eisenhower hoped, be willing to assume an even stronger pro-American stance in the Cold War. That's the positive dimension of the psychological aspect of the Eisenhower Doctrine.

On the negative side, the Eisenhower Doctrine was intended as a form of psychological warfare against Egypt, Syria, and any other Arab country that might be tempted to follow a nonaligned course. In order to get U.S. military and economic aid under the doctrine, each Middle Eastern country would be required to state, publicly and unequivocally, that it regarded international communism as a menace. If a majority of Arab countries could be induced to make such a statement, then those countries that refused to make it would seem isolated and extreme. The only way for them to end their isolation would be to get with the program and condemn international communism. Nasser's whole program of nonalignment would be discredited, and the Soviet Union would be blocked from making any further inroads into the Middle East. Or so, at least, Eisenhower and Dulles hoped.

The Eisenhower Doctrine was not a great success. Although Middle Eastern governments were generally eager to accept U.S. aid under the new program, regional public opinion, especially Arab opinion, was hostile to the Eisenhower Doctrine, which was seen as an effort to impose Cold War thinking on the Arabs by pressuring them to join an anti-Soviet alliance. Nasser's regional popularity, by contrast, soared in the aftermath of the Suez crisis, on account of his having successfully withstood an attack by great powers. Throughout the Arab world, ordinary people began looking to Nasser, rather than to their own governments, as their true leader.

The administration had assumed that the Arab people would be so grateful to the United States for opposing the attack on Egypt that they would want their governments to ally with Washington. This was a serious miscalculation; while Arabs were indeed grateful for Eisenhower's stance, they admired Nasser much more than they admired the United States, and, when asked to choose between allying with Washington and going along with Nasser, they almost always chose the latter.

The pro-U.S. Arab regimes—countries like Saudi Arabia, Iraq, Jordan, and Lebanon—were in a ticklish position. On the one hand, these regimes were eager to receive American aid and protection; on the other hand, they could not completely ignore domestic public opinion, which tended to oppose the Eisenhower Doctrine. The governments of Iraq and Lebanon went ahead and endorsed the doctrine in defiance of domestic opinion, decisions that would lead to enormous turmoil in both of those countries, as we'll see in a moment. The governments of Jordan and Saudi Arabia declined to endorse the doctrine, though they convinced Washington to give them substantial aid anyway. What Jordan and Saudi Arabia basically said was "Look, you know that we support the United States and oppose Nasser, but it's too dangerous, politically, for us to say these things out loud. Can't you accept our quiet support and give us the money anyway?"

Washington essentially accepted their reasoning and gave them aid. The problem, of course, was that this defeated one of the main purposes of the Eisenhower Doctrine, which was to get as many countries as possible on record supporting the United States in the Cold War. From the outset, then, the doctrine failed to produce a solid front of outspokenly pro-American regimes in the Arab world. Worse still, Washington's efforts to reduce Nasser's influence in the region had the opposite effect of making Nasser stronger. A crisis in Lebanon in 1958 nicely illustrates the point.

As I mentioned, Lebanon was one of the few Arab countries to endorse the Eisenhower Doctrine. The Lebanese government's embrace of the doctrine had infuriated the country's political opposition, which favored more cordial ties to Egypt and Syria. These tensions erupted into a full-blown civil war in the spring of 1958. The immediate cause of the conflict was the attempt by Lebanon's president, Camille Chamoun, to amend the Lebanese constitution so that he could stay in office for a second term. The deeper cause of the civil war was a basic disagreement between one Lebanese faction, predominantly Christian, that wanted close ties to the West and another Lebanese faction, predominantly Muslim, that identified with Nasser's brand of Arab nationalism.

Throughout the Lebanese civil war, the pro-Nasser Lebanese opposition received rhetorical support from the Radio Cairo, and material support (in the form of arms and troops) over the border from Syria. Earlier that year, Egypt and Syria had merged to form the United Arab Republic, or UAR, a union that would last until 1961. Nasser was president of the UAR, so he was ultimately responsible for the transfer of arms and troops from Syria to Lebanon. In May 1958, citing massive UAR interference in his country, Chamoun asked the United States if it would be prepared to intervene militarily in Lebanon should he request this, though he held off on issuing such a request just yet.

In considering Chamoun's question, Eisenhower and Dulles agreed that any U.S. intervention in Lebanon would be extremely risky. It could well "create a wave of anti-Western feeling in the Arab world," resulting in the overthrow of pro-Western governments, the closing of the Suez Canal, the sabotage of oil pipelines in Syria, and an oil crisis for the West. On the other hand, Eisenhower and Dulles both felt that refusing to honor such a request would be even worse, since it would show the world that the United States was not prepared to come to the defense of its allies, with disastrous consequences for the Western position in the Cold War. They told Chamoun that U.S. forces would intervene if he requested this, but they also urged him to do everything possible to stabilize the situation, either by crushing the rebellion or by reaching a political settlement, so that intervention would not be necessary in the first place. The Eisenhower administration almost got its wish.

In the early summer of 1958, Chamoun and the Lebanese rebels began moving toward a settlement of their dispute, giving reason to hope that U.S. intervention might be avoided after all. But then, a sudden upheaval in Iraq dramatically transformed the political situation in the region. In July 1958, Iraq's pro-Western monarchy was suddenly overthrown by a group of army officers who appeared to be followers of Nasser, though this turned out to be an erroneous perception. The officers' coup unleashed a frenzy of mob violence. Thousands of ordinary Iraqis took to the streets, venting their fury on the old regime. Members of the Iraqi royal family and government were murdered in cold blood, their bodies mutilated and dragged naked through the streets of Baghdad. Fearing his own regime would be next, Chamoun requested immediate U.S. intervention, and Eisenhower complied by sending 14,000 U.S. marines to occupy Lebanon.

There had never been any doubt that Eisenhower would honor such a request if it was made; to do otherwise, he believed, would be to suffer an intolerable loss of international credibility. The dire consequences of intervention that Eisenhower and Dulles had feared never came to pass. There was intense criticism of the action throughout the region, but the remaining conservative regimes held on to power. In Lebanon itself, the U.S. intervention was a virtually bloodless affair. As the marines hit the beaches, they were greeted not by hostile gunmen but by battalions of soda pop vendors and—so the legend goes—bikini-clad sunbathers.

In justifying intervention, the Eisenhower administration did not fully invoke the Eisenhower Doctrine but mainly relied on Lebanon's right, under Article 51 of the UN charter, to engage in collective security for self-defense. There was no way that Lebanon could be portrayed as facing aggression from "International Communism," as required by the Eisenhower Doctrine, so the doctrine really was not directly applicable. But it was indirectly involved in that the administration believed its global credibility would suffer if it failed to help a country that had, by embracing the doctrine, so closely allied itself with the United States. Ultimately, though, the intervention in Lebanon and its aftermath served to undermine the Eisenhower Doctrine.

The United States made it clear that its marines were in Lebanon, not to prolong Chamoun's presidency but to permit an orderly transfer of power to a new president. And the new president, once in office, repudiated the Eisenhower Doctrine and established friendlier relations with Egypt, thus underscoring Nasser's regional hegemony. In late 1958, the Eisenhower administration made a policy reassessment that, without repudiating the Eisenhower Doctrine itself, explicitly abandoned its underlying anti-Nasserist strategy. The administration instead concluded that Nasser was so politically powerful that the United States had no choice but to seek an accommodation with him. "Since we are about to get thrown out of the area," Eisenhower said, "we might as well believe in Arab nationalism."

Such a conversion became easier to stomach in early 1959, when tensions unexpectedly arose between Nasser and the Soviet Union. The dispute resulted from the Soviets' support for the new Iraqi government, which had allied itself with local communists in opposition to local Nasserists. In this case, then, Nasserism functioned as a barrier to, rather than an avenue of, Soviet encroachment on the region. The result of this surprising development was a U.S.-Egyptian rapprochement that lasted for the rest of Eisenhower's term and into the Kennedy years.

In evaluating the success of the Eisenhower Doctrine, it's important to distinguish between the policy's ultimate objective and the strategy employed to achieve that objective. The objective was to prevent a Soviet takeover of the Middle East, and, since such a takeover never occurred, it has to be said that the objective was achieved. But the strategy to achieve the objective—discrediting Arab figures deemed "soft on communism" by promoting other Arab figures who were conspicuously anticommunist—failed miserably. Fortunately for Eisenhower, that strategy was so ill-chosen in the first place that its failure did not compromise the ultimate objective. In other words, the Eisenhower administration was the beneficiary of its own prior miscalculation.

This sort of irony was typical of the Eisenhower administration's performance in the Middle East, which was highly sophisticated in some ways and strikingly clumsy in others. The Eisenhower Doctrine was a work of considerable subtlety, intricacy, and internal coherence. Yet the whole edifice rested on a basic misreading of political realities in the Arab world, on an underestimation of the power and independence of Nasserism, and an overestimation of the political strength of the United States. Nasser himself was bemused by this contradiction. Once, when discussing the Eisenhower Doctrine with an American friend, he said, "The genius of you Americans is that you never made clear-cut stupid moves, only complicated stupid moves which make us wonder at the possibility that there may be something to them we were missing."

One thing that was definitely accomplished under Eisenhower—though this was more by default than through any brilliance on Eisenhower's part—was that the United States became the dominant Western power in the Middle East. Britain had stumbled so badly in the Suez crisis that it was increasingly relegated to the margins of Middle Eastern politics. In our subsequent lectures we won't be hearing a great deal about the British; from now on the Middle East will be, at least as far as Western powers are concerned, an exclusively American stomping ground.

Lecture Nine
Kennedy—Engaging Middle Eastern Nationalism

Scope:

In this lecture, we examine John F. Kennedy's attempt to deemphasize overt Cold War themes in U.S. policy toward the Middle East—an effort aimed at gaining the trust of Middle Eastern nationalists and, thus, paradoxically, at improving America's Cold War position. In three major policy areas, Kennedy performed a careful balancing act. He tempered public support for the Shah of Iran with quiet encouragement of Iranian reformers; he sought good relations with radical nationalists, such as Nasser, as well as with conservative monarchs, such as Jordan's King Hussein; and he combined pledges of support for Israel's security with pressure on Israel to make concessions to its Arab neighbors. In each case, Kennedy achieved some measure of success in the first two years of his presidency, only to falter in his third and final year, leaving a far less promising situation to his successor.

Outline

I. President John F. Kennedy made a remarkably serious effort to reach an accommodation with the forces of indigenous nationalism in the Middle East.

   A. He did so not for sentimental reasons but out of a conviction that victory in the Cold War would be impossible unless anti-Western grievances in the region could be successfully addressed.

   B. Paradoxically, Kennedy sought to win the Cold War in the Middle East by downplaying Cold War themes and stressing local concerns instead.

II. In inter-Arab politics, Kennedy attempted to strike a balance between placating radical Arab nationalists and supporting conservative Arabs.

   A. Kennedy believed that Eisenhower had made a big mistake in pressuring Nasser and other Arab nationalists to side with the United States in the Cold War. These crude measures had succeeded only in alienating Arab nationalists, pushing them further into the Soviets' embrace.

B. Kennedy believed that the best way to deal with Arab nationalists was to treat them with respect, allow them to make their own foreign policy decisions, and offer them generous assistance in developing their countries internally.

C. In some ways, Kennedy's approach to Arab nationalism resembled Eisenhower's treatment of Nasser in the mid-1950s.

    1. But Kennedy differed from Eisenhower in that he simultaneously tried to move much closer to Israel (a subject to which we shall return).

    2. Another difference was that Kennedy saw his approach to Arab nationalism as part of a broader effort to portray the United States as a friend and supporter of the emerging nations of the Third World.

D. Like Eisenhower before him, Kennedy saw Nasser as the most important leader in the Arab world, and he placed extremely high priority on establishing cordial relations with Egypt.

    1. He began a private correspondence with Nasser in which he treated him with great deference.

    2. He markedly increased U.S. economic aid to Egypt.

E. For a while, Kennedy's approach to Arab nationalism seemed to be working.

    1. Nasser was flattered by Kennedy's attention and toned down his anti-American rhetoric.

    2. Nasser also pledged to refrain from stirring up Arab-Israeli animosities and to allow the status quo regarding the Palestine issue to continue for the time being.

F. But Kennedy's strategy of ingratiating Nasser began to come undone in September 1962, when a civil war broke out in Yemen, pitting a deposed conservative monarchy against a new republican government. The Yemeni civil war quickly expanded into a proxy war between republican Egypt and monarchical Saudi Arabia.

G. The Egyptian-Saudi proxy war over Yemen placed Kennedy in a bind.

    1. He needed to reassure Saudi Arabia that the United States was committed to its security.

    2. But he also wanted to maintain good relations with Nasser.

  H. Kennedy tried to follow a balanced policy.

    1. He sent a squadron of Air Force jets to patrol the skies over Saudi Arabia and serve as a symbol of U.S. support.

    2. At the same time, he formally recognized the republican government of Yemen and pressured the Saudi government to limit its support to the Yemeni royalists.

 I. Kennedy's balanced approach pleased neither Egypt nor Saudi Arabia. Each country accused the United States of siding with the other.

III. Kennedy also tried to strike a balance between ensuring Israel's security and pressuring Israel to make concessions to its Arab neighbors.

  A. Whereas Eisenhower had kept Israel at arm's length, Kennedy established much friendlier relations with Israel.

    1. To some extent, this decision reflected Kennedy's desire to please Jewish voters in the Democratic Party's constituency.

    2. But Kennedy also sincerely believed that the best way to bring peace and stability to the Middle East was to reassure the Israelis that the United States would always strongly support them. Only if Israel received such assurance would it be willing to make the concessions necessary for peace.

  B. There were two principal issues on which Kennedy hoped to influence Israeli behavior.

    1. He wanted Israel to permit the repatriation of Palestinian refugees, something Israel had refused to do since 1948, on the grounds that this would threaten the Jewish character of Israel. Not only had the Arab states called for Israel's repatriation of Palestinians, but in late 1948, the UN General Assembly had passed Resolution 194, calling on Israel to repatriate all Palestinian refugees who wished to return to their homes in present-day Israel and who were willing to live peacefully under Israeli jurisdiction.

2. Kennedy also wanted to prevent Israel from converting its civilian nuclear power program into a weapons program, realizing that Israel's acquisition of nuclear weapons capability would further embitter Arab-Israeli relations.

C. To induce the Israelis to make concessions in these areas, Kennedy agreed to sell them advanced antiaircraft guns. Kennedy refrained, however, from establishing a formal quid-pro-quo between the arms sale on the one hand and the refugee and nuclear issues on the other, on the grounds that a formal linkage might offend Israel's dignity.

D. Unfortunately for Kennedy, this lack of a formal linkage permitted Israel to pocket the inducement without making significant concessions on the refugee and nuclear issues.

1. Israel refused to consider repatriation of Palestinian refugees on the grounds that this would result in the establishment of a hostile fifth column inside Israel. For their part, the Arab states showed little enthusiasm about Kennedy's repatriation scheme.

2. On the nuclear question, Israel appeared to be cooperating with Kennedy, assuring him that the Dimona nuclear reactor was purely for civilian purposes. But by evading U.S. attempts to conduct meaningful inspections, Israel continued to develop a nuclear weapons capability

IV. In U.S.-Iranian relations, Kennedy tried to strike a balance between pressuring the Shah to make internal reforms and shoring up his position within the country.

A. Kennedy worried that the Shah's authoritarian methods were generating unmanageable opposition in Iran.

1. Accordingly, Kennedy quietly urged the Shah to create more space for internal dissent and to institute land reform programs.

2. At the same time, Kennedy saw to it that Iran's internal security forces were well supplied, in case the reforms failed to prevent internal unrest.

B. After some resistance, the Shah introduced electoral and land reforms, but they failed to placate the domestic opposition.

1. Leftist students regarded the reforms as too modest and staged massive demonstrations throughout the country. The government brutally suppressed the demonstrations, further alienating the students.
2. Conservative Shiite clerics saw the reforms as too radical and joined the students in protesting against the government.

V. Thus, by the time of Kennedy's death in late 1963, most of his Middle East initiatives were already stymied.

Suggested Reading:

Bass, Warren. *Support Any Friend: Kennedy's Middle East and the Making of the U.S.-Israeli Alliance.* New York: Oxford University Press, 2003.

Ben-Zvi, Abraham. *Decade of Transition: Eisenhower, Kennedy, and the Origins of the American-Israeli Alliance.* New York: Columbia University Press, 1998.

Questions to Consider:

1. What was John F. Kennedy's criticism of Eisenhower's approach to Middle Eastern nationalism?
2. What obstacles did Kennedy himself face in seeking to improve America's political position in the Middle East?

Lecture Nine—Transcript
Kennedy—Engaging Middle Eastern Nationalism

In this lecture we're going to look at the Middle East policies of President John F. Kennedy. The Kennedy years are fascinating because, in this period, the U.S. government made a remarkably serious effort to reach an accommodation with the forces of indigenous nationalism in the Middle East. It did so not for sentimental or idealistic reasons—indeed, the Kennedy administration prided itself on its pragmatism and hard-headedness—but out of a conviction that victory in the Cold War would be impossible unless anti-Western grievances in the Middle East could be successfully addressed.

I'm going to focus in this lecture on three major policy areas: U.S. relations with Arab nationalism, the Arab-Israeli conflict, and U.S.-Iranian relations. In each of these areas, Kennedy tried to strike a delicate balance between placating radical Arab nationalists like Gamal Abdel Nasser and supporting conservative Arab regimes like Saudi Arabia and Jordan; between ensuring Israel's security and pressuring Israel to make concessions to its Arab neighbors; and between bolstering the Shah of Iran and pushing him to make internal political and social reforms. In each case, Kennedy achieved some measure of success in the first two years of his presidency, only to falter in the his third and final year, leaving a far less promising situation to his successor, Lyndon B. Johnson. Let's start with U.S. relations with Arab nationalism.

Kennedy entered the presidency sharply critical of Eisenhower's policies toward the Arab world. He believed that Eisenhower had made a terrible mistake by pressuring Nasser and other Arab nationalists to side with the United States in the Cold War. These crude measures had succeeded only in alienating Arab nationalists, pushing them further into the Soviet embrace. Kennedy believed that the best way to deal with Arab nationalists was to treat them with respect, to allow them to make their own foreign policy decisions, and to offer them assistance in developing their countries internally. If the United States followed this approach, Arab nationalists would eventually come to see that Washington was on their side and would willingly align with the United States and the West. Paradoxically, then, Kennedy hoped to win the Cold War in the Middle East by deemphasizing that very conflict.

In some respects, Kennedy's approach to Nasser resembled that of Eisenhower in the mid-1950s, before Eisenhower decided to get tough with Nasser. Instead of pressuring Egypt and other countries to join an anti-Soviet pact, Kennedy would try to reassure them that the United States was genuinely interested in their well-being in the hopes that such a "soft sell" would, in the long run, convince those countries to side with the United States. One major difference between Eisenhower's approach of the mid-1950s and Kennedy's of early 1960s was that Kennedy, unlike Eisenhower, also tried to move much closer to Israel, a subject I'll come back to in a moment.

Another way Kennedy differed from Eisenhower was that Kennedy saw his approach to Arab nationalism as part of a much broader effort to portray the United States as a friend and supporter of the emerging nations of the Third World. Kennedy was elected to the presidency just as the decolonization process was reaching its peak. Across Asia and Africa, European nations were liquidating their colonies and granting formal independence to the subject peoples. Indeed, in just one two-month period, September and October of 1960, coinciding with the presidential election campaign in the United States, seventeen African nations achieved their independence.

Kennedy recognized that these new nations represented a rising force in world affairs, and that many of them would be naturally suspicious of the West, given their own painful experience with Western colonialism. Kennedy believed that the best way to allay these suspicions, and thus prevent the new nations from turning irrevocably against the West, was to downplay the Cold War and focus instead on social and economic needs of the newly independent states. Although most Arab states had achieved national independence some years earlier, Kennedy saw them as part of this larger group of emerging nations, and his approach to Arab nationalism was in keeping with his broader strategy of trying to woo the nations of the Third World.

Like Eisenhower before him, Kennedy saw Nasser as the most important leader in the Arab world, and he placed extremely high priority on establishing cordial relations with Egypt. As we saw last time, U.S. relations with Nasser had actually begun to improve in the last couple years of the Eisenhower administration, a result of Nasser's own disagreements with the Soviet Union. Kennedy hoped to take this process much further and to insulate it as much as possible from developments in the Cold War. So even though Nasser's relations with the Soviet Union grew friendly again in the early 1960s, Kennedy did not make an issue of this, as Eisenhower almost certainly would have done.

Instead, Kennedy presented a friendly face to Nasser and did his best to convince him that U.S. support came without strings attached. He began a cordial private correspondence with Nasser and markedly increased U.S. economic aid to Egypt. Most of this aid was dispensed via Public Law 480, or PL 480, a U.S. government program that permitted certain countries to buy surplus American wheat, grain, and other commodities using their own currencies instead of dollars. This was beneficial to poor countries like Egypt that had limited amounts of hard currency. The United States had begun to sell Egypt PL 480 wheat in the closing years of the Eisenhower administration, but the program was greatly expanded after Kennedy became president. In early 1962, the United States signed an agreement with Egypt permitting Egypt to buy $500 million worth of PL 480 wheat over the next three years.

In addition to making Nasser more positively inclined toward the United States, Kennedy hoped that all this economic aid would encourage Nasser to channel his energies inward, to pay more attention to developing Egypt economically than to meddling in the affairs of his neighbors. As one of Kennedy's advisors remarked in 1962, "If Nasser can gradually be led to forsake the microphone for the bulldozer, he may assume a key role in bringing the Middle East peacefully into our modern world." For a while, Kennedy's approach seemed to be working. Nasser was flattered by Kennedy's attention and toned down his anti-American rhetoric. Nasser also pledged to put the Arab-Israeli issue "in the ice box"—that is, to refrain from stirring up Arab-Israeli animosities and to allow the status quo to continue for the time being.

But Kennedy's strategy of ingratiating Nasser and turning his energies inward began to come undone in the fall of 1962. In September of that year, the Imam, or monarch, of Yemen, a small, archaic nation in southern Arabia, was overthrown by nationalist army officers who were sympathetic to Nasser. The officers declared that the monarchy was abolished and that Yemen was to be a republic. The Imam fled to the north of the country, teamed up with loyalist tribesmen, and launched a guerrilla war against the new Yemeni government, attempting to reclaim his throne. The republican government appealed to Nasser for support.

Nasser felt compelled to come to the aid of the Yemeni republicans, partly out of genuine anti-monarchist conviction and partly to maintain his radical credentials in the Arab world. The Yemeni royalists, in turn, appealed to their fellow monarchs in Saudi Arabia, and the Saudis began sending them money and arms. Nasser responded to the Saudi move by sending the Egyptian air force to bomb Saudi towns on the border with Yemen, on the grounds that they served as bases for royalist attacks. Meanwhile, Nasser began calling, in his radio addresses, for the overthrow of the Saudi monarchy.

The Egyptian-Saudi proxy war over Yemen placed Kennedy in a bind. On the one hand, he needed to reassure his ally Saudi Arabia that the United States was committed to the security of its territory and to the survival of its royal family. On the other hand, he was eager to maintain good relations with Nasser. Kennedy tried to pursue these two conflicting goals by following a balanced policy on Yemen. To placate Nasser, he formally recognized the new Yemeni government and pressured the Saudi government to limit its support to the royalists. To placate the Saudis, he sent a squadron of air force jets to Saudi Arabia to patrol the skies over the kingdom and serve as a symbol of the U.S. commitment to Saudi Arabia. At the same time, Kennedy sent a special envoy to the Middle East to try to broker a cease-fire in Yemen.

In the spring of 1963, Kennedy's envoy got all the parties—Egypt, Saudi Arabia, and the two Yemeni sides—to agree to a cease-fire, but the agreement soon broke down and the fighting resumed. Moreover, Kennedy's attempt to find a middle ground between Egypt and Saudi Arabia had pleased neither side; each country accused the United States of siding with the other. By the time of Kennedy's death in late 1963, his attempt to end the Yemeni conflict, and thus keep Nasser's energies directed inward, had failed.

Let's now take a look at Kennedy's relations with Israel. As I mentioned, Kennedy's decision to move closer to Israel distinguished his policies from those of his predecessor. Eisenhower had kept Israel at arm's length, largely for fear of antagonizing the Arab states. Under Kennedy, U.S.-Israeli relations became much friendlier. In a meeting with Golda Meir, Israel's foreign ninister and later prime minister, Kennedy said that the United States "has a special relationship with Israel in the Middle East really comparable only to that which it has with Britain over a wide range of world affairs."

Kennedy repeatedly assured the Israelis that, in the event of an Arab attack, the United States would guarantee Israel's survival and security. He increased U.S. economic aid to Israel and agreed to provide Israel with weapons systems that Eisenhower had denied them. The most significant of these weapons systems was an anti-aircraft missile known as the Hawk, which Kennedy agreed to sell Israel in 1962.

To some extent, Kennedy's friendlier attitude toward Israel can be explained by domestic politics. American Jews have always been more supportive of the Democratic Party than of the Republican Party, and this was much truer in the early 1960s than it would be in later decades. Almost any Democratic president was bound to be more pro-Israel than Eisenhower had been. But Kennedy also was genuinely convinced that the best way to bring peace and stability to the region was to reassure the Israelis that the United States would always strongly support them. Only if they received such assurance, Kennedy believed, would the Israelis be willing to make the steps necessary on their part for achieving peace with the Arab states.

There were two main areas in which Kennedy hoped to influence Israeli behavior. First, he wanted Israel to agree to repatriate Palestinian refugees. During the 1948 war, about 750,000 Palestinians had either fled or been expelled from their homes in present day Israel. Apart from a very small number of Palestinians allowed back into Israel for the purpose of family reunification, all of those refugees had been barred from returning to their former homes. Some of the Palestinian exiles had become citizens of surrounding Arab countries, and some had emigrated to other parts of the world. But as of the early 1960s, half a million Palestinians remained in UN-administered refugee camps in Jordan, Lebanon, and other Arab countries, often living in squalid conditions.

What should become of those refugees was, and continues to be, an extremely controversial issue. The Israelis maintained that the wholesale repatriation of Palestinian refugees would dilute the

Jewish character of Israel and was thus out of the question. They pointed out that, shortly after Israel's creation, hundreds of thousands of Jews from Arab countries had immigrated to Israel. Just as Israel had welcomed and absorbed all of these immigrants, the Arab countries should now grant citizenship to the Palestinian refugees. The Arabs, in other words, should accept the fact that a population exchange had taken place, and not try to undo it by pushing for the return of Palestinian refugees.

The Arab states completely rejected this argument. They pointed out that, whereas the Jews of the Arab world had willingly gone to Israel, the Palestinians had left their homes unwillingly, so it was totally unjust to speak of a population exchange. Israel, they said, was obligated under international law to let the Palestinians back in. Although the Arab countries did grant citizenship to some Palestinians, especially to those who were wealthy and educated, they refused to consider the wholesale absorption of the refugee population. The Arab states were not the only parties calling for Israel's repatriation of the Palestinians.

In late 1948, the UN General Assembly had passed Resolution 194, which called on Israel to repatriate all Palestinian refugees who wished to return to their homes in present-day Israel and who were willing to live peacefully under Israeli jurisdiction. The resolution also called on Israel to pay compensation to those refugees who chose not to return. The U.S. government had co-sponsored Resolution 194 and had voted to renew it every year since. Truman, as we saw, had tried to get Israel to repatriate some of the refugees but had abandoned the effort when the Israelis refused. Eisenhower, though markedly less friendly to Israel than Truman, had not even tried to push the Israelis toward repatriation, convinced as he was that the effort would fail.

But now, Kennedy was determined to solve the refugee problem for once and for all. As long as that problem continued, he believed, no real peace in the region would be possible, and the Soviet Union would continue to exploit Arab grievances against the West. Shortly after taking office, Kennedy asked Joseph Johnson, the president of the Carnegie Foundation for International Peace, to serve as his point-man on the Palestinian refugee issue. Johnson was to look into the matter and come up with a recommended solution. After several months of study, Johnson proposed that Israel be asked to repatriate about 100,000 Palestinian refugees, that the United States offer to help Israel with the costs of repatriating them, and that the Arab states be encouraged to absorb the remaining 400,000. Kennedy accepted Johnson's plan and in the summer of 1962 conveyed it to the Israeli government. Although Israel had rejected repatriation in the past, Kennedy thought he could soften the Israelis up by simultaneously agreeing to sell them the Hawk missiles.

Flexibility on the refugee issue wasn't the only thing Kennedy wanted from the Israelis; he also wanted them to refrain from developing nuclear weapons. Since 1960 it had been public knowledge that the Israelis were constructing, with the help of the French government, a large nuclear reactor in Dimona, in southern Israel. The Israeli government claimed that the Dimona reactor was intended solely for civilian purposes, but the size and type of the reactor caused many observers to suspect that the facility was also intended for producing weapons-grade plutonium, material that could ultimately be used for constructing nuclear bombs. The suspicions were correct. Israel was indeed working to develop nuclear weapons.

Not surprisingly, the discovery of the Dimona reactor caused great consternation in the Arab world. Nasser declared that, if Israel got the bomb, Egypt would get one too, at any cost. Nasser also warned that Egypt might have to launch a preemptive strike against Israel if it acquired a nuclear weapons capability.

This situation was deeply worrying to the Kennedy administration. To be sure, most U.S. officials doubted that Egypt would be able to acquire nuclear weapons of its own, or that it would launch a preemptive strike against Israel, especially now that a third of the Egyptian army was bogged down in Yemen. But Israel's acquisition of the bomb probably would cause Egypt to engage in a major conventional arms buildup, which in turn would allow the Soviet Union to increase its influence in the Middle East, as well as destabilize the region more generally. Kennedy hoped that his decision to sell Hawk missiles to Israel, combined with his stated commitment to protecting to Israel's security, would convince the Israelis to abandon any plans to build nuclear weapons.

But Kennedy failed to achieve his grand bargain with the Israelis. The problem, it would seem, lay in the fact that although the Israelis clearly understood what Kennedy wanted in exchange for the Hawk missiles—the repatriation of Palestinians and an end to Israel's nuclear weapons program—the three issues were never formally linked. Instead, the Kennedy administration would issue one document stating its intention to sell missiles to Israel, a second document stating its desire for Palestinian repatriation, and a third document urging Israel not to develop nukes. Kennedy avoided formal linkage in order to build an atmosphere of trust between his government and Israel's. If the United States treated Israel as an ally rather as an underling, Kennedy calculated, Israel would be more responsive to American wishes. What happened instead was quite different.

The fact that the issues were not formally linked made it possible for Israel to treat each of them separately. Israel gratefully accepted the offer to purchase Hawk missiles but strongly resisted the notion of repatriating 100,000 refugees, arguing that this would result in the establishment of a hostile fifth column inside Israel. To be fair, Israel was not the only intransigent party, as the Arab states themselves showed little enthusiasm for Joseph Johnson's plan, which, after all, sought to repatriate only one-fifth of the refugee population. But Israel's refusal was a serious impediment, one that could conceivably have been overcome, or at least whittled down, had Kennedy established a firmer linkage between the refugee issue and the sale of Hawk missiles. Since Kennedy had offered the missile sale without strings, there was little he could do to compel Israel to change its position.

The Israelis' response on the nuclear question was rather more subtle, but the bottom line was much the same: they successfully thwarted Kennedy's efforts to block their drive to acquire a nuclear capability. On the surface, the Israeli government seemed to cooperate with Washington's nonproliferation agenda. Israel assured the Kennedy administration that the Dimona reactor was purely for civilian purposes and agreed to allow an American inspection team to make periodic visits to the facility to confirm this for themselves. When the American team tried to schedule specific visits, the Israelis would find some reason for delay, insisting that one date was not suitable because it fell during the election season, that another wouldn't work because it coincided with a Jewish holiday, and so forth.

Of course, the Israelis could not put the Americans off indefinitely, and eventually the U.S. inspection team did make it to Dimona. But the Israelis succeeded in establishing extremely rigid ground rules for the inspection—the inspectors could visit only certain areas, and only at certain times—and this prevented the inspection team from gaining a full picture of what was going on at Dimona. After completing their visit, the inspectors issued a report saying they could find no evidence that the Dimona facility was producing enough plutonium for the production of nuclear weapons.

The members of the inspection team may have been fooled, but the CIA remained convinced that something fishy was going on. Aerial photographs taken by American spy planes showed that the Dimona plant was much larger and more complex than what would be necessary for civilian purposes alone. Kennedy, who of course had access to the CIA information, grew increasingly frustrated with Israel's evasiveness, and he began warning the Israelis that, unless they leveled with him about the nature of their nuclear program, relations between the two countries would be gravely jeopardized. This was where matters stood at the time of Kennedy's assassination in November 1963.

Let me now briefly turn to Kennedy's policies toward Iran. In Iran, as in the Arab world, Kennedy hoped to de-emphasize overt concern for Cold War security in favor of social and economic development, assuming that this would, in the long run, benefit America's position in the Cold War. Such an approach ran counter to the authoritarian policies of the Shah of Iran. Ever since being reinstalled in power in 1953, the Shah had portrayed himself as a staunch ally of the United States, willing and able to crush any manifestations of internal dissent so as to keep Iran squarely in the Western camp. The Eisenhower administration had appreciated this stance and had given the Shah almost uncritical support.

Within Iran, however, the Shah's hard-line policies aroused considerable resentment, and by the early 1960s, leftist critics were increasingly willing to raise their voices in opposition. While some of these critics were members of the Communist Party, most of them were republican nationalists of the Mossadeq variety, people who wanted to democratize the government, make it less repressive, and force it to respond to the people's economic and social needs.

Kennedy came into office convinced that the Iranian government had to make some effort to placate these critics; otherwise, the dissatisfaction would continue to grow and provide opportunities for Moscow to increase its influence in the country. Kennedy began pushing the Shah to make internal reforms. At the same time, Kennedy made sure that Iran's internal security forces would be well supplied, in case the reforms failed to placate the population and internal unrest broke out anyway. At the end of the day, Kennedy was no less determined than Eisenhower had been to see to it that the Shah of Iran remained in power.

Essentially, Kennedy was trying to strike a balance between the soft approach of appeasing the Iranian public by means of internal reform and the hard approach of cracking down on public dissent if it got out of hand. The Shah, however, wanted to pursue the hard approach alone, and he tried his best to thwart Kennedy's attempt to follow a more balanced policy. For the first year of Kennedy's term, the Shah kept sending emissaries to Washington to ask for more military aid, arguing that such aid was necessary to protect Iran from communism. The Kennedy administration kept replying that the best way to resist communism was to attend to the social and economic needs of the Iranian people.

Eventually, the Shah got the message, and in 1962 and 1963, he implemented a series of internal reforms that seemed designed to respond to Kennedy's concerns. Actually, the Shah's reform package was too modest for some of his domestic critics and too far-reaching for others. The Shah introduced limited land reforms (limited mainly to breaking up the land holdings of his wealthy critics), nationalized the country's forests, and gave women the vote. Because elections themselves continued to be rigged, and because the Shah refused to ease up on his harsh repression of internal dissent, most critics on the left were unimpressed by the Shah's reforms. Iranian university students were especially unhappy, and, on a couple of occasions in 1962 and 1963, they staged massive demonstrations throughout the country. The government brutally suppressed the demonstrations, killing thousands of students in the process, which of course further alienated the students and their leftist supporters.

Leftists were not the only ones displeased by the Shah's reforms. Conservative Shiite clerics, who up until now had been relatively apolitical, strongly opposed the decision to give women the vote.

They also opposed the Shah's land reforms which, in some cases, placed lands belonging to religious institutions under government control. The clerics joined with the students in protesting against the government. So contrary to Kennedy's expectation, the Shah's reforms angered far more people than they appeased. In this case, at least, there was no easy solution to the problem of winning the allegiance of the indigenous population.

Thus, by the time Kennedy flew to Dallas for that fateful visit in November 1963, most of his Middle East initiatives were stymied. Kennedy had tried to win Nasser's trust by assisting with Egypt's internal development, but now Nasser was engaged in a bitter war in Yemen that placed enormous strain on U.S.-Egyptian relations. Kennedy had tried to cajole the Israelis into repatriating Palestinian refugees and abandoning their effort to acquire nuclear weapons, but Israel had pocketed the inducement—the Hawk anti-aircraft missiles—without giving ground on the two other issues. Finally, Kennedy had tried to improve the Shah's domestic position by demanding internal reforms, but those reforms had made the Shah even less popular than before. This was the situation that Lyndon Johnson inherited when he was suddenly thrust into the presidency in November 1963.

Lecture Ten
Johnson—Taking Sides

Scope:

In this lecture, we see how Kennedy's effort to balance competing interests in the Middle East, already faltering by late 1963, collapsed altogether under Lyndon B. Johnson, who gave up on even attempting a balanced approach. Returning to the three policy areas discussed in the previous lecture, we see how Johnson assumed a frankly partisan stance, siding openly with the Shah of Iran against his internal opposition, with the conservative Arab regimes against Nasserist Egypt, and with Israel against the Arab states as a whole. We end by taking note of America's emerging strategic alliances with Iran, Saudi Arabia, and Israel, alliances that would become more extensive and formalized under President Richard M. Nixon.

Outline

I. Kennedy's effort to balance conflicting interests in the Middle East, already faltering by late 1963, collapsed altogether under Lyndon B. Johnson.

    A. Johnson instead assumed a frankly partisan stance.

    B. He sided openly with the Shah of Iran against his internal opposition, with the conservative Arab regimes against Nasserist Egypt, and with Israel against the Arab states as a whole.

II. Whereas Kennedy had pressured the Shah of Iran to conduct internal reforms, Johnson returned to the posture of nearly uncritical support that had characterized U.S.-Iranian relations in the Eisenhower years. Johnson refrained from pushing for internal reforms and, instead, lavished Iran with military aid.

    A. Johnson's lack of interest in Iranian internal reform may seem out of character given his own passion for domestic reform in the United States. But Johnson was also a great admirer of strength and loyalty.

        1. Whenever a foreign leader showed he was willing to stand up and be counted on the side of the United States, Johnson's impulse was to give that leader unstinting support.

2. The Shah shrewdly played on this facet of Johnson's character, constantly reminding Johnson that Iran was a loyal ally in the Cold War.

B. The Johnson administration supported the Shah for geostrategic reasons as well. By the mid-1960s, it was clear that Britain would soon have to relinquish its protectorates and military bases on the Arabian Peninsula.

1. Who would fill the resulting vacuum in the oil-rich and strategically located Persian Gulf? Would it be the Soviets, radical nationalists, or some pro-Western power?

2. The Shah made it clear that he would be happy to fill that vacuum. From Washington's perspective, he was far preferable to any of the alternatives.

3. This seemed, then, to be a good time to curry favor with the Shah, rather than hector him about the nature of his internal rule.

C. Moreover, by the mid- to late 1960s, the scale of Iran's weapons purchases from the United States was so great that it had a discernible impact on the U.S. economy, creating thousands of defense-related jobs for American workers.

III. In Iran, there was widespread opposition to the Shah's close relations with Washington.

A. This opposition became especially intense after the United States and Iran concluded the Status of Forces Agreement (SOFA) in 1964. Under SOFA, U.S. military personnel suspected of breaking Iranian laws were to be court-martialed by the U.S. military rather than tried in Iranian courts.

B. A broad coalition of left-leaning secularists and conservative Shiites bitterly denounced the agreement as a throwback to the colonial era.

1. A little-known Shiite cleric named Ayatollah Ruhollah Khomeini caused a national sensation by condemning SOFA in a fiery speech.

2. The Shah arrested Khomeini and had him deported. Khomeini ended up in Iraq, where he was to remain until the late 1970s.

3. Iran's internal security forces began arresting, jailing, and torturing suspected dissidents, a regime of repression that would continue for the remainder of the Shah's rule.

IV. U.S.-Egyptian relations rapidly deteriorated after Kennedy's death. Johnson and Nasser had a visceral dislike for each other, and a series of slights or perceived slights brought relations between the two countries to a new low.

A. In 1964, after the United States participated in an operation to rescue white hostages in the Congo, Congolese students attacked and destroyed a U.S. Information Service library in Cairo.

1. Nasser was unwilling to admit that his own police force had lost control of the situation.

2. He refused to condemn the attack or to apologize to the U.S. government.

B. Around the same time, the Egyptian air force shot down a private plane belonging to an American businessman who happened to be a close friend of Johnson.

1. The incident was an accident.

2. The resulting series of diplomatic "misunderstandings" culminated in Nasser's declaring that if the Americans had a problem with Egypt they could "go drink from the sea," the Egyptian equivalent of "go jump in a lake."

C. In response to Nasser's verbal attacks on the United States, the Johnson administration curtailed its food aid to Egypt, further enraging Nasser.

D. As U.S.-Egyptian relations deteriorated, the Johnson administration drew closer to the conservative Arab regimes.

1. The administration sold tens of millions of dollars worth of military equipment to Saudi Arabia and Jordan.

2. The administration also became more supportive of Saudi Arabia in its proxy war against Egypt over Yemen.

3. By 1966, the administration had committed itself to a "two pillars" policy of beefing up support for both Iran and Saudi Arabia.

V. Another beneficiary of Johnson's new approach to Middle East policy was Israel.

A. Johnson viscerally identified with the Israelis, seeing them as latter-day pioneers on the model of his own Texas forebears.

B. During Johnson's administration, the United States first began selling Israel fighter aircraft and tanks, weapons with both offensive and defensive capabilities.

C. Like Kennedy, however, Johnson was concerned about Israel's ongoing efforts to acquire nuclear weapons. He, too, hoped to convince the Israelis to forego the nuclear option by providing them with state-of-the-art conventional weapons.

D. But Johnson was no more successful than Kennedy had been at keeping Israel from developing the bomb. Although the Israeli government insisted that it had no intention of acquiring a nuclear weapons capability, the U.S. intelligence community learned otherwise.

E. The problem for the Johnson administration was what to do with this knowledge.
   1. Forcing an end to Israel's nuclear program would require a public showdown between the Johnson administration and Israel.
   2. This, in turn, would provoke a bitter domestic struggle between the administration and Israel's American supporters. At a time when Johnson was increasingly preoccupied with the war in Vietnam, a public fight over Israel was the last thing the president needed.

F. Aside from occasional protests and pointed queries, the Johnson administration did not make an issue of Israel's ongoing nuclear weapons program.

G. Shrewdly, Israel provided Washington with official assurances that made it easier for the Americans to evade the issue.
   1. Israel's standard statement on the question—"Israel will not be the first to introduce nuclear weapons to the Middle East"—sounded definitive but actually contained significant loopholes.

2. It is believed that Israel acquired its first usable nuclear bomb sometime in early 1968.

H. By that time, of course, the political and strategic landscape of the Middle East had been dramatically altered by the Six-Day War, the subject of our next lecture.

Suggested Reading:

Cohen, Avner. *Israel and the Bomb*. New York: Columbia University Press, 1998.

McAlister, Melani. *Epic Encounters: Culture, Media, and U.S. Interests in the Middle East, 1945–2000*. Berkeley: University of California Press, 2001.

Questions to Consider:

1. Why did Lyndon B. Johnson resume the Eisenhower administration's policy of extending virtually uncritical support for the Shah of Iran?

2. To what extent was the deterioration in U.S.-Egyptian relations in the mid-1960s the result of personal friction between Johnson and Nasser and to what extent was it the result of fundamental differences between U.S. and Egyptian national interests?

Lecture Ten—Transcript
Johnson—Taking Sides

We left off last time with John F. Kennedy's death in November 1963, and the coming to power of Lyndon B. Johnson. As we saw, the careful balancing act that Kennedy had tried to perform over U.S.-Iranian relations, over relations with Arab nationalism, and over the Arab-Israeli conflict had started to come undone even before his assassination. Once Johnson became president, that balancing act collapsed altogether, and Washington abandoned all pretense of even attempting a balanced approach. Johnson instead assumed a frankly partisan stance, siding openly with the Shah of Iran against his internal opposition, with the conservative Arab regimes against Nasserist Egypt, and with Israel against the Arab states as a whole. This partisan approach to Middle Eastern politics would leave a legacy of bitterness and antagonism that remains with us to this day.

Johnson's partisan approach to Middle Eastern politics was the product of both personality and circumstance. Personally, Johnson was far more emotional and thin-skinned than his predecessor had been. Kennedy had possessed an ironic detachment that made it easier for him to deal with volatile and obstreperous foreign leaders. In the Kennedy years, if a foreign leader indulged in anti-American rhetoric, Kennedy tended not to take it personally, assuming instead that the leader in question was playing to his own constituency or engaging in some tactical maneuver. Johnson, by contrast, tended to take anti-American rhetoric at face value and, worse still, to see it as a personal affront to himself. Consequently, Johnson had far less patience with Middle Eastern leaders who criticized the United States, and he responded to them in ways that only increased their criticism.

The problem also had to do with the times in which Johnson served. The mid- to late 1960s were a period of revolutionary ferment throughout the world, and especially the Third World. As we saw in the last lecture, a large number of nations had gained independence in the early 1960s. As the decade progressed, Third World nations became increasingly assertive in world affairs, acquiring a critical mass in the UN General Assembly and other international bodies. Because most of these countries had had bitter experiences with Western imperial domination, and because the United States and its allies were perceived as upholding a status quo that favored rich, white nations over poor nations of color, the tone of Third World assertiveness was increasingly anti-Western and anti-American. The fact that this period also coincided with America's escalation of the war in Vietnam only intensified the criticism directed at the United States.

In the Middle East, too, there was a rising chorus of anti-U.S. criticism. Virtually all Arabs saw the United States as excessively partial to Israel. Arab radicals in particular accused Washington of cozying up to reactionary Arab monarchs who mistreated their own people and hoarded their nations' wealth. In Iran, political dissidents blasted the United States for supporting the Shah, another authoritarian monarch who seemed out of touch with his own people. President Johnson's lack of personal detachment and the rising tide of anti-Americanism reinforced each other. As I suggested a moment ago, the more criticism Johnson received from Middle Eastern leaders and commentators, the more he behaved in ways that generated further criticism, reinforcing his original inclination to give up on trying to win over his critics and to stick with leaders and governments that supported him already.

Let's start with U.S.-Iranian relations under Johnson. As we saw in the previous lecture, Kennedy's preoccupation with internal reforms had greatly irritated the Shah, and there is even some evidence that the Shah was not entirely displeased to hear of Kennedy's assassination. Indeed, Johnson proved to be a much easier president for the Shah to deal with. Johnson essentially returned to the posture of uncritical support for the Shah that had characterized U.S.-Iranian relations in the Eisenhower years. He refrained from pressuring the Shah on internal reforms and lavished Iran with military aid.

This may seem a little odd on the face of it, since Johnson was such a strong advocate of social reforms at home, what with his Great Society programs and civil rights legislation. One would think that Johnson would favor similar sorts of policies for Iran, rather than squandering money on arms and internal security forces. But Johnson was also a great admirer of strength and loyalty. Whenever a foreign leader showed he was willing to stand up and be counted on the side of the United States, Johnson's impulse was to give that leader unstinting support, regardless of how ruthlessly he might treat his own people. The Shah shrewdly played on this facet of Johnson's character, constantly reminding Johnson that Iran was a loyal ally in the Cold War.

Johnson was especially grateful for the Shah's public support for the Vietnam War at a time when even America's closest allies were expressing doubts about that policy. The Shah also played on Johnson's weakness for flattery and attention, never failing to note a birthday, illness, or other personal event. The Shah directed a steady stream of gifts toward the Johnson White House, and saw to it that the president was well supplied with pistachios, caviar, and other Persian delicacies. To a man of Johnson's personal insecurities, such gestures made a real difference. But there were other, more tangible reasons for the Johnson administration to support the Shah.

By the mid-1960s, it was clear that Britain, which had been maintaining a set of protectorates and military bases on the Arabian Peninsula, would soon have to give up these assets because the financial cost was too high. The big question was: Who would fill the resulting strategic vacuum in the oil-rich Persian Gulf? Would it be the Soviets, radical nationalists, or some pro-Western power? The Shah made it clear that he would be happy to fill that vacuum, and, from Washington's perspective, he was far preferable to any of the alternatives. This seemed to be a good time to curry favor with the Shah, rather than hassle him about the nature of his rule.

Moreover, in the mid- to late 1960s the scale of Iran's weapons purchases from the United States was so great that it had discernible impact on the U.S. economy. American corporations like Boeing and McDonald-Douglas manufactured hundreds of millions of dollars worth of military equipment for Iran, creating thousands of jobs for American workers. This was not the primary reason for U.S. support for Iran, but it certainly didn't hurt the Shah's case in Washington.

Within Iran itself, dissatisfaction with the status quo remained at a high level, but the Shah, now confident of Washington's unwavering support, was able to drive much of that dissent underground. Still, a major crisis erupted in 1964, shortly after Johnson became president, when the U.S. and Iranian governments signed the Status of Forces Agreement, or SOFA. SOFA was designed to clarify the legal status of American military personnel who had been stationed in Iran to provide advice and training to the Iranian military. The problem was what to do about the many instances in which American servicemen got into brawls, caused traffic accidents, or otherwise ran afoul of local laws.

Of all these behaviors, reckless driving by American military personnel was probably the most infuriating. As we saw in the lecture on World War II, this problem dated back to the early 1940s. Now, under SOFA, it was agreed that any American soldiers suspected of committing crimes would be court-martialed by the U.S. military rather than tried in Iranian courts. In effect, American servicemen would be exempt from Iranian law. SOFA provoked a furious reaction among the Iranian people, who saw the agreement as a throwback to an earlier period in Iranian history, when Britain and Russia had insisted that their own citizens living in Iran be immune from local law. Once again, Iran seemed to be knuckling under to the demands of an imperial power, surrendering an essential part of its national sovereignty.

As soon as SOFA was made public, a broad coalition of left-leaning secularists and conservative Shiites—essentially the same coalition that had protested against the Shah's reform program in 1962 and '63—began denouncing the agreement. It was in this context that a little known Shiite cleric named Ayatollah Ruhollah Khomeini was suddenly thrust into the national spotlight. Then in his mid-sixties, Khomeini was a highly revered religious leader who had spent most of his adult life steering clear of political controversies. But the Shah's reform efforts of the previous two years, especially land reforms and women's suffrage, had antagonized Khomeini, and now the SOFA agreement angered him further. In late 1964, Khomeini delivered a fiery speech in which he charged that Iran's leaders:

> Have reduced the Iranian people to a level lower than that of an American dog. If someone runs over a dog belonging to an American, he will be prosecuted. Even if the Shah himself were to run over a dog belonging to an American, he would be prosecuted. But if an American cook runs over the Shah, the head of state, no one will have the right to interfere with him…Are we to be trampled underfoot by the boots of America simply because we are a weak nation?

Khomeini's emotional speech touched a chord with the Iranian people, religious and secular alike, and he was widely regarded as a national hero. The Shah, recognizing the threat Khomeini posed to his regime, had the cleric arrested and deported; Khomeini would remain in exile until 1979.

Meanwhile, in early 1965, the Iranian prime minister was shot dead by a right-wing Shiite activist; shortly thereafter, the Shah himself narrowly escaped being assassinated by a left-wing secularist. Taken together, these two acts provided the Shah with a pretext for crushing both the religious and the secular opposition movements. The Shah's internal security organization, a brutal outfit known as SAVAK, began arresting, jailing, and torturing suspected dissidents, a regime of repression that would continue for the remainder of the Shah's rule. Such abuses, however, did not deter Johnson and his advisors from enclosing the Shah in an ever tighter embrace, convinced as they were that U.S. security interests in the Persian Gulf dictated such an alliance. "In effect," a U.S. official remarked in 1968, without evident irony or discomfort, "we are placing our money on a modern Persian Emperor." It seemed a good bet at the time.

Let's now briefly look at Johnson's relations with Egypt. In the last few months of Kennedy's time in the White House, the Yemeni civil war had placed strains on U.S.-Egyptian relations. Soon after Johnson became president, those relations took a nosedive. Johnson and Nasser had a visceral dislike for each other. Johnson saw Nasser as an unscrupulous demagogue who whipped up Arab mobs through hateful and bombastic rhetoric. Nasser saw Johnson as an unsophisticated rube who had no business occupying a position of world leadership. Nasser was especially put off by that famous photograph of Johnson pulling up his shirt to show the scar he had received from his gall bladder operation. Such crude gestures, Nasser thought, were beneath the dignity of a statesman. Very soon after Johnson took power, a series of bitter disputes, many of them more symbolic than substantive, brought U.S.-Egyptian relations to a new low.

In late 1964, a group of Congolese students living in Cairo staged a demonstration to protest U.S. policy toward the Congo. The students gathered at the United States Information Service Library. One of the students planted an incendiary device in the library, and the building went up in flames. The Egyptian government had no complicity in this act, and it would have been a fairly simple matter for Nasser to issue an apology to the U.S. government and perhaps offer to pay compensation for the damage. But Nasser was loath to admit that his security forces had lost control of the situation, so he refused to provide either an apology or compensation, which totally infuriated President Johnson.

Right about this time, late 1964, another dramatic flare-up occurred, this one equally pointless. It all started when the Egyptian air force shot down a private plane belonging to an American businessman, who also happened to be a close friend of Lyndon Johnson; several members of the flight crew, though not the businessman himself, were killed. The shooting down had been an accident, resulting from the pilot's failure to issue a flight plan, but it took a few days to determine precisely what had happened. In the meantime, while the wreckage of the plane was still being sifted over, the Egyptian Minister of Supply summoned the U.S. ambassador to his office and asked whether the U.S. government would be willing to renew the PL 480 agreement.

PL 480, you will recall, was an American foreign aid program that allowed poor countries like Egypt to purchase surplus American wheat, grain, and other commodities with their own currencies. During the Kennedy administration, the United States and Egypt had concluded a three-year PL 480 agreement that was due to expire in 1965. We're now in late 1964. When the Egyptian Minister of Supply asked about renewing the PL 480 agreement, the U.S. ambassador said that this wasn't the proper time to discuss such a matter, in the wake of this tragic accident, or plane crash (it wasn't yet known that it was an accident). During the course of the meeting, the minister of supply offered the ambassador a glass of orange juice. According to one version of the meeting, the ambassador drank the orange juice; according to another version, he politely declined it.

At the time of the meeting, Nasser was traveling by train to deliver a major speech in Port Said, a city in northern Egypt. While en route, he received an extremely distorted account of the meeting. According to that account, the U.S. ambassador not only had flatly turned down the request to renew PL 480 but had rudely refused to drink the orange juice. Nasser, without waiting to get confirmation of this account, went to Port Said to give his speech and included in it a bitter attack on the United States. He passed on to his audience the distorted account of the meeting he had just received, and then breathed defiance against the United States, "Those who do not accept our behavior," he cried, "can go drink from the sea,"—the

Egyptian equivalent of "go jump in the lake." "We will cut the tongues of anybody who speaks badly about us." Nasser went on to insult Lyndon Johnson personally, calling him a "cowboy" who was guilty of "gangsterism."

Nasser's outburst had an extremely negative impact on U.S.-Egyptian relations. The Americans renewed the PL 480 agreement, but instead of signing another three-year contract, they insisted on limiting it to six-month installments; at the end of each six-month period, the Johnson administration could evaluate Nasser's conduct and decide whether or not the contract should be renewed. By this mechanism, the administration hoped to be able to regulate Nasser's behavior, but just the opposite occurred. Nasser was so outraged by this crude attempt to pressure him, that he stepped up his anti-American attacks and drew closer to the East Bloc, accepting ever larger amounts of Soviet economic and military aid. When the Americans responded by cutting back on their wheat supplies, Nasser told them he was no longer interested in any U.S. assistance at all. This was where things stood on the eve of the Six-Day War of 1967, a subject we'll look at in our next lecture.

As U.S.-Egyptian relations deteriorated, the Johnson administration drew closer to the conservative Arab regimes, especially the two monarchies of Saudi Arabia and Jordan. Kennedy had tried to limit U.S. support for these regimes so as to avoid antagonizing Nasser. Johnson, having basically given up on placating Nasser, sold tens of millions of dollars worth of military equipment to the Saudis and the Jordanians. As a U.S. official remarked in 1967, it was time to show "sympathy for good Arabs as against bad Arabs."

As in the case of Iran, the realization that Britain would soon be withdrawing its forces from the Persian Gulf strengthened Johnson's determination to move closer to conservative Arab regimes, especially those located on the gulf. The idea, of course, was to strengthen regional clients and have them fill the power vacuum resulting from Britain's departure. By 1966, the Johnson administration had committed itself to a "two pillars" policy of beefing up support for both Iran and Saudi Arabia, though Iran was always the larger recipient of the two. That same year, the Johnson administration agreed to sell Saudi Arabia $100 million worth of non-lethal military equipment, mainly trucks and jeeps. By 1968, the United States was selling fighter aircraft to the Saudis. As we'll see in a later lecture, the "two pillars" policy initiated by Johnson would be formalized and expanded by President Nixon.

Another major beneficiary of Johnson's new approach to Middle East policy was Israel. "You have lost a very great friend," Johnson told an Israeli diplomat soon after Kennedy's death. "But you have found a much better one." Indeed, the new president viscerally identified with Israel in a way that Kennedy never quite did. Johnson saw the Israelis as latter-day pioneers on the model of his own Texas forebears, and the Israeli government had little difficulty convincing him to turn up the spigot of military and economic aid.

During Johnson's administration the United States began, for the first time, selling Israel weapons with offensive as well as defensive capabilities. In 1965, for example, Johnson agreed to sell Israel over 200 M-48 tanks, and in the following year he approved the sale of 48 A-4 Skyhawk jets. In late 1968, following an intensive lobbying campaign by the Israeli government and its supporters in the United States, which by now included most of the U.S. Congress, Johnson agreed to sell Israel 50 F-4 Phantom jets, the fastest and most sophisticated aircraft in the American arsenal.

Like his predecessor, however, Johnson was concerned about Israel's ongoing efforts to acquire nuclear weapons, and he, too, hoped to convince the Israelis to forego the nuclear option by providing them with state-of-the-art conventional weapons. But Johnson was no more successful than Kennedy had been at keeping Israel from developing the bomb. In the Johnson years American inspectors continued to visit the Dimona facility, and their Israeli hosts continued to prevent them from discovering the true purpose of that facility. The Israelis accomplished this, not by flatly refusing to allow the inspectors to see particular sites, but rather by carefully circumscribing, in advance, the scope of each inspection.

As in the Kennedy years, however, these tactics did not prevent high-level U.S. officials from discovering the true nature of Dimona's activities. Relying on aerial photography and human intelligence, American spy agencies became ever more convinced that Israel was indeed developing nuclear weapons. The problem then became what to do with that knowledge. It became increasingly clear that putting an end to Israel's nuclear program would require a public showdown between the Johnson administration and Israel, which in turn would provoke a bitter domestic struggle between the administration and Israel's American supporters.

At a time when Johnson was increasingly preoccupied with the war in Vietnam, with all the international and domestic headaches that involved, a public fight over Israel was the last thing the president needed. Eventually, the American intelligence community got the message that the Johnson administration did not really want to be officially informed about what was going on at Dimona, because once it had that knowledge it would have to do something about it. It was far easier for the administration to remain officially in the dark about whether or not the Israelis were developing nuclear weapons. Intelligence reports on the subject were buried in the files, and their conclusions seldom made it into the intelligence estimates that were officially conveyed to American policy makers.

The Israelis were aware of Johnson's reluctance to make a stink over their nuclear ambitions, and they shrewdly provided Washington with official assurances that made it easier for the Americans to evade the issue themselves. The standard phrase the Israeli government used, when speaking to U.S. officials, was "Israel will not be the first to introduce nuclear weapons into the area," which on its face seemed pretty definitive. It turned out, however, that the statement contained significant loopholes, and that Israel was using the word "introduce" in a very specific and restricted sense.

In the fall of 1968, a most revealing conversation took place between Paul Warnke, an assistant secretary of defense in the Johnson administration, and Yitzhak Rabin, who was then Israel's ambassador to the United States and who later would serve as Israel's prime minister. According to a memorandum of that conversation, Warnke "observed that he could not find in the record any understanding of what Israel means by the provision 'Israel will not be the first to introduce nuclear weapons.'" Mr. Warnke asked the Ambassador what was meant by this term.

Rabin responds with a long, complicated, Clintonesque answer in which he says it all depends on what one means by the terms "introduce" and "nuclear weapons." As Rabin keeps talking, it becomes clear that he considers that Israel can construct a nuclear explosive device without violating the letter of its pledge to the U.S. government. As long as Israel refrains from publicly announcing that it has nuclear weapons, and as long as it refrains from testing that weapon, then Israel hasn't actually "introduced" nuclear weapons to the Middle East. In other words, Rabin is using the word "introduce" in its literal sense, the way you might use it at a social gathering: "Middle East—nuclear weapon; nuclear weapon—Middle East." If the weapon hasn't been "introduced" in that very public way, it doesn't really exist.

The memorandum of conversation continues, "Mr. Warnke said: 'Then in your view, an unadvertised, untested nuclear device is not a nuclear weapon.' Ambassador Rabin said, 'Yes, that is correct.'" So by the end of this conversation, if not before, it was clear that Israel's pledge would impose few actual limits on its nuclear ambitions. As Warnke himself later wrote of his negotiations with the Israelis, "at the time I believed, and subsequent information has tended to confirm, that Israel had in fact developed a small arsenal of nuclear weapons." Indeed, it is believed that Israel acquired its first usable nuclear bomb sometime in early 1968.

In the ensuing years, as Israel built up its nuclear arsenal, it developed a posture that one historian has referred to as "nuclear opacity," never openly acknowledging that it had nuclear weapons, but leaving its adversaries in no doubt that such a capability existed. The idea was to deter any Arab state from thinking it could annihilate Israel, while avoiding a public declaration that might compel an Arab state to seek a nuclear capability of its own. The problem, of course, was that any Israeli nuclear capability, even an unadvertised one, was inherently provocative, and it was only a matter of time before some other state in the region would seek to acquire its own "weapons of mass destruction."

By the time Johnson left office in early 1969, the outlines of a new American policy were coming into view. Rather than continuing the careful balancing act that President Kennedy had attempted, Johnson had adopted an openly partisan approach, siding with the Shah of Iran against his internal opposition, with the conservative Arab regimes against Nasserist Egypt, and with Israel against the Arab states as a whole. As we'll see in a later lecture, these alliances would be solidified and formalized during the presidency of Richard Nixon, with far-reaching consequences for U.S. policy in the Middle East. We won't go to Nixon just yet; instead, we'll devote our next lecture to examining the causes, conduct, and consequences of the Six-Day War.

In an immediate sense, as we shall see, the Six-Day War reinforced Johnson's inclination to take a partisan approach to Middle Eastern affairs. Over the longer term, it would dramatically transform the political and strategic landscape of the Middle East, creating a new status quo with which the peoples of the Middle East, and the international community as a whole, would wrestle for decades.

Lecture Eleven
The Six-Day War

Scope:

In this lecture, we discuss the 1967 Arab-Israeli War, which dramatically altered the political, strategic, and psychological landscape of the Middle East. We begin by outlining the disputed status of the Strait of Tiran, showing how the interaction of that issue with inter-Arab rivalry created the crisis that ultimately led to war. We then recount Nasser's challenge to Israel's maritime rights in the Strait of Tiran and consider U.S. efforts to manage the resulting crisis. After briefly describing Israel's lopsided victory in the ensuing war, we discuss the diplomatic and political fallout from the war, paying particular attention to the passage of UN Security Council Resolution 242 and to the war's devastating impact on Nasserist Arab nationalism.

Outline

I. The Six-Day War dramatically altered the political and strategic landscape of the Middle East, creating a situation "on the ground" with which the peoples of the Middle East, and the international community as a whole, continue to grapple. It also helped bring about a profound transformation in the nature of Arab opposition to U.S. policy.

II. To understand the causes of the Six-Day War, it is necessary to go back to the Suez War of 1956.

 A. At the conclusion of that war, the international community pressured Israel to withdraw its forces from Egypt.

 B. But Israel gained important concessions in return.

 1. It got a termination of an Egyptian blockade against Israeli shipping through the Strait of Tiran.

 2. It got an end to cross-border raids into Israeli territory from the Gaza Strip.

 C. These gains were secured by the stationing of UN peacekeeping forces on the Sinai Peninsula and in the Gaza Strip.

 D. By the 1960s, the Arab world was divided into two mutually antagonistic camps.

1. A conservative camp, consisting of such countries as Jordan and Saudi Arabia, was strongly pro-American.
2. A radical camp, consisting of Egypt, Syria, and Iraq, was officially neutral in the Cold War but had a distinct pro-Soviet bias.
3. Each camp used the Arab-Israeli issue as a way of discrediting the other.
4. This war of words intensified after a Syrian-Israeli aerial clash in April 1967; Nasser's failure to come to Syria's aid prompted Jordan's King Hussein to denounce Nasser as a cowardly fraud.

III. In May 1967, Nasser requested the removal of the UN peacekeepers from Sinai and Gaza.

A. Nasser's motives appear to have been twofold.
   1. He wanted to pose a credible threat of retaliation in the event Israel launched an attack on Syria, which Nasser feared might be imminent. The peacekeepers stood in the way of a ground offensive against Israel.
   2. Nasser wanted to silence critics in the Arab world who had accused him of using the presence of the UN peacekeepers as an excuse for avoiding conflict with Israel.

B. Nasser realized, however, that a total withdrawal of the UN peacekeeping force would leave a military vacuum in Gaza and Sharm al-Shaykh, a vacuum Nasser would have to fill with his own forces.
   1. And, having occupied Sharm al-Shaykh, Nasser would face enormous pressure to reinstate the blockade on Israeli shipping through the Strait of Tiran.
   2. But if he blocked the strait, the Israelis would go to war against Egypt, because they had made it clear that free passage through the strait was a vital interest for which they were willing to fight.

C. Knowing his forces were unprepared for war, Nasser tried to follow a middle course.

1. Rather than demanding a total withdrawal of peacekeepers, Nasser asked the UN to remove its peacekeeping force only from Egypt's land border with Israel.
2. Unfortunately for Nasser, U Thant, the secretary general of the UN, was unwilling to conduct a partial withdrawal of peacekeeping forces.
3. To save face, Nasser agreed to withdrawal of the UN peacekeepers from all of the Sinai Peninsula and Gaza.

IV. After the peacekeepers departed, Nasser sent Egyptian forces into the Sinai.

A. Once his forces were in the Sinai, Nasser faced enormous public pressure to reinstate the blockade against Israeli shipping through the Strait of Tiran.

B. In late May 1967, Nasser announced the closure of the strait to all Israeli shipping and to vessels of any nationality carrying strategic materials to Israel.

C. Nasser's closure of the strait made it extremely likely that Israel would go to war against Egypt to reopen the strait.

D. If Nasser knew that blockading the strait would bring an inevitable Israeli attack, and if he knew that his army was not ready for war, why did he carry out this action?
   1. In the first place, Nasser concluded that the political price of *not* blockading the strait would have been exorbitant: He would have been ridiculed throughout the Arab world and would potentially lose his position as the standard bearer of Arab nationalism.
   2. In the second place, Nasser evidently assumed that an Israeli attack would not be as devastating as it turned out to be. He had no idea how unprepared for war his army actually was.

V. The Johnson administration was anxious to prevent a war.

A. Although U.S. intelligence estimates indicated that Israel would almost certainly win such a war, there were nagging doubts that the intelligence estimates were mistaken and that the United States would have to come to Israel's aid.
   1. Johnson warned the Israeli government that if Israel fired the first shot and got into trouble in the ensuing

war, it would be impossible for the United States to bail Israel out.

 2. Johnson also promised that if Israel refrained from going to war, he would try to organize an international flotilla to challenge Nasser's closure of the Strait of Tiran.

 B. The Israelis agreed to hold their fire and give Johnson a chance to organize the flotilla.

VI. The Egyptians received similar advice from the Soviet government: If Egypt started a war, the Soviet Union could not come to its aid. Nasser agreed not to fire the first shot.

VII. Although Nasser's posture was now defensive, his public rhetoric, and that of other Arab leaders, was extremely bellicose.

 A. All the rivalries that had recently fractured the Arab world were momentarily forgotten as everyone focused on the coming battle with Israel.

 B. Jordan's King Hussein signed a mutual defense pact with Nasser, placing Jordan's army under Egypt's command.

 C. These developments terrified the Israeli public, arousing fears that the Jews once again faced extermination. There was enormous pressure on the government to do something about the threat.

 D. Moreover, by this time, Israel had conducted a full military mobilization, which disrupted all industrial activity in the country. It was doubtful that the Israeli economy could endure that state of affairs for more than a few weeks.

VIII. Meanwhile, Washington's efforts to organize an international flotilla were getting nowhere. Few countries were willing to allow their navies to take part in an effort to force the Strait of Tiran.

 A. As alternative solutions receded from view, Washington grew somewhat less insistent that Israel refrain from going to war.

B. Through informal intermediaries, Israeli leaders gained the impression that Johnson, while still hoping to avoid a war, would not strongly object if Israel fired the first shot—provided that the United States was not dragged into the conflict.

IX. On June 5, 1967, Israel launched a surprise air attack on Egypt, destroying its air force on the ground.

    A. Deprived of air cover, and confused and demoralized by incoherent orders, the Egyptian army was defenseless against an Israeli ground assault in the Sinai. Israeli forces quickly occupied the entire peninsula.

    B. When Jordan entered the war on Egypt's side, Israeli forces seized and occupied the West Bank, including East Jerusalem.

    C. Israel then turned its attention to Syria, taking from it the strategic Golan Heights.

    D. By the time a cease-fire was reached on June 11, Israel had tripled the territory under its control.

X. There was a marked difference between Johnson's reaction to Israel's behavior in 1967 and that of Eisenhower in 1956.

    A. Whereas Eisenhower had forced Israel to withdraw from Egypt, Johnson merely called for, and achieved, a "cease-fire in place."

    B. This allowed Israel to remain indefinitely in possession of the territories it had seized.

XI. In November 1967, the UN Security Council passed Resolution 242, which was subsequently accepted by Egypt, Jordan, and Israel.

    A. Resolution 242 essentially called for a "land-for-peace" settlement.

        1. The Arab states must recognize Israel's right to exist in security.

        2. Israel must withdraw from territories seized in the Six-Day War.

B. Still, Resolution 242 was an extremely ambiguous document.

    1. It did not say explicitly which should come first: the Arab states' recognition of Israel or Israel's withdrawal from Arab territory.

    2. Moreover, at the insistence of Israel and the United States, the clause dealing with Israeli withdrawal did not contain the definite article. Israel was to withdraw from "territories occupied in the recent conflict," rather than from "the territories."

    3. On the other hand, the preamble to the resolution referred to "the inadmissibility of the acquisition of territory by war."

C. These ambiguities would plague subsequent attempts to resolve the Arab-Israeli conflict, down to the present day.

XII. The Six-Day War was a devastating defeat for Nasserist pan-Arabism.

    A. Under nationalist leadership, the Arabs had been single-handedly defeated by the tiny state of Israel. It was a blow from which Arab nationalism never fully recovered.

    B. The decline of Nasser's brand of secular Arab nationalism left a vacuum that was to be filled by two movements previously marginalized in Arab politics: Palestinian nationalism and political Islam.

    C. There was a growing feeling in the Arab world—and in other Islamic countries—that secular nationalism had failed to deliver the goods and that some alternative form of political organization had to be found.

    D. In the decades to come, these two movements—Palestinian nationalism and political Islam—would play an increasingly prominent role in Arab opposition to American policy in the Middle East.

    E. The Six-Day War also completed the reorientation of U.S. Middle East policy that Lyndon Johnson had begun shortly after taking office in late 1963.

Suggested Reading:

Neff, Donald. *Warriors over Jerusalem: The Six Days That Changed the Middle East*. New York: Simon & Schuster, 1984.

Oren, Michael B. *Six Days of War: June 1967 and the Making of the Modern Middle East*. New York: Oxford University Press, 2002.

Parker, Richard B. *The Politics of Miscalculation in the Middle East*. Bloomington: Indiana University Press, 1993.

Questions to Consider:

1. Could the Johnson administration have done more to avert the Six-Day War in 1967?

2. How, and why, did Johnson's reaction to the Israeli attack on Egypt in 1967 differ from Eisenhower's reaction to the Israeli attack on Egypt in 1956?

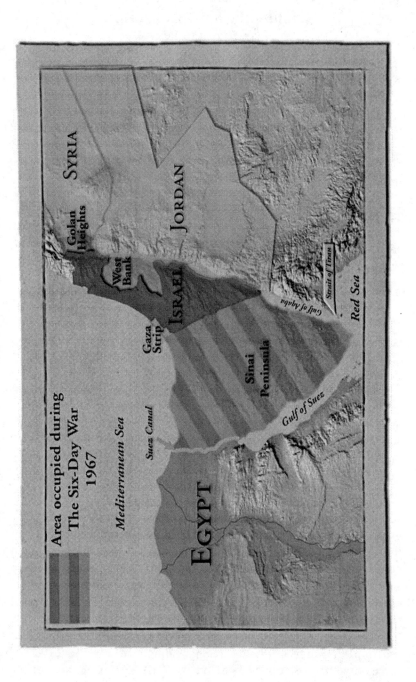

Area occupied during
The Six-Day War
1967

Mediterranean Sea

Suez Canal

EGYPT

Sinai
Peninsula

Gulf of Suez

Gaza
Strip

ISRAEL

West
Bank

Golan
Heights

SYRIA

JORDAN

Gulf of Aqaba

Strait of Tiran

Red Sea

Lecture Eleven—Transcript
The Six-Day War

In this lecture, we'll continue our discussion of Lyndon Johnson's Middle East policies, paying particular attention to the Arab-Israeli War of 1967, also known as the Six-Day War. The Six-Day War dramatically altered the political and strategic landscape of the Middle East, creating a new situation "on the ground" with which the peoples of the Middle East, and the international community as a whole, continue to grapple to this day. The war also helped bring about a profound transformation in the nature of Arab opposition to U.S. policy. To understand the causes of the Six-Day War, it is necessary to go back to the Suez War of 1956. On that occasion, you will recall, Britain, France, and Israel launched an invasion of Egypt, only to be forced by international pressure, especially American pressure, to abandon the attack.

Although the Israelis were obliged to withdraw from Egypt, they got an important concession in return: the termination of an Egyptian blockade against their shipping, and an end to cross-border raids into Israeli territory. In the previous year, 1955, Egypt had tightened a blockade that it had previously imposed against Israeli shipping through the Strait of Tiran, the passageway between the Gulf of Aqaba and the Red Sea. The Egyptian blockade prevented Israel from using Eilat, its only southern port, and thus closed off Israel's most direct outlet to the Indian Ocean. All of Israel's other ports were on the Mediterranean, and because Egypt had already closed the Suez Canal to Israeli shipping, any ships departing from the Mediterranean ports would have to sail all around the cape of southern Africa to get to the Indian Ocean.

Another problem the Israelis had faced prior to 1956 was repeated guerrilla and terrorist attacks on their country from Palestinians in the Egyptian-controlled Gaza Strip, attacks that the Egyptian government either tolerated or sponsored. When Israel attacked Egypt during the Suez War, it occupied the Sinai Peninsula and thus ended the Egyptian blockade of the Strait of Tiran; it also occupied the Gaza Strip, putting an end to the Palestinian attacks. When the Israelis later withdrew from Sinai and Gaza under American pressure, they did so on the understanding that UN peacekeeping forces would be stationed both on the Sinai Peninsula and in the Gaza Strip. The peacekeepers in Gaza would keep that territory from being used as a staging area for Palestinian raids into Israel. The Sinai peacekeepers were stationed in two places: along the land border between Sinai and Israel and in the port city of Sharm al-Shaykh.

The peacekeepers at Sharm al-Shaykh were especially important, since they prevented Egypt from reimposing its blockade on Israeli shipping through the Strait of Tiran. The peacekeepers remained in Sinai and Gaza for the next ten years; indeed, it was their sudden removal in the spring of 1967 that set the stage for the Six-Day War. To understand how this came about, it's necessary to take a look at inter-Arab politics in the years leading up to 1967.

By the 1960s, the Arab world was divided into two mutually antagonistic camps: a conservative camp consisting of countries like Jordan and Saudi Arabia, and a radical camp consisting of Egypt, Syria, and Iraq. The conservative camp was strongly pro-American, while the radical camp was officially neutral in the Cold War, though with a distinct pro-Soviet bias. Each camp used the Arab-Israeli issue as a way of discrediting the other. The radicals would taunt the conservatives by saying, "How can you call yourself true Arabs when you're aligned with the United States, the imperialist nation that brought Israel into being?" The conservatives would reply, "You guys keep talking about how anti-Israeli you are, but you never do anything about it. You're just full of hot air."

This war of words grew especially intense in April 1967, when a border clash between Israel and Syria escalated into a dogfight between the two countries' air forces. The Israelis decisively won that engagement, shooting down several Syrian planes and flying with impunity over the Syrian capital, Damascus. The Syrians pleaded with Nasser to come their aid, but Nasser refused. He knew that Egypt was in no shape to tangle with Israel, especially with a third of the Egyptian army bogged down in Yemen, fighting that obscure proxy war against Saudi Arabia.

King Hussein of Jordan seized on this incident and blasted Nasser for failing to come to Syria's aid. Hussein pointed out that Nasser, by allowing UN peacekeepers to remain in the Sinai Peninsula, was permitting Israeli ships to pass through the Strait of Tiran. "If you were a real Arab patriot," Hussein said, "you'd expel the peacekeepers and re-impose the blockade against Israeli shipping.

Instead you're hiding behind the skirts of the UN." Just to rub it in a bit more, Hussein remarked that Nasser was perfectly willing to send troops to kill fellow Arabs in Yemen but was unwilling to fight against the Arabs' common enemy, Israel. Hussein's accusations were soon echoed by other Arab commentators, even those ordinarily sympathetic to Nasser.

Then, in May 1967, the Syrian government started sounding the alarm about an impending Israeli invasion of Syria. Ordinarily, Nasser would have been inclined to ignore the Syrians, who had a reputation for being somewhat hysterical on this subject. But then the Soviet government privately contacted Nasser and told him that, based on its own intelligence reports, the Syrian claims were credible: Israel was indeed massing its forces on the Israeli-Syrian border. Actually, the Israelis were not massing their forces; the Soviets had either fabricated the report or made a mistake. Nasser had no way of knowing this at the time.

Now Nasser had two reasons to take some countermeasures against Israel: to silence Arab accusations that he was a coward, and to deter what appeared to be an impending Israeli attack on Syria. He decided he needed to make a threatening gesture that would be simultaneously impressive to the Israeli government and to Arab public opinion. At the same time, he would have to be careful not to start a war for which he was unready.

The most credible threat Nasser could pose to deter an Israeli attack on Syria was the threat of conducting a counterattack across the Egyptian-Israeli border. The problem was what to do about the UN peacekeepers. Demanding a total withdrawal of the peacekeepers would leave a military vacuum in Gaza and Sharm al-Shaykh. Nasser would then face enormous political pressure to reoccupy those areas with his own forces; and, having entered Sharm al-Shaykh, he would face even greater pressure to reinstate the blockade on Israeli shipping through the Strait of Tiran. But if he blocked the Strait, the Israelis would almost certainly go to war against Egypt, since they had made it clear that free passage through the Strait was a vital interest for which they were willing to fight.

So Nasser tried to follow a middle course. He asked the United Nations to remove their peacekeeping force from Egypt's land border with Israel, so that Egypt's own forces could take up positions along the frontier, but to keep the force in place in Gaza and Sharm al-Shaykh. This would allow Nasser to make a deterrent gesture against the Israelis without raising the issue of Israeli shipping through the Strait of Tiran. Unfortunately for Nasser, U Thant, the secretary general of the UN, was unwilling to conduct a partial withdrawal of the peacekeeping forces. Nasser had to choose between a total withdrawal and none at all. Having gone this far, Nasser felt he couldn't back down, so he said, "OK, in that case, remove the whole force." The UN peacekeepers were withdrawn from all of the Sinai Peninsula and the Gaza Strip.

For the next three days, as stern calls for Egyptian action emanated from Arab capitals, Nasser hesitated. Although his troops did take up positions along the land border with Israel, they initially steered clear of Sharm al-Shaykh. On May 21, however, Nasser finally ordered his army to occupy Sharm al-Shaykh. The following evening, in a defiant speech at a Sinai air base, Nasser announced the closure of the Strait of Tiran to all Israeli shipping, and to vessels of any nationality carrying strategic materials to Israel. The announcement created enormous excitement throughout the Arab world, reminiscent of the euphoria that had greeted Nasser's nationalization of the Suez Canal Company back in 1956.

Nasser's actions in this crisis have long puzzled historians. If he knew that blockading the Strait would bring an inevitable Israeli attack, and if he knew that his army was not ready to go to war, why did he go ahead and blockade the Strait? As I see it, there are two main answers to this question. In the first place, Nasser concluded that the political price of not blockading the Strait would be exorbitant. Had he failed to take advantage of this opportunity to block the Strait, he would have been ridiculed throughout the Arab world, and he might well have lost his position as the standard bearer of Arab nationalism. There are even some indications that Nasser feared being overthrown by the Egyptian military if he failed to take a tough stand against Israel.

In the second place, Nasser evidently assumed that an Israeli attack would not be as devastating as it turned out to be. While Nasser realized that his armed forces could not defeat Israel outright, he apparently believed they could hold their own in a defensive situation. With sufficient air cover, the Egyptian army could temporarily blunt an Israeli advance across the Sinai desert, until the United Nations had a chance to intervene in the crisis, brand Israel the aggressor, and force it to withdraw to its prewar positions. In other words, Nasser expected the war to unfold in much the same way that the Suez War had unfolded in 1956.

At worst, Egypt's military would get its nose bloodied, and the status quo would be restored, and Nasser would survive to fight another day. At best, Nasser would emerge from the crisis with enhanced regional prestige, as he had done a decade earlier. From Nasser's standpoint, either of these scenarios was preferable to the humiliation that would result from taking no action against Israel. Evidently, Nasser had no idea just how unprepared for war his army actually was.

Once Nasser had announced his blockade of the Strait, it became extremely likely that Israel would go to war against Egypt. Still, the Israelis wanted to know exactly where the Americans stood on the issue, so Abba Eban, Israel's foreign minister, flew to Washington to talk to Johnson and other U.S. officials. In a tense meeting in the White House, Johnson told Eban that if Israel fired the first shot, and then got into trouble in the ensuing war, it would be impossible for the United States to bail Israel out. "Israel will not be alone," Johnson said, "unless it decides to go alone." Johnson also promised that, if Israel refrained from going to war, he would try to get several other nations to join with the United States in publicly challenging Nasser's blockade—that is, by having an international flotilla sail through the Strait of Tiran and dare Nasser to fire on them. By this means, the Strait would be opened for Israel's use as well.

The Israelis agreed to hold their fire for the time being and give Johnson a chance to organize the flotilla. The Egyptians, meanwhile, approached the Soviet government to see what kind of support they could get from their superpower patron. Moscow's advice was similar to Washington's: if Egypt started the war, the Soviets would not be able to bail it out. Nasser agreed not to fire the first shot.

Although Nasser's posture was now defensive, his public rhetoric, and that of other Arab leaders, was extremely bellicose. Indeed, in the days leading up to the Six-Day War, the Arab countries appeared to fall victim to war fever. Although none of the Arab countries was ready for war, Nasser and other Arab leaders whipped up the crowds with strident and at times even bloodthirsty rhetoric, creating the impression that, if war broke out, the Arab states would seek to wipe Israel off of the map. Nasser pledged that Egypt would not fire the first shot, but if war came the Arabs would "restore the situation to what it was in 1948," presumably a reference to the elimination of Israel. Radio Damascus was even less restrained, predicting that if the United States intervened to protect Israel from the Arabs, the righteous Arab masses would "hang the last imperialist soldier with the entrails of the last Zionist."

In the excitement over war, all of the rivalries that had recently fractured the Arab world were momentarily forgotten, as everyone focused on the coming battle with Israel. Arab leaders who had recently castigated Nasser, including King Hussein, now flocked to his side. King Hussein signed a mutual defense pact with Nasser, placing Jordan's army under Egypt's command. It was as if the Arab people as a whole, leaders and citizens alike, had seized on the crisis as a means of overcoming their differences and reasserting a common Arab mission and destiny.

King Hussein's decision to team up with Nasser, combined with the violent rhetoric emanating from Arab capitals, terrified the Israeli public, convincing them that the Jews once again faced possible extermination. Israeli leaders were more confident of Israel's military strength vis-à-vis the Arab states, but they could not ignore public opinion, and there was enormous pressure on the government to do something about the threat, and to do something immediately. Moreover, by this time Israel had conducted a full military mobilization, which disrupted all industrial activity in the country; it was doubtful that the Israeli economy could endure such a state of affairs for more than a few weeks.

Meanwhile, Washington's efforts to organize an international flotilla to challenge Nasser's blockade were getting nowhere; few countries were willing to allow their navies to take part in an effort to force the Strait of Tiran. An alternative approach would be for the U.S. Navy to challenge the Egyptian blockade unilaterally, but Johnson knew that Congress would be unwilling to authorize such an operation, especially at a time when the war in Vietnam was losing popularity at home. As these alternative solutions receded from view, the Israelis went back to the Americans and said, in essence, "We know you can't fight alongside us if we fire the first shot, but can you at least promise that you won't actively oppose us the way Eisenhower did back in 1956?" This time, the Israelis got a more encouraging response, albeit through an unorthodox channel.

Here's how it happened: In late May and early June, the Israeli ambassador in Washington met frequently with Supreme Court justice Abe Fortas, a close friend and advisor of President Johnson. In these meetings Fortas's message to the ambassador was basically as follows: "Mr. Ambassador, the President deeply appreciates the fact that Israel delayed its decision to go to war, which gave him a chance to try to find a peaceful alternative. As of now, that effort seems to have failed, and Israel should decide for itself what the best course of action is." This is not a quotation; it's a paraphrase of what Fortas was telling the ambassador. The Israeli ambassador interpreted this message to mean that Johnson, while still hoping to avoid a war, would not strongly object if Israel went ahead and started one, an accurate interpretation, as it turned out.

So, on June 5, 1967, Israel broke the impasse by launching a surprise attack on Egypt, destroying its air force on the ground. Deprived of air cover, confused and demoralized by conflicting orders issued by incompetent military leaders, the Egyptian army was all but defenseless against the Israeli ground assault in the Sinai. After Israel attacked Egypt, Jordan entered the war on Egypt's side. Israel quickly defeated the Jordanian army as well, taking control of East Jerusalem and the West Bank. Israel then turned its attention to Syria, from which it seized the strategic Golan Heights. By the time the war ended on June 11, 1967, Israel had tripled the amount of territory under its control, taking the Sinai Peninsula and Gaza Strip from Egypt, the Golan Heights from Syria, and the West Bank from Jordan.

Over a million Palestinian inhabitants of the West Bank and Gaza came under Israeli military occupation, while tens of thousands more were forced into exile in neighboring Arab countries, swelling the ranks of a previous generation of Palestinian refugees. The destruction of Egypt's air force was so devastating and thorough, that it was difficult for Nasser to admit that Israel had accomplished it on its own. Early in the war, Nasser publicly charged that the U.S. Air Force had taken part in the attack, and Egypt broke diplomatic relations with the United States on that account. The charge was false, but Nasser stuck to this story for several months thereafter, and U.S.-Egyptian relations would not be formally restored until 1974.

Nasser greatly overstated Washington's support for Israel, but President Johnson's reaction to Israel's behavior in 1967 was markedly different from that of Eisenhower in 1956. Whereas Eisenhower had forced Israel to withdraw from Egypt, Johnson merely called for, and achieved, a "cease-fire in place," which meant that the fighting should stop and each country's forces should remain where they were. This allowed Israel to remain indefinitely in possession of the Arab territories it had seized.

In the fall of 1967, the UN Security Council passed Resolution 242, which would become the basis for virtually all subsequent attempts to resolve the Arab-Israeli conflict. Resolution 242, which was accepted by Egypt, Jordan, and Israel, essentially called for a "land for peace" deal, whereby the Arab states recognized Israel's right to exist in security, and Israel withdrew from territories seized in the Six-Day War. But Resolution 242 was an extremely ambiguous document. It did not say explicitly which should come first: the Arab states' recognition of Israel, or Israel's withdrawal from Arab territory. The Israelis insisted that they did not have give up any of the occupied territories until the Arab states first recognized Israel, while the Arabs demanded an unconditional Israeli withdrawal before there could be any talk of recognition.

Moreover, at the insistence of Israel and the United States, the clause dealing with Israeli withdrawal did not contain the definite article; Israel was to withdraw not from "the territories" but simply from "territories occupied in the recent conflict." The Israelis would claim that 242 entitled them to keep substantial portions of the newly acquired territories. On the other hand, the preamble to the resolution referred to "the inadmissibility of the acquisition of territory by war," which implied that Israel was not entitled to keep any of the land it had acquired. These conflicting interpretations of Resolution 242 would plague all subsequent attempts to resolve the Arab-Israeli conflict.

The Six-Day War itself was a devastating event for the Arab world, and especially for Nasserist pan-Arabism, which could not avoid responsibility for the catastrophe. For all of the previous Arab defeats to Israel, Nasserists and Arab nationalists had provided self-serving excuses. The defeat of 1948 was the fault not of the Arab people themselves, but of corrupt Arab monarchs who had betrayed the Arab cause. The military defeat of 1956 had occurred, not because Egypt was weaker than Israel, but because Britain and

France had entered the war on Israel's side. But 1967 could not be explained away so easily.

Of the three Arab states Israel had beaten so handily—Egypt, Syria, and Jordan—only Jordan was a conservative monarchy; the other two countries were governed by fiery Arab nationalists. It was a blow from which Arab nationalism would never fully recover. Nasser, too, was devastated by the defeat; he would spend the remaining three years of his life desperately trying to regain the territory and honor he had lost.

1967 also came as a terrible shock to Palestinians. Since the early decades of the twentieth century, and especially after 1948, Palestinians had developed a distinct national identity. Still, when it came to confronting Israel, Palestinians had tended to downplay their separate identity in favor of Arab solidarity. The Arab states themselves had encouraged this tendency, telling the Palestinians that the only way for Palestine to be liberated was for the Arab states to band together and vanquish the Jewish state. After 1967, Palestinians became increasingly convinced that collective Arab action was hopeless, and that the only way for them to regain Palestine was to take matters into their own hands and to seek liberation for themselves.

In the late 1960s, the Palestine Liberation Organization, or PLO, which had been created in 1964 to serve mainly as an instrument of Egyptian policy, freed itself from Egyptian control and became an independent political and military force, under the leadership of Yasser Arafat. Operating mainly out of Palestinian refugee camps in Jordan and Lebanon, the PLO was a broad coalition of groups, each with a different strategy for achieving liberation. Some groups wanted to engage in armed struggle against Israel in the newly occupied territories. Others wanted to convince the international community to impose a just settlement of the Arab-Israeli conflict. Still others, on the far left, believed that the only way to liberate Palestine would be to overthrow the conservative Arab regimes and unite the Arab world behind a revolutionary agenda.

Meanwhile, another previously marginalized segment of Arab political life was gaining ground. These were the Islamists, by which I mean individuals and groups committed to organizing political life according to Islamic principles. Of course, Islamists had been active prior to 1967, but they had tended be eclipsed by secular Arab nationalists. By the early 1970s, however, secular nationalism was coming under increasing attack in the Arab world, and not just because of the 1967 debacle, although that was a big part of it.

Nasser and other Arab nationalists had promised a new era in which ordinary Arab citizens would shape their own destiny, and in which the Arab world's resources would be redistributed among the people among vaguely socialist lines. Critics pointed out, however, that while living standards had improved in Egypt and in other countries following similar economic policies, that improvement had been far less dramatic than expected. They also charged that the Arab nationalist regimes, instead of ushering in a new era of democracy and citizen participation, had proved to be just as dictatorial and corrupt as the conservative monarchies they critiqued.

In short, there was a growing feeling in the Arab world, and in other Islamic countries as well, that secular nationalism had failed to deliver the goods, and that some alternative form of political organization had to be found. Many Arabs became convinced that their governments had gotten into trouble because they had abandoned their Islamic heritage and had turned instead to ideologies imported from the West, like liberalism, socialism, materialism, and secularism. Such ideologies, the argument went, had corroded Arab society from within, making it more vulnerable to Western domination.

As pan-Arabism declined, Palestinian nationalists and Islamic activists came into their own. In the years to come, it was these groups would pose the most vigorous challenge to American and Israeli power in the region. Seldom again, after 1967, would there be much reason to expect that the Arab states would band together to oppose a common foe. Arab resistance to American or Israeli schemes would arise on occasion, but it would usually be mounted by non-state actors or by states acting alone.

The Six-Day War also completed the reorientation of U.S. Middle East policy that Lyndon Johnson had begun shortly after taking office in late 1963. From the start, Johnson had moved away from the careful balancing act that John F. Kennedy had performed. Whereas Kennedy had both supported the Shah and pressured him to make internal reforms, Johnson had dropped the reform agenda and hailed the Shah as a staunch ally of the West. Whereas Kennedy had tried to improve relations with Arabs and Israelis simultaneously, Johnson had increasingly embraced the Israelis. Whereas Kennedy had tried to occupy a middle ground between supporting Arab radicals and supporting Arab conservatives, Johnson had openly sided with the conservatives.

Now, with Arab nationalists thoroughly defeated and embittered against the West, the last vestiges of Kennedy's balancing act were cast aside. It was as if American officials said to themselves: "What's the point of even trying to accommodate indigenous nationalists in the Middle East? In the first place, we'll never get their support, and in the second place we don't need their support. Let's stick with those governments that already support us, and are able to maintain stability in the region in a manner that suits our interests." So, by the time Johnson left office in early 1969, three countries were emerging as Washington's primary allies in the Middle East: Iran, Israel, and Saudi Arabia. In the administration of Johnson's successor, Richard M. Nixon, U.S. relations with each of these countries would become much closer and more extensive, with far-reaching consequences for the subsequent political history of the region.

Lecture Twelve
The Nixon Doctrine and the Middle East

Scope:

In this lecture, we discuss the Nixon Doctrine of 1969 and its specific applications to the Middle East. A general response to the relative decline in American power occurring in the 1960s, the Nixon Doctrine called for greater reliance on regional "cops on the beat"—powerful pro-Western governments that could protect American interests in various parts of the world, thus obviating the need for direct U.S. military intervention. Two Middle Eastern nations, Iran and, to a lesser extent, Saudi Arabia, quickly came to be seen as Washington's "cops on the beat." Although Nixon initially intended to keep the Arab-Israeli conflict on a separate policy track, by the early 1970s, Israel, too, had become an American ally within the meaning of the Nixon Doctrine.

Outline

I. During Richard Nixon's first term, the United States forged quasi-alliances with Iran, Saudi Arabia, and Israel. These relationships were buttressed by a new policy formulation known as the *Nixon Doctrine.*

    A. On taking office in early 1969, Nixon was determined to control foreign policy from the White House.

    B. Nixon appointed Henry Kissinger as national security advisor. Ostensibly, Kissinger's role was to receive input from all the executive departments concerned with foreign policy—State, Defense, the CIA, and so on—then make recommendations to the president.

    C. In reality, Nixon and Kissinger largely ignored the executive departments, conducting foreign policy in secret. Nixon appointed William P. Rogers as secretary of state, a lawyer with little knowledge of foreign relations who would be unlikely to interfere in Nixon's and Kissinger's deliberations.

II. Nixon also realized, on taking office, that a new era had begun in which America's power relative to that of other nations had declined.

  A. Western Europe and Japan had recovered from the devastation of World War II and were emerging as powerful economic rivals of the United States.

  B. Communist China had acquired nuclear weapons.

  C. The Soviet Union had achieved rough nuclear parity with the United States.

  D. The domestic American reaction to the Vietnam War made it difficult for the U.S. government to contemplate future military interventions.

III. Nixon realized that the United States must somehow adjust to these new realities.

  A. One way he tried to do this was by placing limits on the sorts of international commitments the United States would assume. In a 1969 speech, Nixon declared that America's allies would have to play a larger role in their own defense. This proclamation became known as the Nixon Doctrine.

   1. Initially, the doctrine was meant to apply mainly to Southeast Asia, an attempt to find some grand strategic framework in which to couch Nixon's new policy on Vietnam.

   2. Over the next few years, however, the Nixon Doctrine began taking on a broader meaning, indicating a genuine pattern for Nixon's approach to world politics.

  B. Under the Nixon Doctrine, the United States became increasingly reliant on powerful pro-Western governments willing and able to protect American interests in various parts of the world.

IV. The principal Middle Eastern power to be cultivated under the Nixon Doctrine was Iran. In 1968, Britain had announced that it would withdraw its military forces from the Persian Gulf in three years' time.

  A. The new Nixon administration was determined to prevent the Soviet Union from filling the vacuum left by Britain.

B. At the same time, the Shah of Iran was growing more assertive in the Persian Gulf, seeking to turn Iran into a regional hegemony.

C. The Shah's ambitions dovetailed with Nixon's foreign policy. By supporting Iran's claims to regional domination, Nixon could ensure that the Persian Gulf remained in pro-Western hands, without the necessity of direct U.S. involvement.

    1. Nixon vastly increased the amount and quality of military aid to Iran, telling the Shah that he could purchase from the United States any type of military equipment except for nuclear weapons.

    2. In thus embracing Iran, Nixon turned a blind eye to the Shah's brutal human rights record.

V. Another Middle Eastern country to gain importance under the Nixon Doctrine, albeit to a lesser extent than Iran, was Saudi Arabia.

A. In some formulations of Middle East policy, Iran and Saudi Arabia were described as the twin pillars on which Washington depended to ensure the status quo, though Iran was always the bigger pillar of the two.

B. By the late 1960s, the emergence of a seller's market for oil permitted Saudi Arabia to raise the price of oil substantially.

    1. One of the main beneficiaries of this development was the Organization of Petroleum Exporting Countries, or OPEC, an oil cartel consisting of the major oil-rich Middle Eastern states, along with some non-Middle Eastern states, such as Indonesia and Venezuela.

    2. With increased oil revenues, the Saudi government was able, in the 1970s, to purchase billions of dollars worth of arms from American contractors, especially in the area of air defense.

    3. This arrangement, known as the "recycling of petrodollars," was highly favored by Washington, Riyadh, and American oil companies.

VI. Initially, Nixon intended to keep the Arab-Israeli conflict on a separate policy track from the Nixon Doctrine.

    A. For the first two years of his presidency, Nixon tried to keep his distance from the Arab-Israeli conflict, on the assumption that the prospects for success in that area were slight, while the domestic political dangers were great.

        1. Nixon initially designated the Arab-Israeli conflict to be one of the few policy areas that his secretary of state, William Rogers, would be allowed to handle.

        2. Policy areas of greater interest to Nixon, including Vietnam and Sino-American relations, were to be managed from the White House by Nixon and his national security advisor, Henry Kissinger.

    B. Nixon's elevation to the presidency coincided with an upswing in Arab-Israeli hostilities. Major challenges came from Egypt to the west and, to the east, from a new phenomenon in world affairs—an independent Palestinian movement.

        1. In early 1969, just as Nixon was taking office, Nasser greatly stepped up Egypt's sporadic artillery attacks and commando raids against Israeli positions in the Sinai, on the eastern side of the Suez Canal.

        2. Israel's initial reaction was to conduct massive air raids against Egyptian artillery positions, surface-to-air missiles, antiaircraft guns, and radar stations. By the end of the year, Egypt's entire air-defense system was in ruins.

VII. The U.S. State Department was alarmed by the escalating violence, and Secretary of State Rogers made the most of this opportunity.

    A. In December 1969, Rogers unveiled a major Arab-Israeli peace initiative that became known as the *Rogers Plan*. It called for an Israeli withdrawal from virtually all of the territories occupied in 1967 in exchange for peace and recognition from the Arab states.

        1. Israel immediately rejected the plan because it violated the principle of direct bilateral negotiations between Israel and the Arab states.

2. Egypt did not reject the Rogers Plan outright but declined to endorse it, either, because the plan demanded specific concessions from Egypt that Nasser deemed unacceptable.

3. Kissinger quietly undermined the Rogers Plan, viewing the plan as giving far too much to the Arabs.

B. The failure of the Rogers Plan, along with a subsequent increase in Arab-Israeli tensions, eroded Nixon's confidence in Rogers's stewardship of Middle East diplomacy.

VIII. In January 1970, the War of Attrition sharply intensified. Though Egypt and Israel agreed to a cease-fire in August 1970, a month later, a major crisis occurred that would further weaken Rogers's position and have a far-reaching impact on U.S.-Israeli relations.

A. A radical faction of the Palestine Liberation Organization (PLO) hijacked several commercial airplanes and forced them to land in Jordan.

B. Seeing this as a challenge to his authority, Jordan's King Hussein moved to crush the PLO, which had established a state-within-a-state in Jordan.

C. A column of Syrian tanks crossed into northern Jordan, apparently in support of the PLO. Nixon and Kissinger believed that Moscow was behind the Syrian intervention.

1. Hussein appealed to the United States for help but was willing, if necessary, to be bailed out by Israeli intervention.

2. Both logistically and politically, it would have been extremely difficult for the United States to intervene militarily in the Jordan crisis.

3. Israel, however, was willing to intervene on Jordan's behalf. In a menacing gesture, a squadron of Israeli jets flew to northern Jordan and swooped low over the advancing Syrian tanks.

4. The Syrian tanks withdrew, permitting Hussein to defeat and, eventually, expel the PLO. The defeat of the PLO came to be known by Palestinians as *Black September*, a name later taken by a new Palestinian paramilitary group that sought to avenge this defeat and call attention to the

Palestinian's plight through a series of spectacular terrorist attacks.

D. The Black September crisis had a profound effect on U.S. policymaking toward the Middle East. Nixon was extremely pleased with Israel's behavior in the Jordan crisis and gained a new appreciation for Israel's potential as a strategic ally of the United States.

1. He saw to it that Israel received increased military and economic aid.

2. He allowed Kissinger, who favored a more pro-Israeli position, to wrest control of Middle East policy away from Rogers.

3. Nixon and Kissinger took a more permissive attitude toward Israel's occupation of Arab lands seized in the 1967 war.

E. Thus, by the early 1970s, Israel, too, had become an American ally under the terms of the Nixon Doctrine.

Suggested Reading:

Bill, James A. *The Eagle and the Lion: The Tragedy of American-Iranian Relations*. New Haven: Yale University Press, 1988.

Christison, Kathleen. *Perceptions of Palestine: Their Influence on U.S.-Middle East Policy*. Berkeley: University of California Press, 1999 (2000).

Parker, Richard B. *The Politics of Miscalculation in the Middle East*. Bloomington: Indiana University Press, 1993.

Questions to Consider:

1. To what transformations in the international position of the United States was Nixon attempting to respond when he issued the Nixon Doctrine in 1969?

2. What circumstances caused Nixon eventually to embrace Israel as a strategic partner under the terms of his doctrine?

Lecture Twelve—Transcript
The Nixon Doctrine and the Middle East

We left off last time with the end of the Lyndon Johnson administration and with the observation that, over the course of his five years in office, Johnson dispensed with the balanced approach attempted by John F. Kennedy and instead became much more closely allied with the governments of Israel, Iran, and Saudi Arabia. In this lecture, as we look at the first term of Johnson's successor, Richard M. Nixon, we'll see how these three alliances became even more firmly established, buttressed as they were, by a new foreign policy formulation known as the *Nixon Doctrine*.

Upon taking office in early 1969, Nixon was determined to control foreign policy from the White House. He ensured his control over U.S. foreign policy by appointing a highly secretive Harvard professor named Henry Kissinger as his national security advisor. Kissinger was a German Jew who, as a boy in the 1930s, had fled with his family to the United States to escape Nazi persecution. He had achieved prominence in the 1950s and 1960s as a political scientist and foreign policy analyst, occasionally serving as a consultant to the U.S. government. Theoretically, Kissinger's function as Nixon's national security advisor was to receive input from all the executive departments concerned with foreign policy—State, Defense, the CIA, etc.—and then make recommendations to the president.

What actually happened was that Nixon and Kissinger largely ignored the executive departments and conducted foreign policy in secret, forcing the bureaucracy to fall in line. Indeed, the man Nixon appointed as his secretary of state, a lawyer and old friend named William P. Rogers, was selected largely because he knew little about foreign relations and was thus unlikely to interfere with Nixon's and Kissinger's deliberations. From the start, Nixon and Kissinger were powerfully drawn to each other. As one journalist said of the Nixon-Kissinger relationship, "Nixon had a consuming need for flattery and Kissinger a consuming need to provide it."

More positively, both men thought in broad conceptual terms. They realized that a new era in world politics had begun, one in which America's power relative to other nations had declined. Western Europe and Japan had fully recovered from the devastation of World

War II and were now emerging as powerful economic rivals of the United States. Communist China had developed nuclear weapons, and the Soviet Union had achieved rough nuclear parity with the United States. America's relative decline as a world power had been both symbolized and hastened by its inability to achieve victory in Vietnam. Nixon and Kissinger realized that the United States must somehow adjust to these new realities. One way they tried to do this was by seeking a new modus vivendi with the communist superpowers.

During Nixon's first term, the United States reached a major arms control agreement with the Soviet Union and, even more strikingly, began the process of normalizing relations with the People's Republic of China. Another way the Nixon administration tried to adjust to changed circumstances was by placing limits on the sorts of international commitments the United States would assume. This latter course was spelled out in a speech Nixon delivered on the island of Guam in 1969. In that speech, Nixon said that while America remained committed to helping with the defense of its allies, the United States "cannot—and will not—conceive all the plans, design all the programs, execute all the decisions and undertake all the defense of the free nations." Other nations would have to play a much larger role in their own defense. This proclamation became known as the Nixon Doctrine.

Initially, the Nixon Doctrine was meant to apply mainly to Southeast Asia. It was an attempt to find some grand strategic framework in which to couch Nixon's new policy on Vietnam, which was to start withdrawing American troops from South Vietnam and to get the South Vietnamese government itself to take more responsibility for waging the war. Over the next few years, the Nixon Doctrine began taking on a broader meaning and to indicate a genuine pattern for Nixon's approach to world politics. During his first term, Nixon not only scaled down the American troop commitment in South Vietnam, though he escalated the war in other ways, but significantly reduced U.S. forces stationed in South Korea, Thailand, and Japan.

The Nixon Doctrine also came to mean that that the United States would become increasingly reliant on regional proxies, powerful pro-Western governments that would protect American interests in various parts of the world. With these "cops on the beat," as the expression went, the United States would be spared the burden of having to intervene with its own forces. This brings us now to U.S. policy in the Middle East, and particularly U.S. policy in the Persian Gulf area.

In 1968, Britain had announced that it would withdraw its military forces from the Persian Gulf in three years' time, giving rise to speculation over who would fill the vacuum created by Britain's departure. The new Nixon administration was determined to prevent the Soviet Union from encroaching on that area. Moscow was already cultivating Iraq, one of the oil-rich states of the gulf, as a client state, and the Americans were concerned about the further extension of Soviet influence. At the same time, the Shah of Iran was growing more assertive. As the date for Britain's departure approached, Iran militarily occupied three small islands, previously controlled by the British, located near the Strait of Hormuz, through which the Persian Gulf feeds into the Indian Ocean. The Shah also revived an old dispute with Iraq over Shatt al-Arab, a tidal river lying on the border between Iraq and Iran. In these ways, the Shah was making a clear bid for Iran to succeed Britain as the next regional hegemon.

The Shah's ambitions jibed well with Nixon's foreign policy. By supporting Iran's claims to regional domination, Nixon could ensure that the Persian Gulf remained in pro-Western hands, without the necessity of direct U.S. involvement. Nixon intensified the policy of generous support for the Shah that Lyndon Johnson had begun, vastly increasing the amount and quality of military aid to Iran. The high point of Nixon's pro-Shah policy came in 1972, when Nixon paid a visit to Iran and, in essence, told the Shah that he could purchase from the United States any type of military equipment except for nuclear weapons. In cozying up to the Shah in this manner, however, the Nixon administration turned a blind eye to the Shah's growing unpopularity at home.

The Shah liked to see himself as a progressive modernizer, bringing the enlightened values of the West to his backward people. It would be more accurate to say that he was an authoritarian modernizer, imposing on his country the physical trappings of modernity—high-rise buildings, massive public works projects, a high-tech military establishment, casinos and nightclubs—without offering any of the civic or political freedoms associated with Western liberalism. This was all deeply resented by the Iranian people, many of whom lived in poverty, gaining little from the country's enormous oil wealth, which instead lined the pockets of foreign corporations, corrupt government officials, and a tiny handful of wealthy Iranians.

Worse still, the Shah had an atrocious human rights record. His internal security police, SAVAK, routinely jailed, tortured, and executed political dissidents, practices toward which the Nixon administration turned a blind eye. In the late 1970s, of course, these circumstances would come back to haunt the United States.

Another Middle Eastern country to take on greater importance under the Nixon Doctrine, albeit to a lesser extent than Iran, was Saudi Arabia. I mentioned in a previous lecture that toward the end of the Johnson administration, the United States had given up on trying to befriend both conservative and radical Arab states and had moved closer to Saudi Arabia. This evolution continued under Nixon, but was now hastened by the requirements of the Nixon Doctrine. Indeed, in some formulations of Middle East policy, Iran and Saudi Arabia were described as the twin pillars on which Washington depended to ensure the status quo, though Iran was always the bigger pillar of the two. Transformations in the international oil market made it possible for Saudi Arabia to take on this new role.

In the first couple decades of the postwar period, the world had experienced an oil glut, allowing for a buyer's market. That is to say, the oil companies could decide for themselves what the price of oil would be, and the oil producing states had little say in the matter. By the late 1960s, global demand for oil began to outstrip available supply, creating a seller's market. Now it was the oil producing states that could dictate the price of oil. One of the main beneficiaries of this development was the Organization of Petroleum Exporting Countries, or OPEC, an oil cartel consisting of the major oil-rich Middle Eastern states, along with some non-Middle Eastern states like Indonesia and Venezuela.

OPEC had been formed in 1960, but it wasn't until the early 1970s, following the sharp rise in the global demand for oil, that the cartel became a major international player. In a historic agreement in 1971, the major oil companies of the West conceded that OPEC could set the price of oil, which, not surprisingly, began to increase substantially. The rise in oil prices provided Saudi Arabia, a major member of OPEC, with a good deal of disposable income, which it could now use to beef up its military.

In the 1970s, the Saudi government bought billions of dollars worth of arms from American contractors, especially in the area of air defense. This process became known as the "recycling of petrodollars," since the huge amounts of money that Saudi Arabia extracted from American oil companies were being funneled back into the U.S. economy by means of arms purchases. This cozy arrangement was, needless to say, much beloved by the American government and corporate sector alike. But like the close relationship with the Shah, Washington's courtship of the House of Saud would, years later, come back to haunt the United States.

Let's now take a look at U.S. policy toward the Arab-Israeli conflict during Nixon's first term. This policy area, too, eventually came to be defined by the Nixon Doctrine, with Israel serving as one of the regional powers operating under U.S. auspices. But this was not how Nixon initially intended it. Indeed, for the first two years of his presidency, Nixon didn't want to have much to do with the Arab-Israeli conflict, since he assumed—realistically—that the prospects for success in that area were slight, while the domestic political dangers were high. So Nixon initially designated the Arab-Israeli conflict to be one of the few policy areas that his secretary of state, William Rogers, would be allowed to handle. By 1971 this area, too, had been wrested from Rogers's jurisdiction and brought under the nearly exclusive control of Nixon and Kissinger.

Nixon's elevation to the presidency coincided with an upswing in Arab-Israeli hostilities. In the Six-Day War of 1967, as we saw, Israel had overwhelmingly defeated the Arab states, taking the Sinai Peninsula and Gaza Strip from Egypt, the Golan Heights from Syria, and the West Bank from Jordan. Shortly after the war ended, violence resumed at a lower level, as some Arab actors revived the struggle against Israel and began trying to dislodge it from the Arab lands it had seized. The major challenges came from Egypt to the west and, to the east, from a new phenomenon in world affairs, an independent Palestinian movement. Let's look at the Egyptian challenge first.

Since the conclusion of the 1967 war, Egypt had conducted sporadic artillery attacks and commando raids against Israeli positions in the Sinai, on the eastern side of the Suez Canal. In early 1969, just as Nixon was taking office, Nasser greatly stepped up these activities, turning them into a major, coordinated offensive along the whole length of the canal that became known as the War of Attrition. By this time, although Egypt had substantially rebuilt its military with the help of the Soviet Union, it still lacked the capability to liberate the entire Sinai Peninsula by force. Nasser was painfully aware of this fact, but he was also determined to prevent the new status quo from being solidified. He hoped that a resumption of hostilities would convince the great powers that the status quo was untenable, causing them to force Israel to withdraw from all of the Arab territories it had occupied in 1967, in accordance with Egypt's interpretation of Resolution 242, (i.e. that Israel must withdraw first, and then there could be talk about mutual recognition.)

Israel's initial reaction to the War of Attrition was to conduct massive air raids against Egyptian artillery positions, surface-to-air missiles, anti-aircraft guns, and radar stations. Indeed, by the end of the year, Egypt's entire air defense system was in ruins. The U.S. State Department was alarmed by the escalating violence, and in December 1969, William Rogers, the secretary of state, unveiled a major Arab-Israeli peace initiative. The *Rogers Plan*, as it was dubbed, called for an Israeli withdrawal from virtually all of the territories occupied in 1967 in exchange for peace and recognition from the Arab states. Israel immediately rejected the plan as violating the principle of direct, bilateral negotiations between Israel and the Arab states. Egypt did not reject the Rogers Plan outright, but declined to endorse it either, since the plan demanded specific concessions from Egypt, such as the demilitarization of parts of the Sinai Peninsula, that Nasser deemed unacceptable. It seemed as if the Rogers Plan had fallen flat.

One person who had quietly undermined the Rogers Plan was Nixon's national security advisor, Henry Kissinger, who saw the plan as giving too much to the Arabs. Kissinger believed that, as long as states like Egypt and Syria maintained close ties to the Soviet Union, the United States should refrain from pressuring Israel to give up the occupied territories. Only when the Arabs had severed their ties to Moscow should Washington make any effort to give them satisfaction.

Shortly after the Rogers Plan was unveiled, Kissinger convinced Nixon that the plan was ill-advised. Nixon was unwilling to repudiate the plan outright, especially in the immediate aftermath of its unveiling, but he did authorize Kissinger to quietly assure the

Israelis that it would never be implemented. Kissinger not only passed on this assurance but encouraged Israel to criticize the Rogers Plan. When Golda Meir, Israel's prime minister, came to the United States for a speaking tour, Kissinger used Leonard Garment, Nixon's liaison to the American Jewish community, as special conduit for off-the-record advice to Meir. "Tell her wherever she goes," Kissinger instructed Garment, "we want her to slam the hell out of Rogers and his plan." Meir was only too happy to oblige.

In January 1970, the War of Attrition sharply intensified. The Israeli air force began conducting what it called "deep penetration" bombing raids over Egyptian territory, which had been rendered extremely vulnerable by the destruction of the Egyptian air defense system. Israeli planes struck military and industrial targets around Cairo and in the Nile Delta. Nasser was shocked by the severity of the Israeli raids, and he secretly flew to Moscow, where he convinced a reluctant Soviet government to supply Egypt immediately with new surface-to-air missiles, known as SAM-3s. Because Egyptians lacked the requisite training in using the SAM-3s, the missiles were operated by Soviet technicians. The SAM-3s were so effective at shooting down Israeli planes that Israel was forced to abandon the deep-penetration raids.

Egyptian construction crews then began moving the missile sites closer to the Suez Canal; the idea was to erect a missile shield that covered the opposite bank of the canal, permitting the Egyptian army to cross it eventually. The Israeli air force ferociously attacked the sites, killing as many as 2,000 Egyptian construction workers. But the construction crews pressed on, and by the summer of 1970, the SAM-3s were about 25 miles west of the canal. Alarmed at this development, the U.S. State Department launched another, more modest initiative, sometimes referred to as the second Rogers Plan. It called on Egypt and Israel to cease all military hostilities for three months' time, and to refrain from changing the military status quo along the Suez Canal. Egypt and Israel both accepted the cease-fire.

Israel and the United States thought that the agreement would freeze Egypt's missile construction, but the Egyptians found a loophole in the agreement that allowed them to install several additional missile sites on the west side of the canal. In a couple other cases, Egypt violated the actual letter of the agreement. By these means, Egypt completed the construction of a vast network of SAM-3 missiles on the western bank of the Suez Canal, with the ability to shoot down Israeli aircraft on the opposite bank. At a huge cost—10,000 Egyptian civilians and soldiers may have died in the War of Attrition—Egypt had laid the basis for a hostile crossing of the canal. This fact would become extremely important during the Yom Kippur War of 1973.

A month after the Egyptian-Israeli cease-fire in September 1970, a fresh crisis occurred that was to have a far-reaching impact on U.S.-Israeli relations. As we saw in the previous lecture, by the late 1960s the Palestine Liberation Organization, under the leadership of Yasser Arafat, had created a state-within-a-state in Jordan, recruiting fighters in the refugee camps and building up a considerable arsenal. Officially, these fighting forces were intended for liberating Palestine, but increasingly the PLO began getting into skirmishes with the Jordanian government. Some of the more left-wing Palestinian groups were convinced that the only way to make progress on the Palestine issue was to overthrow King Hussein, on the grounds that he was a puppet of the United States who would never permit a full-scale offensive against Israel. Arafat himself was not particularly interested in overthrowing the Jordanian government, but his ability to control these left-wing groups was limited.

In September 1970, one of these radical groups, the Popular Front for the Liberation of Palestine, or PFLP, hijacked four commercial airplanes. One of the planes was flown to Cairo, where the hijackers released the passengers and crew and then blew up the plane. The other three planes ended up on a desert runway in Jordan. Once again, the hijackers evacuated the planes and blew them up. The PFLP released most of these passengers immediately but held a small number of them as hostages. The demolition of the planes was broadcast on live television; it was one of the first spectacular acts of international terrorism to unfold before a global audience in real time. Apparently, the PFLP was trying to embarrass and weaken King Hussein by exposing his inability to control events in his own country. Hussein decided that enough was enough and launched a military crackdown on the PLO as a whole.

The Jordanian army quickly gained the upper hand and was poised to crush the PLO. In desperation, PLO leaders took to the radio and appealed for assistance from other Arab countries. Syria, whose radical government strongly opposed the pro-Western Hussein, responded to the appeal by sending a column of tanks over the border into northern Jordan. Now it was Hussein's turn to be desperate. Hussein secretly contacted Washington and begged for assistance against the Syrian attack. Hussein let it be known that, while he preferred that the United States intervene directly, he would, if necessary, allow himself to be bailed out by Israel itself. It was a measure of Hussein's desperation that he was willing consider such a scenario, which would blacken his name throughout the Arab world. But for Hussein, as for most people, survival was the paramount concern, and he was prepared to accept Israel's intervention if U.S. intervention were impossible.

From the start of the crisis, Kissinger was the official who coordinated the U.S. response. Like Nixon, Kissinger was convinced that the Syrian intervention was being masterminded by Moscow, almost certainly an exaggeration of the Soviet position, and that the communist challenge could not go unanswered. But Kissinger also believed that Israeli intervention was the preferred alternative, since that would spare America the necessity of diverting U.S. forces from other theaters, especially Southeast Asia, where the United States was still heavily engaged. With Nixon's approval, Kissinger asked if the Israeli government would be willing to intervene in Jordan on Hussein's behalf, and the Israelis said yes.

A squadron of Israeli jets flew over to northern Jordan and swooped down low over the advancing Syrian tanks. The Israeli jets didn't fire on the tanks, but they made it clear that Israel meant business, and shortly thereafter the Syrian tanks turned back. It's not entirely clear whether the Syrians retreated because of the appearance of Israeli planes or because of the Jordanian counteroffensive. Whatever the reason, the elimination of the Syrian threat made it possible for Hussein to deal a crushing blow to the PLO in Jordan.

In the fall of 1970, to save his organization from utter defeat, Arafat signed a cease-fire agreement with Hussein that called for the PLO to withdraw its forces from the cities and towns of Jordan and stay inside Palestinian refugee camps. In 1971, fighting flared up again between the Jordanian government and the PLO, and Hussein succeeded in expelling the PLO from Jordan altogether. Arafat and his organization moved their headquarters to Lebanon, eventually establishing a state-within-a-state in that country. Hussein was harshly denounced in the Arab world, but his kingdom had been secured. This defeat of the PLO came to be known by Palestinians as Black September, after the month in 1970 in which the crisis began.

Black September also came to be the name of a new Palestinian paramilitary group, which over the next few years would seek to avenge this defeat, and call attention to the Palestinians' plight, through a series of spectacular terrorist attacks. The most notorious of these attacks occurred at the 1972 Olympic Games in Munich, when a group of Black September militants took eleven Israeli athletes and coaches hostage, demanding the release of scores of Palestinians held in Israeli jails. During a subsequent shoot-out with West German police, the militants killed all of the Israeli hostages. Such acts of violence did succeed in bringing the Palestine issue to the world's attention, but they also saddled the Palestinians with a reputation for violence and fanaticism that remains with them to this day.

The Black September crisis had a profound effect on U.S. policy-making toward the Middle East. The first Rogers Plan, as we saw, had failed to gain endorsement by either Israel or the Arab states. The fact that Kissinger had quietly sabotaged it was conveniently ignored. The second Rogers Plan had ended the War of Attrition, but it contained glaring loopholes that the Egyptians had exploited, so Rogers was 0 for 2 in Arab-Israeli diplomacy, the one area of policy he had been allowed to dominate. Kissinger, by contrast, had managed the U.S. response to the Jordan crisis, which was widely seen as a success. Consequently, Rogers was discredited within the Nixon administration and was soon forced to relinquish control over Arab-Israeli diplomacy as well. From 1971 on, Nixon and Kissinger would directly control U.S. policy in that area.

Nixon's and Kissinger's approach to the Arab-Israeli conflict would be far more pro-Israeli than Rogers's had been. The fact that Israel had been willing, during the Jordan crisis, to come to the aid of a pro-U.S. Arab country made a deep impression on Nixon. It suggested that Israel could actively promote American interests in the Middle East, so Nixon now moved closer to Kissinger's pro-Israeli position. Shortly after Syria withdrew its tanks from northern Jordan, Nixon instructed Kissinger to deliver a personal message to the Israeli government. The message read, "The president will never forget Israel's role in preventing the deterioration in Jordan and in blocking the attempt to overturn the regime there. He said that the United States is fortunate in having an ally like Israel in the Middle East. These events will be taken into account in all future developments."

And taken into account they were. Over the next few years there was a steep rise in U.S. aid to Israel, from about $93 million in fiscal year 1970 to $634 million in 1971, and then up to $2.6 billion in 1974. Although the first Rogers Plan, which had called on Israel to withdraw from virtually all of the territory occupied in 1967, remained official U.S. policy, Nixon and Kissinger simply behaved as if it the plan had never been issued. They de-emphasized the whole question of Israeli occupation and treated Israel as a strategic asset entitled to unwavering American support.

So Israel became, along with Iran and Saudi Arabia, a client state of the United States under the terms of the Nixon Doctrine, one of the "cops on the beat" that would discipline and thwart radical and pro-Soviet forces in the Middle East for the benefit of America's strategic and economic interests. But this new approach to the Arab-Israeli conflict would suffer a rude jolt during the Yom Kippur War of 1973, which we'll look at next time.

Timeline

1898 ....Spanish-American War takes place

1906 ....Algeciras Conference held

1914 ....World War I begins; Turkey joins World War I on the side of Germany and Austria

1915–1916 ....Turkey crushes Armenian uprising

1917 ....Britain issues Balfour Declaration

1918 ....Woodrow Wilson issues Fourteen Points; World War I ends

1919 ....Woodrow Wilson sends King-Crane Commission to Middle East

1920 ....U.S. Senate rejects American mandate over Armenia

1923 ....Treaty of Lausanne ends Allied occupation of Turkey

1924 ....Congress passes National Origins Act

1933 ....Hitler takes power in Germany

1938 ....German government launches *Kristallnacht*; American geologists discover oil in Saudi Arabia

1939 ....Britain issues White Paper on Palestine; World War II begins

1941 ....United States enters World War II; United States joins Britain and Soviet Union in occupying Iran

1942–1943 ....Allies undertake North Africa campaign

1945 ....World War II ends

1945–1946 ....Turkish straits crises occur

1946 ....Iran crisis occurs

1947	Harry S. Truman issues Truman Doctrine; UN General Assembly passes partition plan on Palestine
1948	Israel declares independence; first Arab-Israeli War begins
1949	Arab-Israeli armistices concluded
1950	U.S. Treasury Department issues Golden Gimmick
1951–1953	Iranian oil nationalization crisis occurs
1953	Central Intelligence Agency helps overthrow Mohammed Mossadeq
1954	Britain agrees to evacuate Suez Canal Zone by 1956
1955	Egypt concludes major arms purchase deal with Soviet bloc; Eisenhower administration offers to help fund Aswan Dam
1956	Eisenhower administration withdraws Aswan Dam funding offer; Gamal Abdel Nasser nationalizes Suez Canal Company; Suez War occurs
1957	Eisenhower issues Eisenhower Doctrine
1958	U.S. Marines intervene in Lebanon
1962	Yemeni civil war begins
1963	John F. Kennedy assassinated
1964	U.S. and Iranian governments conclude Status of Forces agreement, provoking demonstrations in Iran; Arab League establishes Palestine Liberation Organization (PLO)

U.S. embassy; Soviet Union invades Afghanistan

1980 ....Jimmy Carter issues Carter Doctrine; United States launches unsuccessful attempt to free hostages in Iran; Iran-Iraq War begins

1981 ....Iran frees U.S. hostages

1982 ....Israel completes withdrawal from Sinai Peninsula; Israel invades Lebanon; Sabra and Shatila massacres occur; U.S. Marines land in Lebanon

1983 ....Lebanon and Israel conclude peace treaty; truck bomb kills 241 U.S. Marines in Lebanon

1984 ....Lebanon repudiates peace treaty with Israel; Ronald Reagan withdraws Marines from Lebanon

1985–1986 ..................................U.S. officials agree to sell arms to Iran in exchange for release of American hostages in Lebanon

1986 ....Reagan administration's dealings with Iran become public

1987 ....Palestinian *intifada* breaks out in West Bank and Gaza

1988 ....Iran-Iraq War ends; Palestine National Council "declares" independent Palestinian state in West Bank and Gaza; United States begins political dialogue with PLO

1989 ....Soviet Union withdraws from Afghanistan; Osama bin Laden forms al-Qa'ida

1990	U.S.-PLO dialogue suspended; Iraq invades Kuwait
1991	Gulf War takes place; Madrid Conference held
1992	Pro-Soviet regime in Afghanistan falls; anti-Soviet Afghan factions begin fighting among themselves
1992–1993	United States intervenes in Somalia
1993	First World Trade Center bombing occurs; Israel and the PLO sign Declaration of Principles (Oslo Agreement)
1996	Khobar Towers military complex in Dhahran, Saudi Arabia, destroyed in explosion; Taliban take over in Afghanistan; Osama bin Laden returns to Afghanistan and issues *jihad* against United States
1998	Al-Qa 'ida operatives bomb U.S. embassies in Kenya and Tanzania; Bill Clinton orders air strikes against bin Laden training camps in Afghanistan and against Sudanese pharmaceutical company
2000	Israeli-Palestinian summit meeting at Camp David fails; Second Palestinian *intifada* begins; U.S.S. *Cole* bombed off coast of Yemen
2001	Terrorists attack World Trade Center and Pentagon; U.S. forces intervene in Afghanistan

Glossary

Albright, Madeleine: U.S. secretary of state, 1997–2001.

al-Haq, Zia: President of Pakistan, 1978–1988.

Amin, Hafizullah: Prime minister of Afghanistan, 1978–1979; president of Afghanistan, 1979.

Anglo-Iranian Oil Company (AIOC): British oil company that dominated the extraction, production, and marketing of Iranian oil from 1913 to 1954 (known as Anglo-Persian Oil Company until 1935).

Aqaba, Gulf of: Waterway lying between the Sinai and Arabian Peninsulas.

Aswan Dam project: Egyptian public works project designed to regulate the flow of the Nile, begun in 1960 and completed in 1970.

Azerbaijan Province of northern Iran.

Aziz, Tariq: Iraqi foreign minister during the Gulf War of 1991.

Baghdad Pact (1955–1959): A British-sponsored defense pact whose members were Britain, Iraq, Turkey, Iran, and Pakistan.

Baker, James: U.S. secretary of state, 1989–1992.

Balfour Declaration (1917): Public statement issued by British foreign secretary Arthur Balfour, declaring Britain's support for "the establishment in Palestine of a national home for the Jewish people."

Barzani, Mustafa: Iraqi Kurdish leader, 1930s–late1970s.

Black September (1970): Jordanian-Palestinian clash resulting in the expulsion of the Palestine Liberation Organization from Jordan.

Brandeis, Louis: American Zionist leader; Supreme Court justice, 1916–1941.

Brezhnev, Leonid: General secretary of the Soviet Communist Party, 1964–1982; president of the USSR, 1977–1982.

Brzezinski, Zbigniew: National security advisor to President Jimmy Carter, 1977–1981.

Casey, William. Director of the U.S. Central Intelligence Agency, 1981–1987.

The Dardanelles and the Bosporus (known jointly as the Turkish Straits): Maritime passageways from the Black Sea to the Mediterranean.

Dimona nuclear reactor: Facility in the Negev Desert at which Israel developed its nuclear weapons capability.

Eban, Abba: Israeli foreign minister, 1966–1974.

Eisenhower Doctrine (1957): U.S. policy, embodied in a congressional resolution, designed to help Middle Eastern nations resist international communism.

Fortas, Abe: Supreme Court justice, 1965–1969.

Fourteen Points (1918): Set of principles for establishing a just and stable postwar international order, unveiled by President Woodrow Wilson in a speech to the U.S. Congress.

Gemayal, Amin: President of Lebanon, 1982–1988.

Gemayal, Bashir: Leader of the Lebanese Phalange Party; president of Lebanon, 1982.

Glaspie, April: U.S. ambassador to Iraq at the time of Iraq's invasion of Kuwait in 1990.

Golden Gimmick (1950): Ruling by the U.S. Treasury Department, allowing American oil companies to deduct from their U.S. taxes the amount they paid in royalties to the Saudi government.

Gorbachev, Mikhail: General secretary of the Soviet Communist Party, 1985–1991; president of the USSR, 1990–1991.

Gromyko, Andrei: Soviet foreign minister, 1957–1985.

Haig, Alexander: U.S. secretary of state, 1981–1982.

Hekmatyar, Gulbuddin: Pakistani-supported Afghan resistance leader, 1980s–early 1990s; prime minister of Afghanistan 1993–1994, 1996.

Hizb-i Islami **(Islamic Party)**: Afghan party led by Gulbuddin Hekmatyar.

Hizbullah **(Party of God)**: Iranian-supported Lebanese Shiite organization, founded early 1980s.

Hussein-McMahon Correspondence (1915): Exchange of letters between Henry McMahon, British high commissioner in Egypt, and Sherif Hussein, governor of Mecca, establishing the nature and extent of British support for postwar Arab independence.

Ibn Saud: First king of modern Saudi Arabia, 1932–1953.

Intifada **(1987–c. 1992)**: Palestinian uprising against Israeli occupation of the West Bank and the Gaza Strip.

Intifada **II (2000–)**: Resumption of Palestinian uprising against Israeli occupation of the West Bank and the Gaza Strip.

Karmal, Babrak: Soviet-supported president of Afghanistan, 1979–1986.

Khobar Towers bombing (1996): Deadly explosion at U.S. military headquarters in Dhahran, Saudi Arabia, applauded by Osama bin Laden but probably the work of pro-Iranian Saudi militants.

King-Crane Commission (1919): Commission of inquiry sent by President Woodrow Wilson to ascertain the political aspirations of the native inhabitants of the former Ottoman Empire.

Kristallnacht **(1938)**: Nazi government-sponsored campaign of intimidation and violence against German Jews.

Lausanne, Treaty of (1923): Treaty concluded by Turkey, the Soviet Union, and the victorious allies in World War I, freeing Turkey from Allied occupation.

Lawrence, T. E. ("Lawrence of Arabia"): British military intelligence officer who assisted the Arab uprising against the Ottoman Empire during World War I.

Lend-Lease (1941–1945): U.S. program to loan money, weapons, and war materiel to the Allies during World War II.

madrasas: Religious schools in Pakistan at which future members of the Afghan Taliban were indoctrinated in an austere interpretation of Islam.

Maktab al-Khidmat **(Office of Services)**: Pakistan-based agency devoted to recruiting volunteers for the anti-Soviet resistance in Afghanistan, 1980s.

Meir, Golda: Prime minister of Israel, 1969–1974.

Mossadeq, Mohammed: Prime minister of Iran, 1951–1953.

Mujahidin: Broad coalition of Islamic groups opposing Soviet domination of Afghanistan, late 1970s–early 1990s.

National Origins Act (1924): Act of Congress imposing strict immigration quotas based on national origin.

Nixon Doctrine (1969): Set of principles embodied in a speech delivered by President Richard M. Nixon, urging America's allies to play a larger role in their own defense.

North, Oliver: Marine lieutenant colonel; National Security Council aide who, in the mid-1980s, implemented the sale of U.S. military equipment to Iran and the diversion of arms profits to the Nicaraguan *contras*.

Ocalan, Abdullah: Turkish-Kurdish leader of the *Partiya Karkaren Kurdistan* (Kurdistan Workers' Party), 1980s and 1990s.

Organization of Petroleum Exporting Countries (OPEC): Consortium of oil-exporting countries formed in 1960; members are Algeria, Indonesia, Iran, Iraq, Kuwait, Libya, Nigeria, Qatar, Saudi Arabia, United Arab Emirates, and Venezuela.

Palestine Liberation Organization (PLO): Umbrella organization for a wide variety of Palestinian groups, established in 1964.

Partition Plan (1947): UN General Assembly decision dividing Palestine into two states, one Arab and one Jewish.

Peres, Shimon: Israeli Labor Party politician; headed Israeli nuclear program in the 1960s; served as prime minister from 1984 to 1986 (alternating with Yitzhak Shamir) and from 1995 to 1996; served for several stints as foreign minister.

Popular Front for the Liberation of Palestine (PFLP): Radical Marxist faction of the Palestine Liberation Organization.

Powell, Colin: U.S. Army general; chairman of the Joint Chiefs of Staff, 1989–1991; U.S. secretary of state, 2001– .

Public Law (PL) 480: U.S. aid program, permitting countries to purchase American commodities with their own currencies.

Red Line Agreement (1928): Agreement concluded by American, British, French, and Dutch oil companies pledging to cooperate in exploring for oil in the lands of the former Ottoman Empire.

Resolution 194 (1948): UN General Assembly resolution declaring that Palestinian refugees have the right to return to their former homes in present-day Israel.

Resolution 242 (1967): UN Security Council resolution, passed in the aftermath of the 1967 Arab-Israeli War, calling for a land-for-peace settlement of the Arab-Israeli conflict.

Resolution 338 (1973): UN Security Council resolution mandating a cease-fire in the 1973 Arab-Israeli War and reaffirming Resolution 242.

Rogers Plan (1969): Arab-Israeli peace plan proposed by U.S. Secretary of State William Rogers, calling on Israel to withdraw from the territories it seized in 1967 and for the Arab states to recognize and make peace with Israel.

Rogers Plan II (1970): Cease-fire agreement, brokered by U.S. Secretary of State William Rogers, ending a resumption of fighting between Egypt and Israel over the Sinai Peninsula.

Rogers, William P.: U.S. secretary of state, 1969–1973.

Roosevelt, Kermit: CIA agent who organized an army coup against Iranian Prime Minister Mohammed Mossadeq in 1953.

San Remo Conference (1920): Conference at which the victorious allies in World War I (excluding the United States) awarded Middle Eastern mandates to European powers.

SAVAK: Internal police force of Mohammed Pahlavi, Shah of Iran.

Schwarzkopf, Norman: U.S. Army general; commander of coalition forces during the Gulf War of 1991.

Shamir, Yitzhak: Conservative Israeli politician; served as prime minister from 1983 to 1984, from 1986 to 1990, and from 1990 to 1992; served for several stints as foreign minister.

Sharm al-Shaykh: Egyptian port city located at the southern tip of the Sinai Peninsula, overlooking the Strait of Tiran.

Shatt al-Arab: Tidal river, disputed by Iraq and Iran, feeding into the Persian Gulf.

Shultz, George: U.S. secretary of state, 1982–1989.

Status of Forces Agreement (1964): U.S.-Iranian agreement providing that U.S. servicemen accused of breaking Iranian laws be court-martialed by the U.S. military rather than tried in Iranian courts.

Sykes-Picot Agreement (1916): Secret agreement between Britain and France dividing up the territory of the soon-to-be-defeated Ottoman Empire.

Taraki, Nur Muhammad: Soviet-supported president of Afghanistan, 1978–1979.

Thant, U: Secretary-general of the United Nations, 1962–1972.

Thatcher, Margaret: Prime minister of Great Britain, 1979–1990.

Thomas, Lowell: American publicist who popularized the exploits of Colonel T. E. Lawrence ("Lawrence of Arabia").

Three Mile Island accident (1979): Accidental release of radioactive water from a nuclear reactor in Pennsylvania, undermining public confidence in nuclear energy.

Tiran, Strait of: Maritime passageway from the Gulf of Aqaba to the Red Sea.

Truman Doctrine (1947): Foreign policy declaration, delivered by President Harry S. Truman in a speech to the U.S. Congress, pledging American support for "free peoples" resisting attempted subjugation by armed minorities or by outside pressures.

Valentino, Rudolph: American movie star and sex symbol of the 1920s, often appearing in Arabesque settings and roles.

Vance, Cyrus: U.S. secretary of state, 1977–1980.

Weizmann, Chaim: Scientist and Zionist leader; first president of Israel, 1948–1952.

World Islamic Front for Jihad against Jews and Crusaders (formed 1998): Broad coalition of anti-Western Islamic terrorist groups formed by Osama bin Laden.

Yamani, Ahmad Zaki: Saudi minister of petroleum and mineral resources, 1962–1986.

Yousef, Ramzi: Pakistani-born operative working for Osama bin Laden's al-Qa'ida network; mastermind of the first World Trade Center bombing in 1993.

Biographical Notes

Yasser Arafat (b. 1929). Chairman of the Palestine Liberation Organization (PLO) and president of the Palestinian Authority in the West Bank and the Gaza Strip. In the 1960s, Arafat headed al-Fatah, a Palestinian resistance group. In 1969, Arafat took al-Fatah into the PLO and became chairman of the larger organization. In the 1970s and 1980s, Arafat built up support within the PLO for a two-state settlement of the Israel-Palestine dispute, a process culminating in the PLO's recognition of Israel and renunciation of terrorism in 1988. In 1993, Arafat negotiated an accord with Israel that led to limited Palestinian self-rule in the West Bank and the Gaza Strip, an achievement for which he was awarded, along with Israeli Prime Minister Yitzhak Rabin and Foreign Minister Shimon Peres, the 1994 Nobel Peace Prize. In 1996, Arafat was elected president of the Palestinian Authority. A failed 2000 summit meeting with Israeli Prime Minister Barak, however, led to renewed violence between Palestinians and Israelis.

Hafiz al-Asad (1930–2000). Syrian general and minister of defense, who became president of Syria after a coup in 1970. Throughout his long rule, one of Asad's main goals was regaining the Golan Heights, which Israel had seized in the 1967 Arab-Israeli War. Neither in the Yom Kippur War of 1973 nor in negotiations with Israel in the 1990s did Asad succeed in recovering the Golan. In 1976, Asad sent Syrian peacekeeping troops to Lebanon and, thereafter, was heavily involved in the political affairs of that country. In Syria, Asad was an authoritarian ruler whose brutal crushing of a Muslim Brotherhood uprising in 1982 received widespread condemnation. Following his death in 2000, Asad was succeeded as president by his son Bashar.

Mustafa Kemal Ataturk (1881–1938). Founder and first president of the modern Turkish republic. In the 1900s and 1910s, under the name Mustafa Kemal, he served as an officer in the Ottoman army. His distinguished military leadership during the First World War, while failing to prevent Turkey's ultimate defeat, gained him a wide following among the Turkish army and public. Following the Ottoman Sultan's capitulation to the Allies in 1918, Kemal established a rival Turkish government that, over the next four years, succeeded in freeing Turkey from Allied occupation, though Turkey's imperial holdings were lost. In 1922, Kemal abolished the

©2003 The Teaching Company Limited Partnership

sultanate and, in the following year, became president of the new Turkish republic, a position he held until his death in the late 1930s. Under the new surname Ataturk ("father of the Turks"), he launched ambitious programs to Westernize, modernize, and secularize Turkey.

Menachem Begin (1913–1992). Prime minister of Israel from 1977 to 1983. Born in Russia, he led a Zionist youth movement in Poland before World War II and, in 1942, settled in Palestine, where he led militant opposition to the British Mandate authorities. After the establishment of the state of Israel, Begin sat in the Knesset and led the right-wing opposition to the Labor Party. In 1977, Begin's Likud party was victorious in national elections, and Begin became prime minister. In 1978, he negotiated the Camp David peace accords with Egyptian President Anwar al-Sadat, agreeing to withdraw Israeli forces from the Sinai Peninsula in exchange for Egyptian recognition of Israel. Begin shared the 1978 Nobel Peace Prize with Sadat. The failure of the 1982 Israeli invasion of Lebanon, however, led Begin to resign from office in 1983.

Osama bin Laden (b. 1957). Saudi leader of al-Qaʻida, a Muslim terrorist organization he founded in 1989. The son of a wealthy businessman, in the 1980s, bin Laden participated in the Muslim resistance to the Soviet invasion of Afghanistan. Following the stationing of American troops in Saudi Arabia in 1990, bin Laden turned against the Saudi government. Over the next several years, based first in Sudan, then in Afghanistan, bin Laden's al-Qaʻida organization sponsored a series of escalating attacks on Saudi and American targets. Among the operations linked to al-Qaʻida are the 1993 World Trade Center bombing, the 1998 embassy bombings in Kenya and Tanzania, the 2000 attack on the U.S.S. *Cole*, and the 2001 terrorist attacks on the World Trade Center and Pentagon. After 9/11, the United States intervened in Afghanistan and successfully defeated the Taliban and al-Qaʻida forces. Bin Laden himself eluded capture, however, and continues to issue threats against the United States and its allies.

John Foster Dulles (1888–1959). An international lawyer who began his career in public service as counsel to the American delegation to the Paris Peace Conference of 1919. He was an early U.S. delegate to the UN General Assembly and, in 1951, negotiated the peace treaty between the United States and Japan. In 1953,

Dulles became Eisenhower's secretary of state; in this role, he strenuously fought communism and worked to promote U.S. security through the maintenance of strategic alliances and reliance on nuclear deterrence. Dulles helped fashion the Eisenhower Doctrine of 1957, which aimed at strengthening Middle Eastern states' resistance to communism through the furnishing of economic and military aid.

Hussein I (1935–1999). Became king of Jordan in 1953 after his grandfather was assassinated by a Palestinian extremist and his father was declared unfit to serve. Hussein himself faced several assassination attempts, because his pro-Western positions set him at odds with radical Arab nationalists. Though relatively conciliatory toward Israel, Hussein led Jordan into the 1967 Arab-Israeli War, in which Israel seized the West Bank from Jordanian control. In 1970, Hussein defeated PLO forces stationed in Jordan and, in the following year, expelled most of those forces from the country. In 1988, Hussein forfeited Jordan's claims to the West Bank and, in 1994, signed a peace treaty with Israel.

Saddam Hussein (b. 1937). President of Iraq from 1979 to 2003. Trained as a lawyer in Egypt, he was instrumental in the 1968 revolution that brought his Ba'th party to political power in Iraq. During the Iran-Iraq War of the 1980s, Hussein gained notoriety for using chemical weapons against Iranian soldiers and Iraqi Kurdish civilians. In 1990, he ordered the invasion of Kuwait, but his forces were subsequently compelled to withdraw from Kuwait in the Gulf War of 1991. After the Gulf War, Hussein faced continued international pressure to disarm Iraq of all weapons of mass destruction; this pressure included the imposition of economic sanctions against Iraq and the threat of military attack by a U.S.-led coalition.

Ayatollah Ruhollah Khomeini (1900–1989). An Iranian Shiite cleric who served as Iran's political leader from the late 1970s to the late 1980s. Khomeini received religious training in theological schools and, in the 1950s, was named *ayatollah* (sign of God), a position of supreme religious leadership. In the mid-1960s, Khomeini was exiled from Iran for his harsh criticism of the shah's policies. First in Iraq, then in France, Khomeini continued his political and religious critiques of the shah, developing a strong following inside Iran. After the shah fled Iran in 1979, Khomeini returned to establish an Islamic republic, consolidating his position by supporting the Iranian students' seizure of the U.S. embassy in Tehran. Khomeini was Iran's supreme leader for the next decade, during which he waged a bloody and draining war with Iraq.

Henry Alfred Kissinger (b. 1923). U.S. secretary of state from 1973 to 1977. Born in Germany, Kissinger immigrated to the United States in 1938. An influential political scientist, he taught at Harvard University and consulted widely before becoming Richard Nixon's assistant for national security affairs (1969–1973), then secretary of state. Kissinger's foreign policy achievements included negotiating the Strategic Arms Limitation Talks (SALT) with the Soviet Union and engineering America's rapprochement with the People's Republic of China. He won the Nobel Peace Prize in 1973 for negotiating the cease-fire with North Vietnam, part of a more general U.S. disengagement from Indochina. In the same year, Kissinger negotiated a cease-fire to end the 1973 Arab-Israeli War. Kissinger continued to serve under President Gerald Ford; since 1977, he has lectured, written, and consulted.

Gamal Abdel Nasser (1918–1970). First president of the republic of Egypt. In 1942, as a young army officer, he founded the secret Society of Free Officers to oppose corruption and foreign domination in Egypt. In 1952, he led the army coup that deposed King Farouk. In 1954, he became premier and, in 1956, was unopposed as candidate for president. His policy of Arab socialism emphasized land reform and economic development; he advocated Arab national pride and took a neutral position in the Cold War. After nationalizing the Suez Canal Company in 1956, Nasser successfully resisted an invasion by Great Britain, France, and Israel. He served as president of the United Arab Republic, a union between Egypt and Syria that lasted from 1958 to 1961. In 1967, Nasser expelled UN peacekeeping forces in the Sinai Peninsula and closed the Strait of Tiran to Israeli shipping, touching off the Six-Day War, in which Israel seized the Sinai Peninsula and Gaza Strip from Egypt. In his last years in office, Nasser drew closer to the Soviet Union.

Muhammad Reza shah Pahlavi (1919–1980). Became shah of Iran in 1941, after Britain and the Soviet Union deposed his father, Reza shah Pahlavi, who was suspected of collaboration with Germany. During a 1953 conflict with Prime Minister Muhammad Mossadeq, Muhammad shah briefly fled the country, but he was restored to power by a U.S.-backed coup. His "White Revolution" of the 1960s offered moderate reforms, but the unequal distribution of oil wealth alienated many of his subjects, and Muslim clergy criticized his pro-Western stance. In the 1970s, the shah relied increasingly on SAVAK, his secret police, to repress discontent. Rioting drove the shah from Iran in 1979, and the exiled religious leader Ayatollah Ruhollah Khomeini returned to govern the country. The shah died in exile in Egypt.

Yitzhak Rabin (1933–1995). An Israeli general and twice prime minister of Israel. Before the establishment of Israel, Rabin fought in the Jewish militia and the British army in Palestine. He served in the Israeli army from the 1948 Arab-Israeli War and became army chief of staff in 1964, a position he held during the 1967 Six-Day War, in which his leadership was widely celebrated. In March 1974, Rabin, a member of the Labor Party, became Golda Meir's labor minister, then, upon her resignation, prime minister until 1977. While serving as defense minister in a Labor-Likud coalition government from 1984 to 1990, Rabin led a harsh crackdown on the Palestinian uprising in the Israeli-occupied territories. Rabin became prime minister again in 1992 and, in 1993, approved the peace agreement with the PLO, an achievement for which he shared the 1994 Nobel Peace Prize. Rabin was assassinated in 1995 by an Israeli student with links to right-wing extremists.

Anwar al-Sadat (1918–1981). President of Egypt from 1970 to 1981. As a young man, Sadat was friendly with Gamal Abdel Nasser and shared his commitment to Egyptian nationalism. During World War II, he collaborated with the German army and was imprisoned for two years by the British. He was involved in the army coup that deposed King Farouk in 1952 and went on to hold several positions in Nasser's government, including vice president from 1969. When Nasser died in 1970, Sadat became president and led Egypt to limited success in the 1973 war with Israel. In 1978, he concluded the Camp David peace accords with Israel and was awarded, along with Menachem Begin, the Nobel Peace Prize that year. Sadat was assassinated in 1981 by Muslim extremists.

Ariel Sharon (b. 1928). Prime minister of Israel. Sharon was an effective military leader in the 1948 and 1956 Arab-Israeli Wars and gained fame with his successes in the 1973 conflict with Egypt. Sharon then left the army and helped establish the right-wing Likud party. Following Likud's electoral victory in 1977, he held a number of government posts. In 1982, as defense minister in the government of Menachem Begin, Sharon engineered the Israeli invasion of Lebanon, during which he was harshly criticized for allowing the massacre of Palestinian civilians in the Sabra and Shatila refugee camps by Lebanese Christian forces. Sharon held a series of cabinet posts in the 1980s and 1990s. His armed visit to the al-Aqsa Mosque in Palestinian East Jerusalem in 2000 set off a violent insurrection in the West Bank and Gaza. In 2001, Likud prevailed in national elections and Sharon became prime minister. Sharon has since pursued a hard line with the Palestinians, forcibly reoccupying much of the Palestinian territory vacated by his predecessors.

Bibliography

Essential Reading:

Bass, Warren. *Support Any Friend: Kennedy's Middle East and the Making of the U.S.-Israeli Alliance*. New York: Oxford University Press, 2003. An extensively researched and elegantly written account of U.S. Middle East policy in the early 1960s; makes a strong case that the U.S.-Israeli "special relationship" began during the Kennedy years .

Bergen, Peter L. *Holy War, Inc.: Inside the Secret World of Osama bin Laden*. New York: Simon & Schuster, 2001 (2002). An intelligent and accessible study, based on years of research, of the emergence and ideology of Osama bin Laden.

Berman, Aaron. *Nazism, the Jews, and American Zionism*. Detroit: Wayne State University Press, 1990. A well-researched and deftly written study of the transforming effect Nazi policies had on the development of American Zionism.

Bill, James A. *The Eagle and the Lion: The Tragedy of American-Iranian Relations*. New Haven: Yale University Press, 1988. An essential (though occasionally tedious) excavation of U.S.-Iranian relations from the 19th century through the 1980s; strongly opinionated but exhaustively researched.

Christison, Kathleen. *Perceptions of Palestine: Their Influence on U.S.-Middle East Policy*. Berkeley: University of California Press, 1999 (2000). A study of American attitudes toward the Palestine issue since the late 19th century; strongly opinionated but well researched and nuanced.

Hahn, Peter L. *The United States, Great Britain, and Egypt, 1945–1956*. Chapel Hill: University of North Carolina Press, 1991. A well-researched and evenhanded study of U.S. and British dealings with Egypt in the first postwar decade; argues for the preeminence of strategic considerations in Anglo-U.S. policy.

Hiro, Dilip. *Desert Shield to Desert Storm: The Second Gulf War*. New York: Routledge, 1992. A meticulously researched and comprehensive account of the Gulf War by a seasoned observer of Middle Eastern and international politics.

Hourani, Albert. *A History of the Arab Peoples*. London: Faber and Faber, 1991. A masterful and accessible survey of several centuries of Arab history by one of the most distinguished historians of the Middle East.

Lenczowski, George. *American Presidents and the Middle East.* Durham: Duke University Press, 1990. An accessible and generally evenhanded survey of U.S. policy toward the Middle East from the 1940s through the 1980s.

Mansfield, Peter. *A History of the Middle East.* London: Penguin Books, 1991. A concise, comprehensive, and evenhanded survey of several centuries of Middle Eastern history.

Morris, Benny. *Righteous Victims: A History of the Zionist-Arab Conflict, 1881–1999.* New York: Alfred A. Knopf, 1999. An extensively researched and wide-ranging history of the Arab-Israeli conflict; remarkably successful in illuminating the perspectives of both Arabs and Israelis.

Neff, Donald. *Warriors against Israel.* Brattleboro, VT: Amana Books, 1988. An accessible, well-researched, and dramatic account of the 1973 Yom Kippur War.

———. *Warriors at Suez: Eisenhower Takes America into the Middle East.* New York: Simon & Schuster, 1981. One of the most accessible and comprehensive accounts of the Suez crisis of 1956.

———. *Warriors over Jerusalem: The Six Days That Changed the Middle East.* New York: Simon & Schuster, 1984. A lively and well-written account of the 1967 Arab-Israeli War.

Oren, Michael B. *Six Days of War: June 1967 and the Making of the Modern Middle East.* New York: Oxford University Press, 2002. An accessible and intelligent account of the Six-Day War, based on extensive research in newly available American, Israeli, and Egyptian materials.

Parker, Richard B. *The Politics of Miscalculation in the Middle East.* Bloomington: Indiana University Press, 1993. A meticulous study of several Middle Eastern crises from the 1960s to the 1980s; especially successful at integrating material from interviews with former U.S., Israeli, and Arab officials.

Randall, Jonathan. *After Such Knowledge, What Forgiveness? My Encounters with Kurdistan.* New York: Farrar, Straus and Giroux, 1997. An eye-opening if occasionally overwrought exposé of the great powers' mistreatment of the Kurds.

Smith, Charles D. *Palestine and the Arab-Israeli Conflict*. 4th ed. New York: St. Martin's Press, 2001. A concise, accessible, and evenhanded survey of the Arab-Israeli conflict.

Spiegel, Steven L. *The Other Arab-Israeli Conflict: Making America's Middle East Policy, from Truman to Reagan*. Chicago: University of Chicago Press, 1985. An insightful and detailed analysis of U.S. policy toward the Arab-Israeli conflict; highly successful in presenting American and Israeli perspectives, less so in explaining Arab points of view.

Telhami, Shibley. *The Stakes: America and the Middle East: The Consequences of Power and the Choice of Peace*. Boulder, CO: Westview Press, 2002. A forcefully argued but balanced essay on the policy implications of recent American actions in the Middle East.

Yergin, Daniel. *The Prize: The Epic Quest for Oil, Money, and Power*. New York: Simon & Schuster, 1991. Extensively researched and wide-ranging history of international struggles over oil; especially successful in explaining the dynamics of the oil industry and in bringing the history alive through lively narrative.

Supplementary Reading:

Ashton, Nigel John. *Eisenhower, Macmillan and the Problem of Nasser: Anglo-American Relations and Arab Nationalism, 1955–59*. London: Macmillan, 1996. A well researched and sharply analytical study of Anglo-American policies toward Arab nationalism in the mid- to late 1950s.

Benson, Michael T. *Harry S. Truman and the Founding of Israel*. Westport, CT: Praeger, 1997. A one-sided but illuminating account arguing for the salience of moral considerations in Truman's support of the Zionist cause.

Ben-Zvi, Abraham. *Decade of Transition: Eisenhower, Kennedy, and the Origins of the American-Israeli Alliance*. New York: Columbia University Press, 1998. A stimulating (though at times overstated) account of the evolution of U.S.-Israeli relations from the 1950s to the 1960s; argues that the U.S.-Israeli "special relationship" has its origins in the Eisenhower years.

Bryson, Thomas A. *American Diplomatic Relations with the Middle East, 1784-1975: A Survey*. Metuchen, NJ: The Scarecrow Press, 1977. An informative if pedestrian survey of U.S. official involvement in the Middle East over two centuries.

————. *Seeds of Mideast Crisis: The United States Diplomatic Role in the Middle East during World War II.* Jefferson, NC: McFarland & Company, 1981. A workmanlike but informative account of American diplomacy in the Middle East during World War II.

Cohen, Avner. *Israel and the Bomb.* New York: Columbia University Press, 1998. A meticulously researched account of Israel's development of a nuclear weapons capability in the 1950s and 1960s.

Cohen, Michael J. *Truman and Israel.* Berkeley: University of California Press, 1990. An extensively researched study of the domestic influences on Truman's decision to support the Zionist cause.

Cooley, John K. *Unholy Wars: Afghanistan, America and International Terrorism.* London: Pluto Press, 2002. A wide-ranging and sharply critical study of U.S. policy toward Afghanistan during and after the Soviet invasion of that country, to be used with some caution on account of its heavy reliance on unverifiable sources.

Daniel, Robert L. *American Philanthropy in the Near East, 1820–1960.* Athens, OH: Ohio University Press, 1970. An extensively researched study of American missionary, educational, and philanthropic activities in the Middle East in the nineteenth and twentieth centuries.

DeNovo, John A. *American Interests and Policies in the Middle East, 1900–1939.* Minneapolis: University of Minnesota Press, 1963. A well researched, wide-ranging, and informative study of American involvement in the Middle East in the early decades of the 20th century.

Draper, Theodore. *A Very Thin Line: The Iran-Contra Affairs.* New York: Hill and Wang, 1991. A meticulous excavation of the Iran-contra scandal by a prominent social historian.

Esposito, John L. *The Islamic Threat: Myth or Reality?* New York: Oxford University Press, 1999. A comprehensive survey of Islamist politics in the modern era, taking special pains to stress their complexity and diversity.

Fromkin, David. *A Peace to End All Peace: Creating the Modern Middle East, 1914–1922.* New York: H.Holt, 1989. A lively, expansive, and richly detailed account of Western powers' remaking of the Middle East during and immediately after World War I.

Gerges, Fawaz A. *America and Political Islam: Clash of Cultures or Clash of Interests?* Cambridge: Cambridge University Press, 1999. A careful and nuanced study of U.S. policy toward political Islam in the 1990s, successfully refuting accusations of appeasement on the one hand and unrelenting hostility on the other.

————. *The Superpowers and the Middle East: Regional and International Politics, 1955–1967.* Boulder, CO: Westview Press, 1994. An extensively researched and perceptive study of U.S. and Soviet interactions with Middle Eastern states, stressing the initiative of local actors.

Goode, James F. *The United States and Iran, 1946–51: The Diplomacy of Neglect.* New York: St. Martin's Press, 1989. A critical assessment of U.S. policy toward Iran in the early Cold War years, arguing that Washington failed to foster liberal forces within Iran.

Heiss, Mary Ann. *Empire and Nationhood: The United States, Great Britain, and Iranian Oil, 1950–1954.* New York: Columbia University Press, 1997. An intelligent and well-researched study of Anglo-American responses to the Iranian nationalization crisis of the early 1950s; especially illuminating in its discussion of Anglo-American cultural perceptions of Iran.

Hodson, Joel C. *Lawrence of Arabia and American Culture: The Making of a Transatlantic Legend.* Westport, CT: Greenwood Press, 1995. A well-researched and accessible study of the life of T. E. Lawrence and the impact of his legend on American culture in the 1920s.

Huntington, Samuel. *The Clash of Civilizations and the Remaking of World Order.* New York: Simon & Schuster, 1996. A provocative and influential essay arguing for the salience of ethno-cultural identity to international conflict.

Khadduri, Majid, and Edmund Ghareeb. *War in the Gulf: The Iraq-Kuwait Conflict and Its Implications.* New York: Oxford University Press, 1997. A perceptive and well-researched study of the Iraq-Kuwait dispute and the subsequent Gulf War; especially effective at elucidating inter-Arab politics.

Kuniholm, Bruce R. *The Origins of the Cold War in the Near East: Great Power Conflict and Diplomacy in Iran, Turkey, and Greece.* Princeton: Princeton University Press, 1980. A meticulously researched study of great power rivalry in the Middle East during and immediately following World War II, portraying U.S. behavior as a justified response to Soviet expansionism.

Little, Douglas. *American Orientalism: The United States and the Middle East Since 1945*. Chapel Hill: University of North Carolina Press, 2002. A collection of well-researched and trenchant essays on the evolution of American policies and attitudes toward the Middle East.

Lyttle, Mark. *The Origins of the Iranian-American Alliance, 1941–1953*. New York: Holmes & Meier, 1987. A study of early U.S. involvement in Iran that stresses Anglo-American cooperation and criticizes U.S. policy for being unnecessarily confrontational toward the Soviet Union.

Makovsky, David. *Making Peace with the PLO: The Rabin Government's Road to the Oslo Accord*. Boulder, CO: Westview Press, 1995. An insightful and accessible account of the diplomacy leading up to the Oslo peace agreement, based on extensive interviews, especially with Israeli officials.

McAlister, Melani. *Epic Encounters: Culture, Media, and U.S. Interests in the Middle East, 1945–2000*. Berkeley: University of California Press, 2001. A collection of imaginative and provocative essays on the Middle East's cultural impact on the United States.

McDowell, David. *A Modern History of the Kurds*. London: I.B. Tauris, 2000. A comprehensive and accessible study of Kurdish history in Syria, Iran, Iraq, and Turkey (especially the latter two countries) over the last century.

Miller, John, Michael Stone, and Chris Mitchell. *The Cell: Inside the 9/11 Plot and Why the FBI and CIA Failed to Stop It*. New York: Hyperion, 2002. A fast-paced account of al-Qa'iada's campaign of terror over the decade preceding 9/11, and of the U.S. government's often ineffectual efforts to thwart it.

O'Ballance, Edgar. *The Palestinian Intifada*. New York: St. Martin's Press, 1998. A thorough and judicious treatment of the first Palestinian intifada by a seasoned chronicler of international conflict.

Quandt, William. *Peace Process: American Diplomacy and the Arab-Israeli Conflict Since 1967*. Berkeley: University of California Press, 2001. A sober, balanced, and well informed account of U.S. sponsorship of the Arab-Israeli peace process since 1967.

Rashid, Ahmed. *Taliban: Militant Islam, Oil and Fundamentalism in Central Asia*. New Haven: Yale University Press, 2000. An extensively researched and judicious study of the rise and rule of the Taliban in the 1990s, with special attention to the international dimensions of the extended Afghan crisis.

Rubin, Barry. *The Great Powers in the Middle East, 1941–1947*. London: Frank Cass, 1980. A thorough, workmanlike study of Western powers' political involvement in the Middle East during and after World War I.

Shaheen, Jack G. *Reel Bad Arabs: How Hollywood Vilifies a People*. New York: Olive Branch Press, 2001. An extensive and lively compendium of film portrayals (mostly negative) of Arab people and culture over the last century.

Said, Edward W. *Orientalism*. New York: Vintage Books, 1979. A provocative and highly influential critique of portrayals of the Middle East in Western intellectual traditions.

Smith, Gaddis. *Morality, Reason, and Power: American Diplomacy in the Carter Years*. New York: Hill and Wang, 1996. A general overview of Jimmy Carter's foreign policies, with excellent chapters on Camp David, Iran, and Afghanistan.

Usher, Graham. *Dispatches from Palestine: The Rise and Fall of the Oslo Peace Process*. London: Pluto Press, 1999. An indignant but well researched analysis of the Oslo peace process of the 1990s, highly sympathetic to Palestinian national claims but sharply critical of both Yasser Arafat and successive Israeli governments.